D1457692

[Photo Lafayette

THE AUTHOR

WINDING LANES

*A Book of Impressions
and Recollections*

BY

THE REV. J. H. HOWARD, M.A., D.D.

AUTHOR OF

"Which Jesus?" : "Jesus the Agitator," &c.

CAERNARVON
THE CALVINISTIC METHODIST PRINTING WORKS

DEDICATED TO

DR. CYRIL HAMILTON OWEN
AND
DR. DONALD OWEN

WHOSE FRIENDSHIP I TREASURE

CONTENTS

Chapter   *Page*

Author's Note   11

1. Parentage . . . without pride or prejudice 13

2. Boyhood . . . no idyll 20

3. Llansamlet . . . laughter and tears   ... 32

4. The Chapel on a Hill 57

5. How not to prepare for the Ministry   ... 75

6. Swansea sidelights   99

7. Cwmavon among the mountains 108

8. Birkenhead . . . a grey spot on the Mersey 121

9. Colwyn Bay . . . the garden with few
      weeds   135

10. Beyond Offa's Dyke   170

11. God's own country . . . in parts   ... 190

12. Liverpool . . . home of extremes   ... 226

13. The Welshman at home 245

14. Types   255

Index   273

WINDING LANES

CHAPTER ONE

PARENTAGE . . . . WITHOUT PRIDE OR PREJUDICE

PRIDE of lineage never thrilled me, and I cannot understand others being excited over so doubtful an asset. If we go back far enough, we shall find that all of us come from the same ancestors who were quite unconcerned about family crests. Anthropology should cure Germany even of racial conceit, and a perusal of our beginnings as recorded in the opening chapters of Genesis is a sure corrective for all childish boast of ancestry. A man preening himself on his family tree illustrates an arrested historical sense, and glories in the disgrace of a full-grown person dependant on his parents.

We dare not arrogate to ourselves any credit or blame for our parentage and birth, since we had no say in those matters of origin. Our lot fell in pleasant or less favourable circles in accordance with an Order not quite unrelated to the sins and virtues of unnumbered generations. Better, therefore, to take the past as read, and be thankful that it was not much worse.

Heredity is a factor we cannot deny. Proclivities, tendencies, nebulous memories, instinctive reactions, and unaccountable intuitions convince me that amongst my progenitors were bandits and bards, mystics and murderers, saints and sinners, and, maybe, some who found the secret of peace. There are skeletons unfit for the light of day in the majority of family histories. Wisdom leaves the work of excava-

tion to Egyptologists; the sleeping Pharaohs are far
away, and saints nearer home should not be disturbed.
Spirits called from the mighty deep can prove trouble-
some to those who invoke them.

Yet, I have gleaned a few facts concerning my family
which are interesting to me, and may be so to others.
My father, Joshua George Howard, claimed to be a
direct descendant of the renowned prison reformer,
John Howard, on his paternal side. His mother came
from a long line of Army families, more or less distinguished. The ancestral home was in King's Lynn,
Norfolk, and my father was the only child of John and
Lydia Howard. The family were fairly rich, and the son
qualified for a Commission in the Navy, as his father
had done before him. Lydia Howard was left a widow
when in her early thirties, and she devoted her life to
her son and heir, my father, who was then seven years
old. Evidently, mother and son were strongly attached
to each other; but a tragic break took place when the man
of twenty nine insisted upon marrying Catharine Bowen,
a beautiful Roman Catholic of poor parentage and scant
education. Ultimately, my father was disowned and
disinherited, and, so far as I can ascertain, mother and
son never met afterwards. Not until thirty years had
elapsed, and only when on her deathbed, did the ar-
istocrat forgive that runaway match; by then it was too
late for reconciliation, since both my parents had been
dead for eighteen years.

Seven years after the break with his mother, my
father was fatally injured on board his ship. He had
served in India; and in China, under Gordon, during
the Taiping rebellion. The medal pinned to his coat by
that intrepid general for " a deed of conspicuous
bravery " is an heirloom I cherish. He was thirty-six
when he died leaving a widow and three boys:—George,
aged five; William, four years old, and myself, nearly
two. In the only photograph of him that remains, he
seems tall, well-proportioned, and has a full beard.

After disinheriting my father, my grandmother adopted a girl cousin of ours; upon this child was lavished the affection and wealth denied to a son. The new favourite was educated at a High School, and, after completing her education, she was sent on a world tour with a paid companion. Every luxury that money could procure was hers—servants, horses, and a country residence of her own. Once only did I see the young lady; she was tall, graceful, athletic, with blue eyes, and a deep mellow voice. Needless to add, she was elegantly dressed. My grandmother had planned a brilliant match for her ward, and hoped to get her " presented " at Court about the time of the catastrophe which shattered more schemes and social ambitions. One morning, the lady casually informed her guardian, that, on the previous day, she had been married at a Register Office. The distressing ordeal of disowning and disinheriting was repeated in that home, and our cousin's name was forbidden in the presence of her former benefactress.

My grandmother did not acknowledge her son's wife, and refused all appeals for help. Yet she bought a grave, and paid for my father's funeral at St. Peter's, Cockett. But when my mother died, just ten months afterwards, the mother-in-law refused her body burial at Cockett. Consequently, my parents lie in different graves. Jealousy did not stop at the cemetery gates.

It was to me that my grandmother expressed her genuine remorse for the triple tragedy wrought by her pride and prejudice. She had deprived her son of his patrimony, broken my mother's heart, and penalised a young girl for following the dictates of affection. Her last pathetic request was to be buried with the son she had disowned. Divided in life, we attempted to reunite them in death; but even in the grave she would not meet her son's wife.

My mother must have been a remarkable personality to draw her husband away from his aristocratic circles. Often have I wondered where lay her power to

awaken such love, and stir so savage a hatred; no
weakling could do that. But orphanhood has compensa-
tions in life. All through the years I have cherished an
ideal mother who is unsullied by time and change; and
I have sensed her presence when watching my children
being fondled by their mother. A mother in the heart
can be as wonderful as a parent on the hearth. Is this
the Mother of the Holy Shrine? It may explain a strain
of mysticism in my own nature. Catharine Bowen was
an ardent Roman Catholic, and her husband followed
into the communion of that Church.   Perhaps I in-
herited an unconscious bias towards the Mother-Church
of Christendom, and that is why I feel no stranger in her
sanctuaries. When travelling on the Continent, I have
frequently attended Catholic services, and experienced a
sort of hypnotic rest that bides no question or revolt. I
sympathise with Orchard, Manning, and Newman in
their flight from Protestant doubts, discussions, splits and
schisms. The human heart craves for the final word,
and the note of authority; man needs rest for the mind as
well as for the soul; he longs for the changeless, the
everlasting Yea, and an ultimate to lean upon. The
Church of Rome professes to offer all this; and scores
of times have I wished I could accept her creed. But
I cannot subscribe to the central doctrines of papal
infallibility, purgatory, masses for the dead, and the con-
fessional. To me, they are direct negations of History,
Reason and Revelation.

After a Sunday morning service at Tours Cathedral,
in August, 1924, an elderly priest and I drifted together.
We discussed the Mass and the Creeds, the Church and
the Priesthood, Catholic France and Protestant England,
until late in the afternoon. When we were about to part,
the old cleric placed both hands on my shoulders in
blessing, and said: " My son, your heart is at the Shrine
of Holy Mother-Church; but your proud intellect makes
you a Protestant heretic. May God have mercy on your
soul, and grant you peace."

Not only did my grandmother repudiate my mother in life and in death, she also left us children to the care of others. But, six years after my mother's death, our irate relative relented a little, claimed my two brothers, and placed them with certain rich friends at King's Lynn. Then, when both proved refractory, she apprenticed them to sea. But during those years my grandmother would do nothing for me, because, in features, I resembled my mother who was still the object of her scorn, although dead.

Once again Lydia Howard was to suffer disappointment. My brother George deserted his ship in Australia, and William did likewise at Cuba. For two years both were regarded as dead; but, ere long, a letter arrived from each asking for passage money to enable them to return home. William added a characteristic note to his request, intimating that unless the money was forthcoming soon, he contemplated marrying two charming negresses who could add lustre to the aristocratic Howard family! My grandmother telegraphed the money within forty-eight hours after receipt of that fantastic letter. George was equally successful in his assault upon the grandmother purse. Both were then settled in the old Salutation Inn, Aberdare, under the care of Mrs. Stanton, mother of Charlie Stanton, who became miners' agent, and a Member of Parliament for Merthyr Tydvil. From that time on, my grandmother lost all interest in my brothers, and they worked in the coalmines about Aberdare. She resolutely ignored me during those years. Not until my fifteenth birthday did she invite me to visit her, at Swansea; and then she gave me a shilling and a frown, whilst muttering loud enough for me to hear: "The boy is so like his wretched mother." But, just a week before her death, at Swansea, when I was twenty-one years old and about to begin my collegiate course of preparation for the Ministry, she sent for me, alone. It was then she informed me about the outstanding facts of her life, and the history of my parents. As I have

B

already mentioned, her last request was to be buried with my father.

My mind often reverts to the last week of grandmother's life. It was my first conscious contact with death and with remorse. I have witnessed several similar scenes since; but never has the poignancy of dissolution impressed me so much. For weeks, if not months afterwards, I lived in the fear and under the shadow of death; I dreaded darkness and sleep, and was haunted by terror of the unknown. Not until I watched a fellow-student greet death with a smile, nearly five years after my elderly relative had passed on, did I lose the terror of that "black-robed messenger of the King." Today, I can almost call death a friend, and the grave incites in me a reverent curiosity.

Lydia Howard overbore people nearest and dearest to her. She was a born leader, and could not take second place in a crowd, or in the life of her son. It was her habit to give unstintingly to those she loved; but a divided loyalty would not be tolerated by that proud soul. A beautiful presentation Bible in my possession contains the following inscription:

"LYDIA HOWARD,

Presented by the Committee for conducting the
Festival in the Parish of Ashford on the
occasion of the marriage of the Prince of Wales.
In gratitude for services rendered.

10th March, 1863."

That gives some indication of her social activities. My father's tombstone is a monument to his mother's exacting demands upon affection.

Possibly a kindred unyielding nature was shown by her youngest grandson when I resolutely refused two out of her three requests at our final interview. She failed to persuade me to take Holy Orders in the Anglican Church;

and when she pressed me to accept more than sufficient money for a six years course at any college of my choice in Oxford University, I refused all pecuniary help from one who had spurned my mother in the hour of her dire need. Today, I think that I was too stubborn; gracious acceptance is, sometimes, a nobler virtue than refusal. I feel that I missed an opportunity of practising forgiving love, which might have eased the last hours of a frustrated soul in the throes of remorse when wishing to atone for injustice done before facing the great Beyond.

CHAPTER TWO

BOYHOOD . . . . NO IDYLL

HEAVEN did not lie about my infancy. My earliest memories are of hunger, loneliness, and the exasperation of a not-wanted child in the various houses of my mother's poor relatives who must have lived in the hope of my grandmother coming to their financial aid. Ultimately, I was placed in the Cottage Homes, Cockett, near Swansea, and remained there for seven years. My first Master was a Mr. Grossmith, an old bachelor Army officer with a sergeant-major voice and manner. He could shout like a fog-horn, and, sometimes, coo as softly as a dove. Both notes accompanied the swish of a birch upon a bending sinner. This was of frequent occurrence, and, usually, preceded the evening meal when all the boys were assembled. Our old warrior enjoyed his part in those thrashings. It was, evidently, better to give than to receive,—as I could testify from bitter experience.

Well do I remember the funeral of that Master. The procession of half-terrified children sang "Down in the valley with my Saviour I would go," as we followed the coffin draped in an Union Jack. That mournful dirge will ever be associated in my mind with the first military burial for me to witness.

Our next Master was a Mr. Morgans, who was a married man. I have no recollections of his wife; but her husband was tall and soldierly. He always seemed to be labouring under a grievance, and found vent for his feelings by taking it out of five or six boys at a time. Delinquents were assembled straight after breakfast, and placed in a row before the others. The Master harangued them about honour, justice, and playing the game in life.

Then they were put through the dispensation of the birch. To sit at ease in Zion or anywhere else was an unlikely prospect for a few days after that laying on of hands. Birching seemed to be a pastime to Mr. Morgans; he resorted to it for almost every offence, until the Guardians interfered. Caning on hands only was allowed afterwards, and many were the stratagems devised by boys to mitigate the sting of a rod. One rub of resin was supposed to deaden the smack, and, in some cases, it might even snap the instrument of torture. The most effective method I practised more than once was that of elevating the hand to meet a descending cane. A wielder of the rod could not object, even if he discovered that trick.

The greatest evil of corporal punishment is not the pain inflicted, but the spirit of bitterness that is engendered; in time, a child regards an inflicter of punishment as an enemy to dread, and hate, and thwart. Again, it must be difficult for a master to keep on thrashing boys without despising them, and, at the same time, himself developing the spirit of a tyrant. The sergeant-major is not loved in the Army; an executioner is usually shunned by society.

But Mr. Morgans had his good points; he introduced many reforms into the administration of the Homes. He secured a trained gardener, a horse, and cart, and plough for the heavy work which used to be done by children on the farm. Under his regime, butter was given us in place of dripping; cocoa became an article of diet, and we were shod in boots instead of clogs. The Master interested himself in our games, watched over our studies at school, and encouraged initiative. Many of his former wards have had cause to thank the Master for his foresight and after-care when they had to face the great world outside.

The "Mother" in our cottage was a widow, Mrs. Lloyd. A daughter lived with her, and made frequent use of some boys as go-betweens in her varied, and, sometimes exciting courtships outside. The matron was a masculine sort of woman who ruled us with a firm hand. But, occasionally, she would unbend and act the real nurse to a child in pain. For some inexplicable reason I became her favourite, much to my surprise and to the chagrin of less fortunate boys. Her mood varied with the moon, or the weather, and I was petted or thrashed according to the prevailing whim. It was an unenviable position; but there were many advantages, and I have some pleasant memories of the irascible matron of that cottage.

Our day began at 6.30 a.m., by which hour we were fully dressed and washed. Each boy had some allotted task before breakfast, at eight o'clock. Weeding, digging, cleaning styes and stables required to be done daily; whatever the season or weather there was work awaiting every capable boy and girl, and the Master saw to it that we were fully employed until the gong sounded.

The morning meal of porridge, or bread and cocoa, was nutritious, if not plentiful. We got no second helping, and I cannot remember feeling satisfied before leaving the table. Perhaps that explains my freedom from indigestion. More people suffer through surfeit than are starved.

We marched in procession to school, about half a mile away, by nine o'clock; and returned for the mid-day meal of bread and broth, or meat and potatoes, by 12.30. Then back to school by 2 o'clock, and home for the evening meal of bread and milk, or cocoa, by six. We saw no more food until the following morning, unless our occasional depredations upon the sometimes unlocked larders proved successful. There were evening tasks on the farm, and play-time out of doors in the summer. We were in our dormitories at seven in winter, and by eight during the summer months.

Our most joyous time was spent at St. Peter's national school. There we found another world, and associated with children from outside; we attended the same classes

without distinction. Of course, we formed cliques and
gangs, and took sides. Cockett versus Forest Fach was
the order at games and, especially, in fights. Geography
determines many things in life and in theology. There
was, at least, one clash weekly, between the two divisions
—usually on Friday evenings after school. That was
the nearest approach to present day all-in-wrestling. No
missile was debarred, and every trick was permissible.
Blood flowed freely at times; black eyes and scratched
noses were week-end fashions. But nobody carried a
grudge to school on Monday morning. We shook hands
and remained friendly until the following Friday when
the struggle for supremacy was resumed.

St. Peter's was typical of the national schools of that
period. The building still remains, with very few altera-
tions, as a Council school. At the time of writing,
David Jones, the then schoolmaster, now in his eighties,
lives in honourable retirement. He was a strong, stern,
and cynical man who had received the appointment
when in his early twenties, and ruled a Staff of two assistants and two pupil teachers. The ritual of thrashing
was a serious affair in the old school, and Jones was an
artist at the task. He never hurried over it; but seemed
to extract the utmost thrill from the ordeal. So long as
one remained a mere spectator it was an education to see
the master arranging forms, testing a birch, taking a
practice swish, deliberately placing the culprit in position,
and then, with a sigh, setting to work accompanied by
the shrieks of his helpless victim. After David Jones
had finished chastising a boy, that lad might stand in the
way of sinners, and even walk in the path of the ungodly,
but he would not sit in the seat of the scornful for many
a day.

What a change has come over our school system since
those hectic days. Corporal punishment is discouraged,
if not quite forbidden, now; a cane is a curio; the birch
has vanished; an ordinary teacher dare not reprimand a
pupil, and parents, sometimes, prosecute a headmaster for

caning a child.   The new system is kinder and more
humane ; perhaps children also are more amenable to
persuasion than to compulsion.   Anyhow, persuasion
was rarely tried on us.   David Jones justified his liberal
use of the rod as a means of beating sin out of a boy,
and forcing knowledge into him.

Notwithstanding my many birchings at the hands of the
headmaster, we became very friendly as time went on. In
fact, I was selected to do some delicate work on his behalf.   Jones had fallen desperately in love with one of
his pupil teachers,—Miss Louisa Bamford.   I was commissioned by both to exchange their written communica-
tions ; this took place often for a considerable time.
Mine was a delightful position of trust, and not unre-
munerative ; many a penny did I receive, and, one day,
a whole sixpence was given me.   In my case, that was
wealth indeed.   But my boast aroused the cupidity of one
school-mate, who successfully relieved me of the burden
and peril of filthy lucre.

My kind patrons got married before I left school,
and remained the efficient Heads of St. Peter's for forty
years.

Some of my schoolmates, who were not Home boys,
achieved eminence in after life.

William John is miners' agent, and Member of Parliament.   At present, he is Secretary of the Welsh Parliamentary Party, and President of the Welsh Baptist Denomination.   John remains a loveable man, and is honoured by his Party.

W. H. Mainwaring also is miners' agent and Member
of Parliament, and has proved himself to be one of the
keenest minds in the Federation.

After a successful time at the Bar, and in Parliament,
Walter Samuel is County Court judge, and a prominent
figure in the public life of Wales.

The four of us were schoolmates who gravitated to
the mines, still retaining our friendship.

My most intimate friend at school was Abraham Thomas, who used to bring me chunks of cake the morning after each baking day at his home in Cwmbwrla. One day he obtained permission for me to visit his people. That was my first remembered sight of a real home. Since then, I have been guest at cottages and mansions in several countries, and am blessed with a good home of my own. But never was I so thrilled by a home circle as when my school chum's mother gave me the kiss of welcome to her modest hearth. That house was a plain workman's cottage devoid of luxury and costly furniture; yet, it was like heaven to a homeless boy who could remember no mother's kiss; a new world seemed to open before my astonished soul.

Abraham Thomas qualified for the teaching profession; but he died a year after leaving college; and I have failed to trace his family.

Although school friendships usually remain amongst the sweetest memories of life, one remembers comparatively little about those early days. Three incidents are embedded in my memory. In themselves, they seem trivial; yet each proved significant in after years, since I trace to them my three-fold hatred of deceit, of injustice, and of brute force.

One lad informed a few of us that he had found a tom-tit's nest containing four eggs. Two boys handed over a halfpenny each, whilst another and I gave the lucky one two marbles apiece to share in the find. We were all sworn to secrecy, and promised not to touch the eggs. On the following Friday evening, after school, five boys stood in awe before the nest and counted its contents. Last to leave the spot, was the proud, yet suspicious discoverer; he was taking no risks, but saw us all safely away from the neighbourhood of that El Dorado. He then resorted to an adjacent tuck-shop, and leisurely spent his easily won gains. But the four contributors to that lad's fortune desired more than a peep at the nest; and we met. It was only natural to demand a re-

count of the eggs, and to hold them for a moment or
two; there was one egg apiece staring us in the face.
After some hesitation, I agreed to extract the spoils, and
share them out. I leave readers to imagine the scene
when those "eggs" were found to be four balls of
putty!

A very dishevelled, sore and unhappy egg conjurer
dragged himself home the following evening after four
impoverished and disillusioned boys had satisfied their
desire for revenge upon him.   I have often wondered
what became of that illusionist.

The gangster spirit is no American monopoly; it has
operated in schools ever since Tubal-Cain assembled his
first Arts class (Genesis iv.), and is likely to persist so
long as boys mass together.   Gangs at St. Peter's national
school had little to learn from Dillinger, or Al Capone,
so far as organisation went.   After acquiring experience
in a few subordinate gangs belonging to lower forms, I
was initiated into gang number One; this was the ambition of every aspiring bandit in the school.   Oaths of
fidelity, obedience, and absolute secrecy were sworn, and
written in blood,—drawn from a slashed arm.   We had
stringent rules, grades of office, and a leader wielding
the powers of life and death; his word was final on all
questions, and we had no right of appeal; it was a pure
dictatorship as absolute as anything devised by Fascism
or Communism.   Fines, punishments, tortures even,
were threatened to traitors and rebels.   I was sentenced
to death once, and went in fear of my life for several
weeks.   Luckily, the selected executioner resigned from
the gang, and nobody would take on the mission he had
shirked.

An order would be circulated during the dinner hour,
and the gang met in the churchyard, immediately after
school.   The roll was called; and woe betide absentees!
Our leader then issued instructions, and, after rehear-
sing our parts to his satisfaction, we dispersed in groups
of twos and threes.   We raided orchards, stole turnips,

robbed hens' nests, fired gorse, smashed gates, dressed like ghosts to frighten people at night, and, collectively, avenged any slight put upon one of our number. Robin Hood was our patron saint, or ideal. We sincerely believed in robbing the rich to help the poor. As a matter of fact, our real heroes were robbers like Jack Sheppard, Dick Turpin, and Charles Peace, whose "*penny-dreadful*" biographies we knew by heart.

Ten days after my initiation, I realised the illusion of our Robin Hood pretentions. Four of us were ordered to raid a tuck-shop kept by an elderly widow. According to plan, two boys engaged the attention of the lady whilst fellow-conspirators filled their pockets with stuff at the other end of the shop. As soon as the signal was given, I grabbed the article nearest to hand, made for the door, and ran for all I was worth to our meeting place in the churchyard. Sweat was pouring down my face, and I trembled like a leaf whilst hiding behind a tombstone. In due time, the other raiders arrived, and I envied their coolness and nonchalance. Then came the order to pool the results of the smash-and-grab. One robber proudly displayed four bars of chocolate; three other boys brought forth handfuls of jujubes, chewing gum, and toffee. When I, shakingly, turned out my pockets, all I could show was a piece of soft sandstone. I had passed through the tortures of hell for that! Our disgusted leader literally kicked me out of gang number One, minus my share in the loot. But I was cured, for ever, of any stealing propensities that might have been lurking in my soul. Amongst my long catalogue of sins thieving does not find a place.

My last school fight also took place at the old churchyard. By then, I had attained the proud eminence of Cockett champion, and usually led our side in the weekly attack on a Raven Hill rabble. The greatest event in the school year for us boys was an annual fight between the respective champions of Cockett and Raven Hill.

For weeks before the appointed day, our school seethed with excitement; betting was heavy, and varied, almost daily, according to reports, "straight from those in the know." Marbles, tops, buttons, and pennies figured in the turnover; and we had smart bookies in the various gangs. Teachers could sense a prevailing tension, but were powerless to interfere; enquiries met with a conspiracy of silence and assumed ignorance; leakage of information could be traced, and would result in condign punishment. My rival for whole-school supremacy was Dan Evans,—the most affable bruiser ever known. Later on, he became a prominent member of the Swansea Town Council, and filled the Mayoral chair with grace and dignity. In reality, Dan and I feared each other. We had fought our way up to championship form and class by process of elimination; he was champion of his side, and I of mine. But there cannot be two leaders in a pack; duality of control will not last in school or State. So, much as we dreaded the ordeal, a fight was inevitable. On the great day, supported by twelve backers each, we met in the undeveloped part of the churchyard. Our crowd knew nothing about Queensbury rules; it was to be a fight to the finish with bare knuckles, and uncontrolled by a referee. There could be no peace without victory in that school; one fight lasted for three evenings in succession; night and mutual exhaustion were the only interruptions possible.

Dan was taller than I. He deliberately took off his coat, rolled up his sleeves, displayed his wonderful arm muscles, and then went prancing among his excited supporters who showered upon him advice and promises. I was in a blue funk myself. I had never seen such brawn and pugnacity, and I had visions of leaving the scene of my former triumphs a beaten cur. Pretending that my opponent was not worth a fuss, I refused to discard my coat, but took care that a line of retreat was kept clear. With no attempt to spar for an opening, I rushed in, and blindly let out a fierce right-hander which took

Dan off his guard, came in contact with his prominent nose, and knocked him down. There was nobody to separate us; so I jumped on to his chest and pummelled him until he acknowledged defeat. In less than three minutes the fight was over, and I rose to be acclaimed champion of the whole school. Then we ran wild, as my exhilarated backers, with one whoop, fell upon the opposing twelve, and drove them off the field. Little did Dan and his team realise that my lucky blow was the convulsive reflex of fear. He was a much better boxer than I, and could easily have put me to sleep in a proper fight. But, during the remainder of my stay at St. Peter's, I was feared and flattered by the whole school, and remained the acknowledged champion. It was a very unpromising beginning for the pacifist I became.

I was now to leave school, and no caged bird longed for freedom more than I did. Not a tear could I shed; neither did one sigh of regret escape me, when, finally, I said goodbye to that school. Upon reaching the age of thirteen, children of the Homes were given out to families who applied for boys or girls,—not, of necessity, with the object of adoption, but, usually, for the purpose of apprenticeship, or cheap labour. Farmers thus got young workers, housewives secured domestic servants, and ordinary working-class families augmented their income. Occasionally, a childless couple sought a boy or girl to fill the gap in a maternal heart, or on a bereaved hearth.

Forty years ago, very little after-care was exercised by the Guardians, and there were many scandals. But things have altered much for the better since those days.

I was allotted to a miner, Thomas Davies, and his wife, Mary, who, fortunately for me, sought a boy for adoption; and so began my great adventure in life. My equipment consisted of a passion for reading, an insatiate curiosity, and a grim determination to finish with school. Suicide seemed preferable to return at the end of the three-months trial period. I took with me a prize Bible, and six "penny-dreadfuls" which were gifts from school chums. Personally, I cannot disparage the latter sort of literature. It introduced me to a romantic world when pennies were scarce, and libraries seemed far beyond my reach. We read the badly printed booklets in all sorts of places, even in church; they gave us glimpses of freedom, abandon, and romance, heroism and defiance of fate, whilst we chafed at restrictions and shut doors. True, our heroes, apart from the Bible, were outlaws. But what boy is not a bandit, a rebel, a pirate at heart! As a corrective to natural law-breaking propensities, the "penny-dreadful" always ended with the punishment of crime. Even the envied rider of glorious Black Bess could not escape the gallows. Whatsoever a man soweth, that shall he reap.

After a forty year interval, it is difficult to recall my real feelings when leaving the Homes. An average man cannot delve very deeply into the subconscious. A so-called crisis is blurred with time, and loses its sharpness. What seemed momentous ten years ago may not cause a tremor today. Great controversies grow stale and uninteresting in a short interval. Mankind is blessed with a capacity for oblivion, and that is essential to sanity. Deity knows all; man must forget much. But we wish to remember the best, and to perpetuate the good. "God gave man memory so that he might have roses in December." We do not, willingly, re-live sorrow; time can rob pain of its sting; but memory enhances joy and increases the pleasure of long ago. The good men do lives after them —in the memory of posterity; it is the evil that lies buried with their bones. We try to speak well of the dead; epitaphs, usually, record virtues, real or imaginary; anger and censure should expire at the grave; harmony travels far; discords drop on the way. Said Tagore of two men who fell in a duel:

"They fought and they died, and God covered the spot with green grass and daffodils."

I love to recall the friendliness shewn me during my youth; and thrill yet at the memory of a pat on my shoulder when the world seemed black; the faded petals of a rose received from a teacher are still in one of my Bibles; many a romance have I read into those dead leaves. Heaven seemed very far from my boyhood; but sympathy brought it near sometimes. I cannot say with Tom Hood:

> "But now t'is little joy,
>   To know I'm farther off from Heaven
>   Than when I was a boy."

In fact, I felt much older at ten than when fifty years of age; because, it seems, of a morbid habit of asking questions for which there are no satisfactory answers: What is life? What is death? Do people live in the grave? Why should I repeat the Creed when I can make no sense of it? . . . . The Devil was more real to me than God, and appeared to be much more powerful. How could I love, or respect, a divine Detective and implacable Punisher of childish delinquencies? I dreaded Hell, but felt no desire for Heaven, and thought that the Creator needed forgiveness more than those who were the victims of fate. Of course, I had a false conception of life and of God, and have unlearnt much since then. But, I always try to give children kind thoughts about the Heavenly Father.

One disadvantage of institutionalism is the absence of disinterested love during the formative years of youth. Another is the inferiority complex instilled and encouraged; a child is taught to salute visitors, and doff cap to squire and parson as though they belonged to a superior plane of existence. But I have ever been a rebel at heart, and, in secret, despised patronage in Church and State. Consequently, my greatest handicap in life has not been lack of self-confidence, or an inferiority complex.

CHAPTER THREE

LLANSAMLET . . . LAUGHTER AND TEARS

ONE memorable afternoon I was called from a game of
football, and introduced to Mrs. Mary Davies, who
wished to make me her adopted son. That was my
first sight of the most remarkable woman to influence my
destiny. Hope and fear fought for mastery as I half
listened to what was being said to me at the time; at last,
the longed-for day had arrived. Occasionally, one
seems to live a whole decade in a moment or two; such
were my feelings as a new world opened before my imagination. For the first, but by no means the last time,
I was clairvoyant, and saw, beforehand, much that
since has happened.

Was it luck, or fate, or a beneficent Being that allotted
me to Mary Davies? Things happened so haphazard at
those Homes. On the whole they worked out fairly well
for boys, but, sometimes, results proved disastrous to
girls. When, later on, I engaged in rescue work at Swansea, I found three ruined women who had been former
inmates of the Homes, and they told sordid stories of
deception and desertion by people who once "adopted"
them.

I can vividly recall that first walk from Cockett to
my new home at Bonymaen, Llansamlet. I had not
been so far away before, and was very excited and
curious. Mary Davies knew little English, and not one
word of Welsh had I. Our attempts at conversation were
rather pathetic, and I noticed suspicious twitches on the
lips of my new benefactress as she tried to understand
and answer me; more than once she surreptitiously
wiped her eyes. But my questions came fast and insistent,
and must have been baffling to that simple soul; a smile

would be her only reply sometimes.   That was quite
enough until something else caught my eye or fancy.
And so we covered the five-mile walk,—a strangely-as-
sorted pair, but very happy; and I ever so anxious to see
my new home.

At last we came within sight of the semi-detached
cottage which was to shelter me for the next ten years.
It was, and still is in the midst of fields, within sight of
the English Channel, and with towns, great steel and
copper works, and high hills on the horizon. To my boyish mind the house resembled a magical palace. It was
there my soul awoke; and I loved even the smoke that
used to roll up in great clouds from the Landore furnaces,
much to the detriment of foliage and vegetation. There
was beauty for me in all things, and I expected to find
fairies everywhere, and at all times.   Yet, Bonymaen
was not, by any means, a model village, so far as social
amenities went. We had no street lamps to hide the
bespangled sky; watertaps were unknown in our houses,
and on the roadsides; the well that supplied us, and
seldom ran dry, lay nearly a mile away.

On alternate days, the women, in batches of three
or four, resorted there for a supply of fresh water; the
well was their meeting place for exchange of news. With
earthenware pitchers proudly borne on their firm-set
heads, and silhouetted against a purple sky-line during
the hour of sunset, they often resembled a placid scene
from biblical times. Much of the dignified carriage and
gracefulness of Bonymaen women resulted from the
custom of carrying things on their heads; they needed no
lessons in poise.

I loved our open spaces and winding paths that displayed no threatening warnings to wanderers. The little
wire fencing seen was merely for demarcation; and our
few hedges were jumped easily by boys and sheep. One
newcomer horrified the whole village when he introduced
barbed wire on his farm; the cause of offence was soon
removed.

c

We seldom locked our doors even at night. I cannot remember seeing a key to our back door; there was a bolt to the door at the front; but that door was not opened in any house, except for a funeral or a wedding. Neighbours walked in without so much as knocking; they simply called a name as they crossed the doorstep, and were sure of a welcome; we knew nothing about the artificialities of town folk.

Thomas Davies, the husband of Mary Davies, was a monoglot Welsh collier, of strong physique, a regular chapel-goer who conducted family worship, morning and evening, without a break, so long as he was able to read and pray. I knew his prayers off by heart; but would dread to descend the pit unless I heard those prayers said by that modest man before starting out for the day's toil in the mine. I do not remember him losing a day's work through sickness, until his break-down, about five years before his death, when I insisted upon his leaving the pit for good—which he did. He was painfully regular in all his habits, and rarely varied his routine. His farthest railway journey from home was to Swansea, three miles away. Although his earnings did not exceed two pounds a week, he saved enough money to buy two cottages at a cost of three hundred pounds, and also subscribed to a sick and burial club. He was not a lovable man, but readily helped those in need. Whilst sparing of speech, he could be stern, and his reprimand stung to the quick. Once only do I remember him really angry; it was after I had coaxed Mary Davies to buy me a watch, which, in his opinion, cost too much. He reduced my pocket money for the following two months; but his wife more than made it up on the quiet. I ought to add that six-pence a week was my allowance for a long time—three coppers and a threepenny bit, "And mind not to change it if you wish to become rich."

Thomas Davies worked underground for fifty-five years; he was bow-legged through being so continuously

in crouching positions along low seams; experienced two
explosions, and had been carried home twice after accidents. His was a small circle; home, work, and
chapel comprised his whole world. He read no
newspapers, either English or Welsh. The only monthly
magazine that came to the house was "*Trysorfa'r
Plant*" (The Children's Magazine); our whole library
consisted of the Big Bible, a Hymn Book, Barnes' Commentary, and an illustrated Pilgrim's Progress — all in
Welsh. I greatly grieved the godly pair when I brought
home a half-penny English weekly paper called "*Boys'
Friend.*" It was English, and had never been recom-
mended in chapel. The little Paper always disappeared
from my pocket by Sunday morning, and then, on
Monday, it would be facing me at my bedside.

Such was the typical Llansamlet collier of fifty years
ago. From a worldly standpoint almost illiterate, but
steeped in the culture of the soul, strong in the Faith of
his Fathers, puritanical in morals, and dependable in an
hour of crisis. When I decided to train for the Ministry,
Thomas Davies offered to sell, or mortgage, his two cottages, and so risk the savings of a lifetime to pay for my
education. Fortunately, the need for that sacrifice did
not arise; but he was unaware of the fact at the time.
How many people owe their chance in life to men and
women who had few opportunities themselves! I
revere the memory of the stern old puritan who did so
much for me, and wished to do more.

I could not do justice to the character and influence
of Mary Davies. Three women have dominated my life,
—my grandmother, Mary Davies, and my wife. The
one whom I must call foster-mother was a gentle
soul, who rarely raised her voice in anger; when
agitated, she spoke in a deeper note suggestive
of tears; a smile transfigured her face as if light radi-
ated from some inner source; and it was infectious like
that of an infant in arms. During girlhood, she had
served with the nobility, and gentility seemed natural to

her. Mary Davies would have made a wonderful Mother Superior at a convent; people confessed to her as a matter of course, and neighbours confided in her without expecting any response in kind; her piety was spontaneous, not forced or unnatural. That tender lady loved children; her only child died when six months old; I was the third boy for her to adopt.

Charles Rowlands passed on at the age of 21.

John Williams was in training for the teaching profession when he died on his eighteenth birthday.

Death had robbed Mary Davies of three loved ones; but her maternal heart craved for another whom she could love; and upon my undeserving head was poured the pent-up affection of a wonderful woman.

I shall always wonder at the faith and venture of Mary Davies and her husband. They knew nothing about my parentage, my temperament, my proclivities for good or evil; they saw before them a lonely boy in need of the love stemmed in their own hearts three times by death; and that love was given me unstintingly until I laid them both to rest alongside the three whose place I had tried to fill.

Llansamlet lies between Neath and Swansea. It remains practically unaffected by the English influx that has so anglicised those two growing towns. We were a world on our own, and essentially Welsh in tongue and sentiment. Save within the Council school, hardly a word of English was spoken throughout the village. The district is no health resort; yellow smoke then emitted day and night from the Landore and Upper Bank spelter and copper works destroyed vegetation; the little grass that survives is anaemic and pale; very few animals find pasture there; even sheep expired from the fumes. But, strange to say, humans flourish through it all; epidemics are unheard of in Llansamlet; longevity is quite common; one can find plenty of people in their eighties at Bonymaen, and centenarians are not unknown amongst that people. There was an old saying that Llansamlet folk were too full of sulphur to die a natural death, and that they had to be disposed of by forcible methods.

We were a hardy community, and nearly self-supporting. Grocer shops are still few and far between in the village; greengrocers and fruiterers lived at Swansea; they could not make a living in our midst; meat vendors had a very lean time of it, because our women folk bought their weekly joints of meat in the Swansea market, where they were renowned for driving hard bargains. A Llansamlet housewife would not dream of giving the price first demanded; and we knew that butchers always asked natives of Bonymaen for more than they expected to receive. Mary Davies used to walk round the market twice before fixing upon the joint she fancied, and would argue, then, for fully twenty minutes over the price. She left the stall after her modified offer had been rejected, and pretended to go elsewhere to buy; then back again we went, and the process of bargaining would be repeated, unless the joint had, by then, been sold, as sometimes happened. At last, they split the sum in dispute, and, soon, all was serene; tuppence or more had been saved on a joint worth three or four shillings; a bargain had been concluded, and each side was satisfied.

I remember one woman trying to beat down the price of a railway ticket, and then walking three miles rather than give the additional half-penny asked for by the booking clerk. Mary Davies once asked a postmistress to sell her three penny stamps for tuppence, and it took me a long time to convince her that such bargains were impossible at a post office.

Llansamlet women baked their own bread in outside brick ovens heated with logs of wood. "Shop loaves" would be a reflection on the industry of a housewife. We also grew our own vegetables; and potatoes, sufficient for the whole year, were stacked under mounds of earth. We reared two pigs yearly for home consump-

tion. A pigsty was a necessary adjunct to a Llansamlet dwelling as is a garage today for a town house;
it was certainly more profitable. One colliery proprietor
complained that he could not hope to break a colliers'
strike in Llansamlet because each family had three
mounds of potatoes and two pigs to fall back upon.

The pig was as important in our village as he is in
Eire; he was the gentleman who paid the rent, or interest on the mortgage; and he furnished the table most
days of the week when fresh meat was beyond our reach
and means. For us children, there were two stages in
the drama of the sty. I used to accompany Mary Davies
to Neath fair in the early Autumn, and to Llangyfelach
fair in the Spring. At each place, a piglet was bought,
after the usual process of bargaining; a rope was tied to
one hind leg, and we drove the awkward animal home.
On such days I received extra pocket money, and gorged
myself with figs, gingerbread and coco-nut. Buying a
pig was a great event to be celebrated worthily. Neighbours would welcome us home, guess the price and
weight of the new occupant of the sty, and wish its
owner a good season.

The climax of pigdom, for us, was the rite of killing.
Our village butcher was a collier named Henry Clement
who dispatched squealers in his spare time at two shillings
a head, plus a pint of beer at the kill, and another pint
on the day of cutting up the carcase. Those were the
only times alcohol appeared in our house, and it was for
the sole use of the man with the knife. Once, Henry
Clement gave me a sip on the quiet, and I was violently
sick in consequence.

I often lamented the death of the animals I had
helped to fatten; I used to grow fond of them, and hold
imaginary converse above the trough, and when cleaning out the sty. May not the most wayward of creatures
appreciate the friendly spirit of a boy? I cannot understand the catastrophe of the Gadarene swine; to
say the least, it was a waste of good meat; the swine-

herds were thrown out of work without a dole, and,
maybe, many friendships ended beside that diving pool.

The spare ribs (*mângig*) were cut into pieces of one,
two, or three pounds in weight. Those portions we gave
to neighbours; and I proudly carried the laden basket
round as though I were Santa Claus; naturally, I reaped a
copper and small silver harvest that day, and could save
up for the next fair.

Then came the day for salting the meat; two or three
neighbours helped with this, and a high tea followed.

How neighbourly we were in Llansamlet! A domestic
event interested every family in the village. We did not
pry into each other's business from mere curiosity, but
shared in the joys, the sorrows, the failures and successes
of all our people. In conversation we used no
" Mister " or " Miss," etc. ; the Christian name was suffi-
cent, and that without any suspicion of undue familiar-
ity. One peculiarity was the custom of retaining a
married woman's maiden name in addition to the name
of her husband, and then linking a child's Christian
name to the names of both parents. For instance, I was
called "Thomas Davyth's Mary Morgan's James"
(*James, Mari Morgan, Tomas Dafydd*), and am remembered so still by many.

A wedding excited the whole community, and that
for weeks before, and after the great event. The mother
of a prospective bride would invite women neighbours
to a " pastry tea." They came in groups of four, or
more, at a time, daily, for a whole week. No charge was
made; but a large plate remained prominent near the
door, and each woman would place her money gift upon
it. " *Gwystlon* " was the term applied to these donations, which were gifts repaid or donated. The object of
the feast was to call in old " *gwystlon*," and to accept
new ones which were repaid whenever a wedding or
funeral took place at the donor's home. No written
accounts were kept; but neglect of repayment would disgrace a family forever.

After the wedding, our newly married pair held another week of less elaborate teas for people near their own age, and gifts, in smaller amounts, were contributed in the same way. Thus was the home furnished and paid for. The hire-purchase system was unknown in our village at that time, although the Scotch draper was a familiar visitor.

Sometimes, beer was brought to the *"gwystlon"* suppers which were attended by the male population, and there were high jinks which brought the family into disrepute; then our chapel authorities interfered. One sedate villager was accused, at a church meeting, of being drunk in a *"gwystl"* supper; proofs were plentiful; he had been seen offering to fight the bridegroom and trying to kiss the young bride; then he careered homeward singing and disturbing neighbours in the early hours of the morning. Evidence was conclusive, and a majority of the elders wished to excommunicate the culprit. But, before they came to a decision, our senior elder, Thomas Beddoe, asked the sinner: "If we reprimand and suspend you for three months, will you promise to become a total abstainer?" After a long pause, the delinquent anxiously asked: "But what am I to do with the half-bottle of beer that is still in the house, Thomas Beddoe?"

Intermarriage was common at Llansamlet; nearly all the families were related to each other, somehow; and we pitied the stranger who interfered in our quarrels! Belated marriage, sometimes, caused trouble amongst chapel folks.

It was our habit to rejoice with those who did rejoice, and weep with others when in sorrow. Sickrooms were besieged by neighbours anxious to help; delicacies and messages of comfort arrived from all quarters. We had no district nurse; our only medical man lived two miles away, and we had no telephone to connect us with him. But every able-bodied neighbour offered to watch beside a sufferer during the night, and to minister to his or her needs.

Mary Davies was ever at hand. She soothed the last hours of scores, and saw them enter the Dark or pass on to the Light of some Beyond. After such times she would be very silent, but quite tranquil; and we moved about the house with softer tread. Death to her had no terror; but the poignancy of separation opened an old wound in her heart, and left a far-off look in her eyes, as though she were glimpsing a land of far horizons where dwelt a baby-girl of long ago.

For two nights preceding a funeral we held prayer-meetings, or 'wakes,' in the house of mourning. These lasted about an hour and a half, and that, sometimes, in a two or four-roomed cottage, packed out, and with many people standing about the doors, as well as around the house. There was great fervour, much weeping and wailing, and, not infrequently, women would faint and be carried out during the service. I know now that it was unhealthy and unwittingly cruel. But nobody dared suggest dispensing with the 'wake,' even for an ungodly and non-chapel-going family in sorrow.

On the day of burial, all blinds in houses along the route were drawn. Workmen either lost a day's work, or returned home in time for the service; we had prayer and singing at the house, and then formed a procession of two deep. An average funeral procession meant about two hundred people; there was no horse-drawn or motor hearse in the village; we carried the coffin on a bier. A master of ceremonies for the occasion, under the supervision of an undertaker, saw to the order of carrying and changing; with occasional pauses, we sang doleful hymns all the way to chapel. Then followed a full service, for an hour or more; a special preacher officiated, and he delivered a sermon appropriate to the occasion, after which we filed out to the grave-yard. If it was a fine day, more addresses and prayers followed before the committal and the last hymn of farewell.

The rural Welsh funeral is a protracted and exhausting ordeal. I have attended a burial which lasted nearly two hours in so modern a town as Colwyn Bay; on that occasion several women fainted. In fact, the Welsh seem to love funerals. They are the only nation I know of who rhapsodise over death and sing about the grave. Many Welsh hymns and songs end with death, or the glory of grief. An average Welsh minister is more eloquent at burials than in weddings; funeral orations come readier from him than speeches of felicitation at the festive board. "The Celt is always accompanied by a shadow."

The only occasion for men to wear gloves in Llansamlet, during my time, was at a funeral; then one saw old colliers entering church with gloved hands held out in front. The gloves, perhaps, did service for several families, over many years, and the fingers had never been fully filled; their ends drooped half-way down the palm as though in harmony with their environment.

Practically all our male population were engaged in the coal industry. There was no other opening for boys nearer than Morriston or Landore, where the great tin, copper, steel, and spelter works then flourished. We had nothing but coal excavated from pits and levels; naturally, boys gravitated to those places for employment, Even in coal we were a world of our own. We produced nothing but house-coal. The steam and anthracite coal-fields were elsewhere—in West Carmarthenshire, in Aberdare, and the Rhondda Valley. Consequently, we had no use for the safety or Davy lamp, but used candles and naked oil lamps, and were rarely troubled by gas. Neither did we fear unemployment; the great Combines had not arrived. A dissatisfied miner could go from pit to pit, and was always sure of employment. Workmen were more scarce than work, and a manager was glad, usually, to engage additional men and boys. Neither had the Machine come to displace human labour, and to revolutionise the whole industry. Hours were long,—at least ten a day; but we worked leisurely, and were not driven like cattle. Production always was of great importance; yet it was not the supreme consideration, as it is to-day. Colliery proprietors and workmen knew each other; they were neighbours, lived in the village, attended the same chapel, spoke the one language, and were interested in each other. The manager was approachable, and that without a go-between agent or committee; we were a family with mutual interests at the pit.

We had difficulties and problems then as now. Trade-unionism, collective bargaining, federations, etc., have done incalculable good, and are essential in an age of Trusts, Combines, and post-war Rationalisation of Industry. But missing are the human touch and neighbourliness of long ago, and we can see no prospects of regaining these for industry.

So long as we had regular employment and decent wages we rarely concerned ourselves about dividends and the surplus wealth of the owners. And some colliery proprietors grew exceedingly rich in those days; seams were cheap to work, especially in the levels; wages were low, and the demand for coal great; tremendous fortunes were amassed in an incredibly short time. Occasionally, colliers united to form a Company with a few hundred pounds capital between them. A group would lease or sink a level; they, with their families and friends, worked in relays day and night; and, in about eight or ten years they were able to retire as rich men. At the bigger pits, like Pwll Mawr, Tŷ-Draw, Pwll Charles, or Tirgwyllt, our wages varied with a sliding scale decided monthly according to the market price of coal. Every man and boy watched that scale jealously, and we demanded the last penny due to us. Changes in the scale occurred so frequently that local strikes continually broke out. The greatest sinners were boys, and not the men.

Every collier had his boy helper in the Tŷ-Draw pit; and, if the boy could not do without the collier, neither was the collier able to carry on for long without his boy, who was paid by the Company according to tonnage, just like the miner. For many years colliers were paid monthly. In my time pay-night was every fortnight; now it is weekly. Sometimes a boy's pay-sheet or envelope was a shilling or so short. A hurried meeting of carters would be called; an appointed spokesman approached the cashier; then, if that proved ineffective, we went in a crowd to the manager. Unless the money due was handed over by Saturday morning, all the boys refused to descend the pit, and no coal would be produced for that day. We took a holiday—and a good thrashing, perhaps, at home. I am surprised now at the leniency of our officials. A stoppage like that, to-day, would expose men to large fines, dismissal, and, maybe, jail. But we returned to work on the following Monday as though nothing had happened, and that would be the end of the business.

I remember being spokesman for carters at an interview with the manager, Ben Powell, a boisterous, but good-natured tyrant. "What do you want, boy?" asked the boss. "A rise, sir," was my stammering reply. With surprising agility the old man placed his boot where chairs are more appropriate, and literally raised me off the ground, saying at the same time: "There's a good rise for you, my lad," and that was all I heard as I limped after my cowardly crowd in their headlong flight for home.

We knew nothing about syndicalism and the general strike in those days. But a local strike of a few weeks, and even of several months, happened there sometimes. We did not resort to incendiarism or machinery smashing through. Pump and "safety men" remained at work, and paid a share of their wages into the Lodge funds for the support of strikers. There was no personal animosity; officials and owners were unmolested, and, with the workmen, continued to attend chapel. Such was not the case in other coalfields, where mounted police and soldiers had to be called in. Later on, I took part in the ferocious "hauliers' strike" at Aberdare, and I remember the Tonypandy riots, and the Llanelly clash. But Llansamlet was noted for peaceableness and its law-abiding colliers even during times of industrial unrest, strikes, and lock-outs.

I began my life underground as a door-boy. Less than a century ago girls of six or eight used to do this work. Only boys were engaged, in my time, for this lowest paid job in the mines. The next step up was carting; then tramming, and, ultimately, hewing coal. A hewer could develop into a contractor. Our first official was the fireman; next in prestige came the gaffer or under-manager, and at the apex was a manager, who had the last say in everything pertaining to the pit. Today, an Agent supervises the managers of a combine of pits.

How little ordinary citizens know about the life of miners! Sailors, soldiers, quarrymen, fishermen, and the men of the hoe have their poets, pictures, and publicity. But where is the dramatist of the mine? the artist of the collier? the poet of the pit? Winifred Owen, James Welsh, Lewis Morris, Galsworthy, and Cronin have done a little towards familiarising people with the lives that are lived in the bowels of the earth; but it takes a horrible explosion at Gresford or Newhaven or Duckmanton to disturb the complacency of the British Public concerning the labours and sacrifice of the men who heat our homes, drive our machinery, and propel our ships across the seas. Coal is the basic industry of Britain, and the collier is the worst paid and hardest worked of her citizens. About a thousand miners are killed outright in our mines, yearly; and eight thousand, and more, receive injuries. They work in wet places, with

insufficient or foul air, amidst danger to life and limb
every moment, and that for a wage less than is given to
a lamplighter, a porter, a scavenger or a game-keeper.
Policemen, postmen, and teachers are awarded pensions
after a stated period of service, and rightly so.   But
there is no provision for a collier who may have spent
sixty years working in the mines of Britain.   Belgium
pensions miners at 55, and their wives at 50; and yet
scores of thousands of British colliers died to save Belgium in 1914—1918!   Belgian miners are much better
off than British colliers.

I doubt whether door-boys are employed in the mines
to-day.   Our work was light, but important.   We opened
and closed wooden doors to let through trains of tubs
drawn by horses, or by wire ropes from an engine in
some other part of the pit, above or below.   It was necessary to shut those doors tight lest air should escape.   We
were very lonely, and had much time to ourselves.
Drowsiness was our weakness, and hauliers kept us
awake by telling creepy stories about ghosts and the
Devil.   Colliers are as superstitious as sailors.   Maybe
they have more cause for belief in the supernatural or
unnatural, since they work down in the heart of the
earth where man faces the unknown, and hears sounds
that are inaudible to people on the surface.   Those noises
were embedded in the forests of aeons ago, and after
centuries of silence, are now being released.   Is not the
earth a huge gramophone-record retaining every whisper,
each note, and all the utterances of the world?   Tele-
pathy also is familiar to miners, especially when working at night.   We could hear men hewing within a few
yards of us, whilst we knew at the same time that they
were sound asleep at home.   One could recognise a collier's grunt, and his knock of pick and sledge-hammer.
"Why does'nt that fool stay at home!" was the usual re-
mark in cases of that sort.   Sometimes we heard absent
men speaking near us.   One trammer reported that a
deacon was praying by him.   Lewis Morris (1754) at-

tributed noises heard in the lead mines of Cardiganshire to spirits called "knockers." He held a firm belief in their existence and beneficence (L.M. Letters. Vol. I., pp. 311-312; 321-322).

Here is a story believed in Llangyfelach. A collier named Small called as usual for his safety lamp. "I advise you to go home, Small," said the fireman. "Why?" asked the miner, "is the face too dangerous?" "There is no gas there this morning," replied the official, "but I think you had better go home, Small." After much pressure on the part of the man and some of his mates, the fireman said, "Small, I met you being carried out this morning!" That was quite enough for the man. He immediately went home, resigned from that pit, and found employment at Aberdare, about thirty miles away, where he worked for seven years. Ultimately, Small returned to Llangyfelach, and to the old pit. But on his very first working day he was carried out of the pit a mangled corpse.

We were not afraid of the squealing rats that scrambled over our clothes, or stole our food and candles. They seemed to be the scavengers of the mine. But one white rat was sure sign of an accident! A swarm of rats on the move was dangerous; discretion proved the better part of valour in such an emergency, because, in a crowd, rodents will attack man and beast. When a great number of rats make for the surface colliers prepare for some impending catastrophe at their pit. Just as sailors say that rats leave a sinking ship, we were told that, before an explosion, rodents make for the top. That actually happened at Morfa and Senghennydd when several hundreds of men and boys lost their lives.

After working as door-boy for nearly a year at 7s. 6d. per week, I was put to cart. The vehicle used was a wooden box on iron shoes, and shaped like a coffin. The seam we worked was a two-foot vein; so the cart was of shorter height, and five feet long; it held about two hundredweight of coal. One filled it to the brim, and then hitched his lashing to a hook, and, on all fours, dragged the box at a fair speed for about a hundred and fifty yards, more or less. The lashing was of leather, tied round the waist, and a chain that passed between the legs. In so confined a space boots would be burdensome, and were therefore discarded. For five years, whilst carting and tramming, I wore no boots when at work. Occasionally, one stepped on nails; but we thought nothing of that, and could run, bare-footed, on the roughest surface. Bare-footed youngsters who gambol about our streets do not suffer so much as pampered people think; there is a wonderful exhilaration in freedom from the thraldom of leather; open air is good for the foot as well as for the face. I never suffered from catarrh when I worked without footwear.

Carters were the most irresponsible set in the whole pit, and they gave endless trouble to their seniors and to the officials. We were always devising mischief and strikes. But an average boy is easily frightened by anything out of the ordinary.

My collier had left a candle alight in the " face " after finishing his day's work, and preparing for me a heap of loose coal to cart. All the boys in my level came together for a chat whilst awaiting tubs. One lad told a weird story about a haunted house, and I was very frightened when I returned to my cart and started for the " face." I can still recall the cold shivers running down my spine, and the yell I let forth at seeing a light galloping down to meet me. Back I rushed to the level where the other boys had been attracted by my shouts. I told them of the terror that had nearly overtaken me. One lad wished to rush the place; another advised calling the fireman; the only pious youngster amongst us suggested prayer and singing "Abide with me." At last, all together, we set forth to investigate the strange phenomenon, and kept on shouting our very loudest to keep up our courage. In the end, the candle, still alit, was espied being nibbled by a complacent rat on top of the gob. For years afterwards I was teased about that "corpse candle."

I shall ever remember the first fatal accident I witnessed. My collier was Edward Jones, a strong, vivacious, reckless man, aged thirty. Usually his language was lurid; but he would not swear in my hearing. The reason he gave his pals for this restraint was that he expected me to become a preacher some day, and that he had no desire to contaminate my mind. Jones lived a fast life, and was always in a hurry to leave work. One day, when about to fill his last tub for the shift, he would not spare time to prop the roof, and so took a foolish risk. There was a crack, a crash, a roar, and my collier lay buried under tons of rock. Death must have been instantaneous; it took an hour to extract the body, and two men were injured before we succeeded. My own escape was nothing less than miraculous, and it impressed me very much. Can I ever forget that covered still form, which, a few hours before, had been brimming over with fun and health! Work was stopped throughout the pit as we brought the corpse to the surface, and no more coal came up for the day. Then went the silent procession of begrimed men and boys to the home of the widowed mother bereaved for the second time by the call for coal. Our pit had claimed Edward Jones's father seven years before. There was no loud wailing at the cottage; our women suffered, in silence, a grief too deep for tears even,—a sort of stupor of sadness much more heart-breaking to witness than wailing hysteria. Great is the price of coal in life, and limb, and agony of soul.

The three most prolific causes of accidents in mines are falls of roof, explosions, and foul air. Not infrequently, men like Edward Jones lose their lives through sheer and inexcusable negligence. When I worked in the Shepherd's Pit, Cwmamman, near Aberdare, a very gase-

D

ous mine where over eight hundred workmen were employed, I saw colliers smuggling matches down the pit, and actually smoking, and in so doing endangering all those precious lives. There was no need to dismiss me from that mine.

Tramming was a very laborious task; we had no ponies in our pit; so men had to push as well as fill the tubs. The average amount of coal trammed by one man was between twenty and twenty-five tons in a shift of about ten hours. We had very little time for food; a trammer pushed the tub with one hand and ate from the other at the same time, unless, of course, both hands were fully employed on a gradient. Cold tea or water was swallowed whenever convenient; but a sit-down meal, or lie-down rest was quite impossible. Things became a bit easier when horses were brought in; but with the animals came hauliers, and they added a new terror to the life of the pit; hauliers were renowned for swearing. Some men sincerely believed that a horse could not, or would not, work unless sworn at. During the religious revival of 1904-1905 people had ocular evidence of this. Converted hauliers would not swear, neither did they use a whip; and their sagacious horses took advantage of such unprecedented forbearance; they refused to work for less than a full-throated curse or swear-word. What, in such a case, was a distracted haulier to do?

The great day for a collier is when he is given charge of a stall of his own; he is then a full-grown miner, and must be able to prop the roof, and co-operate with others. The old block-and-stall system, when we left pillars of coal to hold up the roof, has been discarded; a whole " face " is now worked clear by rows of colliers; props and cogs take the place of pillars. The " iron man " scoops coal where we used to hew laboriously; one machine, now, can do the work that was done formerly by twenty men or more. But the new method has its peculiar dangers to life; noise and rush make it impossible to hear warning sounds in the roof; hence the increase of accidents.

I spent three years at hewing coal, and earned good wages; but my propping of the roof rarely satisfied me; confidence there is essential to one's peace of mind and safety. I never fully achieved it, and was really glad to leave the pit.

Colliers are a wonderful class of workmen; they keep loyal to each other and to their leaders. Tin workers, etc., have rigid class distinctions; three or four trade-unions operate, sometimes, at the same works. Colliers maintain one Federation, and every attempt to form a rival organisation has failed, and must fail; equality and fraternity are more than catch-phrases amongst miners. That is why Socialism makes such progress in colliery districts. Colliers are naturally pious although prone to profanity; religious revivals that swept great parts of Britain in the past quickly spread amongst miners; such was the experience of Whitefield, Wesley, and Evan Roberts. Nonconformity, especially, finds a natural home and nursery with colliers.

The heroism of the pits is one of the unsung sagas of the centuries. What a drama was enacted in Tŷnewydd pit when brave men rescued seven entombed miners who had been facing death in a barrier of water held back by a few feet of air for seven days! One could multiply instances like that.

How kind they are to one another! They share their last crust, and are always ready to throw open their homes to the needy; adoption of orphans is very prevalent amongst them. Miners are easily exploited, and there is no end to their forgiveness; they sing like angels, and can blaspheme in poetry.

A colliery village after an explosion is an awesome spectacle:—children standing about in a hush, dry-eyed women stunned into speechlessness, the soft movements of doctors and nurses passing in and out of the cottages whose blinds are drawn, the processions of stretcher-

bearers with their covered burdens, the agonising vigil at
the pit head, the half articulate sob of despair as a cage
discloses its grim secret of mangled bodies. I
have witnessed it all more than once,—the calvary of
the collier. And the stolid courage of women is as
wonderful as the bravery of their men.

Many are the victims of the mine. Explosions account for about one-tenth of the total; more than half
of the accidents, I believe, could be prevented. And it
is time to counteract diseases incident to coal-cutting;
myosis is common; silicosis is more prevalent still. A
medical man told me that the lungs of one miner were
hard walls of congealed coal-dust.

I doubt if a beneficent Creator ever ordained that
human beings should labour in the darkness and dangers
of the mine, and that industry must despoil the face of
the fair earth with ugly tips and belching furnaces, and
that children shall live in the sordid surroundings to be
found in some old colliery districts. Think of the
monotonous long rows of cottages, back to back, with
no gardens, no green fields near, no baths within, and
the beds occupied by relays day and night. One outside privy has to serve three or four families in some
places. What surprises most observers is the high
moral tone and sense of decency, the culture and peaceableness found under such conditions. If I had to live
in Mid-Rhondda or Ynysddu, with my present experience, I should certainly be a revolutionary. Maerdy is
called " Little Moscow"; but, why " Little "?

This brings up the question of leadership.

The easiest way to prominence in Trade Unionism is
through agitation. A man makes himself a nuisance to
those in authority, and they, then, try to stifle criticism
with patronage, and by admitting the firebrand into their
councils. Frequently, office and responsibility will
bring the agitator to heel, and, soon, he becomes as active
in defence of officialdom as he was previously in at-

tacking it. In the Miners' Federation, A. J. Cook was a rare example of continuity of revolt.

I knew several of the old Welsh miners' leaders during 1895—1926.

Mabon (William Abraham) hailed from Cwmavon, and often occupied my pulpit at Tabernacl. He possessed a powerful voice, and did not need the help of loud-speakers when addressing crowds. Mabon dominated a situation by his natural wit and raciness of speech. He was a born leader of men, and averted several strikes through sheer common sense. For many years his leadership was unchallenged by masters and workers, and, so far as I know, he was the only democratic leader to add his name, temporarily, to the Calendar. " Mabon's Day " was a monthly holiday throughout the South Wales coalfields for long. Mabon started the agitation for an eight hour day " from bank to bank." The leader had his critics, who, in time, became vocal. There was one libel action when substantial damages were awarded the veteran. Mabon died a rich man.

John Williams, Gower, was accommodating, and could always find a way to compromise; he succeeded in maintaining the peace for years; everybody liked him, and he paved the way for one of the finest Parliamentarians of our generation—David Grenfell.

William Brace came into prominence through his attacks upon the old school of leaders. We called him the " Dandy " of the Federation. His ferocious moustache, mellow voice, and grammatical English (a rare accomplishment in a miners' agent then) were real assets for an aspirant to office. I believe that Brace was the first monoglot Englishman to attain leadership amongst the miners of South Wales; but he soon made headway, and did much to oust the old brigade. He also introduced new aggressiveness into Labour, made more use of the daily Press, and relied less upon the Liberal Party to further the cause of the miner; he was in close touch with Keir Hardie, and, consequently, was held in suspicion by the Mabon school. Brace took office under Government, during, or immediately after the war, and so was lost to Labour.

I spent much time during holidays with Tom Richards, who was one of the most unselfish and disinterested of men. He had no axe to grind, no selfish purpose to serve; he lived for the Labour Movement. He was a deeply religious man, a deacon in his church at Beaufort, and, later on, at Cardiff, a lifelong total abstainer, a serious thinker, and a powerful orator who could sway a crowd anywhere. As President, and when Secretary of the Federation, he became a mighty force in the country, and was sure of a full House whenever he stated the cause of the miner in the House of Commons. Richards told me once that when a party of Welsh M.P.'s visited France, Mabon led them in singing Welsh airs and hymns. The then French President requested an encore of one piece. To the joy of the leader and the amusement of all the singers, that request was for another rendering of "*Sosban Fach*"— the war cry of Llanelly Rugby footballers.

I met Keir Hardie once; and he made a lasting impression upon my mind. Rugged, bearded, wearing a cap, slight of frame, with challenging eyes, he was one of the most perplexing personalities of our period, and did more pioneering work for his class than any man belonging to the Labour Movement. Hardie was the real founder of the Parliamentary Labour Party which made possible the first British Labour Government. He aroused bitter enmity and made strong friendships wherever he went. At one time, he was, undoubtedly, the best hated man in British public life. Pulpit, Press and Platform attacked him without restraint; there was real malignity behind the abuse poured upon his shaggy head; it was a coalition of hatred and of scorn. Conservatives, Liberals and Trade Unionists competed in a campaign of calumny; there has been nothing like it in our generation,—not even during the years of war hysteria.

One Sunday I heard a Welsh minister preaching about, or against, the Devil. The name of Keir Hardie figured prominently in that discourse, and I failed to understand whether Hardie was supposed to be the Devil or that the evil One was Keir Hardie; they got so mixed. For about two decades that was typical of the prevalent attitude towards the unselfish Scot in South Wales.

W. F. Phillips, a brilliant, but not over modest fellow-student of mine, engaged Hardie in public debate once. The patience and forbearance of the Labour leader as he dealt gently with an inexperienced and presumptuous youth surprised the whole of Wales; Phillips was first to express his appreciation of so much magnanimity at the hands of the finest debater I ever heard.

Keir Hardie was born in a single-roomed cottage on a Lanarkshire coalfield, and was one of nine children to inhabit that single room. His mother taught him to read. When six years old he was at work, and, temporarily helped to maintain the family with his wage of 4s. 6d. a week. For several nights he nursed a brother who was ill with fever; this made him twice late for work in the morning. On the second occasion he was dismissed, and deprived of a fortnight's wages.

When nine years old he was working twelve hours a day in a coal mine. Before reaching his twentieth birthday he had educated himself to read Latin and speak French.

" For many years, mocked by the parasites he threatened, doubted by the workers he wished to help, flayed by the Press, excommunicated by the society church, feared by his contemporaries in the House, shunned by all who wished to remain respectable, this remarkable man went up and down Great Britain fanning the Labour smoulderings into flame" (J. R. Clynes.)

Hardie gave away two fortunes, and died worth half his year's salary as a member of the House of Commons. The war broke his great heart.

Was it mere coincidence that the three leading pacifists of their generation died about that time?

August Bebel,—mighty orator, trusted leader of the working classes in Germany, unsparing and fearless critic of the Big Navy school in the Land of the Kaiser, —died of heart failure August 13th, 1913.

Jaurés, the foremost socialist and pacifist of France, was assassinated on July 31st, 1914,—a few days before the declaration of war; his assailant, although arrested, was not punished.

J. Keir Hardie, pioneer of Socialism and absolute pacifism in Britain, passed on, September 2nd, 1915. He was a man of faith, vision and indomitable courage. His successors must face other difficulties in the crusade of democracy; but the example of Hardie will remain their perpetual inspiration.

The most disastrous leader miners had in our time was A. J. Cook. As Secretary of the Federation, he would not compromise, and critics admit his integrity. But he was deficient in all that makes for a good negotiator. Logic he despised, and a catch-phrase or resounding slogan always signified more to him than any argument. When the miners threw over Frank Hodges for Cook they committed industrial suicide; and the general strike, engineered chiefly by Cook, split the Federation, and put back the Labour Party for a decade or more. Nevertheless, the miners remained loyal to their Secretary until his early and tragic death. Cook was a sincere though stubborn soul.

THE CHAPEL ON A HILL

CHAPTER FOUR

THE CHAPEL ON A HILL

SOCIAL and religious life in Llansamlet revolved about chapels; and especially around Capel-y-Cwm, the oldest in the village.

Howell Harris, the noted Welsh revivalist, started the Cause in an old farmstead, about 1742, on the side of a hill. So prominent a site for a Nonconformist chapel was exceptional at the time; the early dissenters erected their little Bethels away from the public highways; secrecy was a serious consideration in times of persecution. But, evidently, Cwm Nonconformists were defiant and aggressive; they selected a position that was visible on all sides over a large area. More significant still, the site had been utilised, previously, for cock-fighting.

Salem, the second and enlarged edifice, was circular, and had high backed pews with doors, a seating capacity for 500, oil lamps, no heating apparatus, no cushions, and no carpets except one small strip on the stairs of the high pulpit. "Woe to them that are at ease in Zion" did not apply to Capel-y-Cwm. The heat of the over-crowded chapel in summer made us uncomfortable. Intense cold during the winter months rendered it advisable to huddle together for warmth. We spent long hours in that sanctuary, Sundays and week-nights, and were glad of somewhere to meet our friends. The village had no theatre, no cinema, and no lamps to illumine our unpaved and rough roads. The chapel was a centre of light and interest to which the whole village gravitated; there we sang and prayed, worshipped, and found romance.

Our congregation was divided,—males sat on one side of the chapel, and females on the other; families even were separated in this way.

For a long time, we had no musical instruments of any sort. A precentor gave the key-note from a pitch-fork which he struck audibly on his upraised knee, or against the side of a pew, and we sang in harmony. There were many "slurs" in the old tunes; the elderly folk loved them, and often improvised new ones. William Williams, our precentor, would run the scales of the modulator, up and down, between lines, sometimes, as he turned, alternately, to face each side of the congregation. One of his deputies was quite as wonderful; that man could make every hymn, whatever its metre, go to the tune "Old Hundred." If there happened to be a surplus line, it would be squeezed in somehow.

I remember a time when only two hymn-books were available in the whole chapel,—one in the pulpit, and the other for the use of a precentor. Our congregation knew their hymns so well, books were not essential at a service.

Preaching was the most talked of part in our chapel life. I listened to sermons that lasted an hour and a half, at Cwm, and that when I did not understand the language. We read that John Jones, Talysarn, preached for two hours, occasionally, and three times a Sunday. When on itinerary, the early Methodist preachers did this daily for weeks at a stretch, and travelled on horseback from place to place. Field-preaching was no strain upon them. We are told that John Jones, of Blaenannerch, when in the "*hwyl*" could be heard half a mile away.

Welsh people are passionately fond of preaching; it thrills them as opera or pageantry does other nations. All the emotions are brought into the service of the pulpit in Wales; oratory, drama and music find scope in Welsh preaching. For long we had no other outlet for the born actor, the national leader, the moulder of public opinion.

Even to-day nothing can draw and retain a Welsh crowd like a preaching festival when favourites ascend the pulpit. Preacher "fans" will travel many miles to hear well-known pulpiteers. The sermon remains chief feature of a religious service with us.

Let it not be imagined though that our folk overburden their preachers with worldly wealth. Some of our great pulpiteers have lived in poverty, and died in debt. But, when a minister's need becomes known, the whole nation, irrespective of sect, comes to his help, or to the aid of his family.

At the Old Chapel on a Hill during my boyhood the supreme favourite preacher was Edward Matthews, of Ewenny,—a rugged, heavy, slow man with a leonine sort of head, side whiskers, bushy overhanging eyebrows under which one saw dreamy eyes that sometimes flashed with hidden fire. He was unique in the Welsh pulpit because of his style of oratory, and for sermon composition. Unlike his rival, David Saunders, Matthews did not intone; his was conversational preaching with an occasional shout that thrilled an audience. The typical Matthews sermon was pure drama ending in a mighty climax which left a crowd gasping or shouting with the joy of some great discovery. I heard him twice, and was too young and insufficiently conversant with the Welsh language to appreciate the light and shade, the humour and pathos, the sarcasm and wooing notes of that exceptional preacher. But I could follow the Shepherd in His eager search for the wanderer, the anxiety displayed by our congregation as we all accompanied Him, and the wild ecstasy of finding a lost sheep. I know of nothing even to-day in sermonic literature equal to that discourse on the "Lost Sheep" for drama. But to have heard it from the lips of Matthews was an unforgettable experience.

Matthews occupied our pulpit three Sundays every year. Although he would be announced to preach for the Sabbath only, people flocked to chapel on the

Saturday night, and demanded a service. The same happened each visit.

I sometimes think that South Walians worshipped that man.

Owen Jones, from Penycae, and two friends stood outside Taibach chapel on a Sunday morning after Matthews had delivered one of his great sermons.

"Boys!" exclaimed the old man, "do you really think that Jesus Christ was a greater preacher than our Matthews?"

Probably we hear our best preachers before we reach the age of twenty-one. I listened to mighty preaching at Capel-y-Cwm; but then the environment was so congenial! A man who failed to preach there would be inefficient everywhere for preaching.

A remarkable institution in Welsh Nonconformity is the Big Pew (*Set Fawr*) situated between pulpit and the ordinary pews in a chapel. The origin of this enclosure is wrapped in mystery, and one can only guess its object. Occupants of the Big Pew are influential people, and leaders of a church. Of late years, women elders have been admitted to what used to be a male preserve. Elderly folk are not yet reconciled to the invasion; they look askance at women elders and female preachers. Did not Paul say "Let women keep silence in the church"? It is almost blasphemy to insinuate that the great apostle had been disappointed in love, or suffered at the hands, or from the tongue of a garrulous wife, as did Socrates and John Wesley.

Some historians regard the *Set Fawr* as an improved penitential form. If that is correct there has certainly been an improvement in the seating comfort accorded occupants. The Big Pew is the most luxuriously furnished part of a modern chapel.

Personally, I think the *Set Fawr* is a remnant of the old body-guard that formerly stood between a preacher and hostile crowds when unlicensed or itinerant preaching was illegal. The early Methodist evangelists stood in special need of such support. Grunts of approval or encouragement are still fashionable, especially in South Wales; more so amongst militant Baptists and Congregationalists than with staid Presbyterians. North Walians are usually silent and sedate; an "Amen" or "Glory" shout would cause something like a sensation in North Wales; but South Walians expect audible support from the Big Pew; silence indicates doubt or disapproval.

Sometimes a vocal affirmation is given in the wrong place, as that veteran, the Rev. Philip Jones found once. He was reading the first Psalm, and a Baptist listener interposed the customary "Yes! Yes!" All went well until the minister came to the verse: "The ungodly are not so." "Yes! Yes" exclaimed the Baptist. "No! No!" exclaimed the reader to the accompaniment of general laughter from the congregation, " the ungodly are not so. Man, do you know better than the Psalmist?"

A preacher may expect help too much from the Big Pew, and show his disappointment and disgust if it does not come. The late Rev. Philip Gelly could not get a single word of encouragement out of the occupants of a Big Pew at one fashionable church. In the course of his sermon he endeavoured to show the difference between what was possible and that which is likely; and this is how he illustrated the point: "It would be quite possible for the people of this Big Pew to say one "Amen" to the sermon; but such an unheard of event is unlikely."

Another witty preacher begged a mother not to take her crying babe out of the chapel,—it was the only sound of life in the place: "And if you wish the little one to sleep, bring him into this Big Pew, they are all asleep here."

A mischievous son of one minister is said to have undertaken to keep the occupants of their Big Pew awake by shooting peas at their bald heads; and, when the horrified father called upon his offspring to desist, the lad replied, "You go on preaching, dad, and I'll keep them awake."

The prevalent impression is that those who sit in the Big Pew are defenders of the Faith and custodians of church discipline. I know from experience that criticism of a man's orthodoxy emanating from the Big Pew is something to be respected by young preachers.

A minister noticed that his senior elder always slept under the pastor's sermons, but knew also that the brother was most alert in the presence of visiting preachers. One day he voiced his grievance to the well-known critic: "Ah, Pastor, you need not worry," said the somnolent one, "you see, when those strangers occupy our pulpit I must watch and listen carefully lest they poison the minds of our people with some heresies; but when you preach, I can relax; your preaching will disturb nobody."

The origin and function of the Big Pew are among the mysteries of history. English Nonconformists have no use for the institution. But the laudable ambition of an average Welsh Presbyterian is to face the congregation as an acknowledged leader of his church; like membership of the House of Lords, it is a seat for life.

Who can say whether the Big Pew or the Pulpit has been the greater force in the moulding of Dissent!

We had a wonderful set of men in our Big Pew at Capel-y-Cwm when I first went to the church. I think they were eleven in all—like the apostolic band, without Iscariot. We counted four ordained ministers in the group.

Ezeciel Thomas was considered a scholar, and had published one commentary on the Epistle to the Hebrews, a very original, fanciful, inaccurate, but refreshing booklet. On the strength of this he was appointed co-examiner with Principal Thomas Charles Edwards in the Synodical examination of candidates for the Ministry. Whoever was responsible for that arrangement must have possessed a keen sense of humour, because the two examiners represented different worlds. The cultured Principal of Aberystwyth University College was an authority of European fame on the Epistle to the Hebrews; his commentary in the Expositor's Bible series still holds the field for scholarship and exposition.

The chief text-book for that Synodical examination was the Epistle to the Hebrews. One candidate quoted the "learned commentary of the Rev. Ezeciel Thomas" in practically every answer.

"And would you believe it," said Principal Edwards to a friend afterwards, "the old prophet Ezeciel insisted upon awarding 125 per cent. marks to that man! It was useless telling my fellow examiner that 100 per cent. meant full marks; 125 and no less would he give the young rascal."

Ezeciel Thomas was very restless, and rarely would walk sedately. He was buried near the doorstep of the chapel he loved so much. When they lowered the coffin the bearers found that it was too long for the grave, and since rain was pouring at the time, they left it on edge until the sexton could improve matters and put the old patriarch to rest for once. But the saying goes that the coffin never was laid flat down, and that the old preacher is already half way through the resurrection.

Thomas Richards had been in two pit explosions; his face was marked with blue scars and looked rather unsightly; but, like Thomas John, Cilgerran, who was said to be positively ugly, Thomas Richards was transfigured when deeply stirred in the pulpit. He had wonderful Scriptural knowledge, could quote the Bible upon almost any subject, and preach a whole sermon by stringing verses and hymns together. I heard him quote nothing else. He was so unassuming and reserved that people sometimes underrated him. Dr. Saunders sent him to preach in his stead at an Association in Machynlleth. Nobody there knew the man from Llansamlet, and he seemed so insignificant that those responsible for the arrangements put him to preach at 6 a.m., when the congregation would be sparse. But Richards had a pentecostal time; his listeners were deeply moved, and the service ended in a great outburst of singing and weeping; the whole town was stirred. Consequently, the deacons arranged that Richards should preach again at the evening service. But the wise minister had fled.

During a three weeks' preaching tour in the company of William Jones, Morriston, Thomas Richards delivered thirty-five sermons without one repeat, and made no use of written notes.

Richard Howells was refined, gentle, winsome, and had a sweet tenor voice which he used with effect when in the *"hwyl."* Unlike two other monoglot ministers at Cwm, Howells possessed a smattering of English which he practised on me in church meetings with amusing results sometimes, especially when he rendered spontaneous translations from Welsh for my benefit. He translated well-known hymns, very freely. Just like the one I heard of

> *" Gwnes addunedau fil*
> *I gadw'r llwybr cul,*
> *Ond methu 'r wyf."*

thus

> " A thousand vows I've made
> To keep the narrow path;
> It can't be done."

I retain sweet memories of the minister who did his best to initiate a monoglot English boy into the mysteries of religion and the Welsh language.

Thomas Howell Jones was quite unique in his day. His '*hwyl*" was sweeping in range and effect; he could manipulate a rich baritone voice at will. Prayer was his forte rather than preaching; he was called " Thomas the Man of Prayer " throughout South Wales. An Associa-

tion seemed incomplete without him to take the devotional part; popular preachers like Owen Thomas and Henry
Rees used to request his help, and, very often, the prayers
of Jones were remembered much longer than the sermons
of the great orators. At one Cilfynydd Association my
old friend was put to preach, a most unusual event. But,
for once, he had a greater time at preaching than in prayer. His theme was "The Accusing and Redeeming
Blood." The climax to that sermon was one illustration
taken from an assize trial for murder, when the most
damning evidence against a prisoner was an article of
clothing besmeared with the blood of his victim. Our
preacher drove his point home by waving a red handkerchief before that vast congregation, and shouting along
the whole range of the modulator: "The Blood! The
Blood! The Blood!"

Such a scene was unprecedented at that chapel;
scores of people professed conviction.

Jones was in much demand at funerals, and it was said
that he could sing (intone) the worst sinners into heaven.
He was requested once to preach a memorial sermon to a
suicide; the text he chose was: "Judge nothing before
the time."

The old preacher read but few books; yet he frequently purchased expensive volumes for me.

There were other ministers belonging to the Cwm—
men like the saintly Lewis Morgan; Samlet Williams,
musician and prolific author; beloved John Richards;
versatile David Hughes, and his son. But these were
not among the occupants of the Big Pew in my time.

Our elders were as wonderful as the ministers. In
the very centre sat Thomas Beddoe, with a long white
beard, stooping shoulders, and a voice that usually trembled. He was senior elder, not only by age, but because
of his influence in the church. Beddoe always spoke
last, and nobody dared say a word on any subject after
he had finished. However stormy the meeting, our

E

senior elder would close by saying: "Pray for the peace of Jerusalem." To us children, God was a glorified Thomas Beddoe, and I have hardly grown through that idea even yet. How some impressions of early years cling to one! After all, are we very far from reality if we read Deity into the noblest found in mankind? "Behold the Man"—and we worship the God-man or Man-God!

Evan Jenkins was a tailor living in Swansea; twice a Sunday he walked the four miles back and fore to Capel-y-Cwm; also on Monday evening for the prayer meeting, and Thursday to the "Society" or Church Meeting. Like many pliers of needle and thread he was a poet, and composed hymns which he recited, and we sang, at week-night services. One of those hymns found its way into the official hymn book of the Denomination: *"Duw-ioldeb yn ei grym"* (504).

Others amongst our elders were strong characters and influential men. But the most remarkable was Evan Sims; he was rather small of stature, and seemed shorter than he was because of an habitual stoop and downward glance. When I first knew him he looked old, with a full beard and longish hair (donkey crop) turned grey; and yet he could not have been fifty. A grocer by trade, his shop was remarkable for the things excluded from it; tobacco was taboo: "If God had intended men to smoke there would be chimneys on their heads." Vinegar found no place in that shop: "It reeks with alcohol." For many years tea could not be procured there either:—"It pollutes water, and is unhealthy."

Sims was troubled by beggars, of whom there were two classes, viz., the profane and the pious. The first question asked every one of them was: "Have you prayed to-day?"

Members of that profane fraternity would reply: "Naw, I never pray." Then Evan would say: "If you want help, come into the house and begin praying now." Sometimes, that drove the hardened sinner away;

occasionally, a mendicant was reminded of prayers learnt at a mother's knee. But the pious beggar would answer glibly: "Yes, Boss, I prayed this morning."

Sims understood human nature fairly well, and, innocently, would retort: "Come in, it will do you no harm to pray again." On one occasion a tramp was overheard to sigh: "Good God, what shall I do." The old grocer rejoined: "That's a good start my man; come in to breakfast."

A rough specimen of humanity was invited to stay with Sims overnight, and he determined to have a cosy time at the expense of the elder. During family worship that night Sims prayed for his guest by name; that made the sinner perspire. But when his host proceeded to plead for the family (which had been deserted), and to commit wife and children to the loving care of a Heavenly Father, the visitor groaned, and tears began to flow. Then Sims fervently besought grace, pardon and cleansing for the man, and the opening of the door of mercy for a prodigal's return. This proved too much for the stranger who rushed out of the house as though the Furies pursued him. Speaking of his experience to a pal, he exclaimed: "Man, it was an awful place, and too hot for me!"

Sims himself knew very little about business; his wonderful wife took care of him, the shop and the children, whilst her husband gave his time and energy to the chapel.

He was reared in the chapel house where ministers are entertained, and many were the stories he related about that period.

The old "chapel house" was a meeting place for ministers and elders. Long pipes and shag tobacco were supplied at that period, and in the older times, ale as well. The *tobacco of the Cause* was always available in Capel-y-Cwm during my youth, and there I first learnt to smoke; but we were not supposed to carry any of the weed away with us.

It was in such an environment Sims had been reared.
He kept school in the chapel vestry for a time, and taught
children reading, writing, and the rule of three. In addition, he did letter writing on behalf of his illiterate
friends.   A man possessing such accomplishments was
important in the village, and would be commissioned to
deal with correspondence for his neighbours.   One
much sought scribe carried on the courtship correspondence of a young friend, and ended up by himself marrying the lady he had been paid to win for another.

Whilst Sims was schoolmaster and single, he slept in
the vestry; the bier was his couch.   A few of his men
friends who used to visit him of an evening determined
to cure him of this habit; so, one night, a length of strong
rope was tied to two legs of the bier, and the plotters
waited outside until Sims extinguished his candle.   No
sooner had the schoolmaster fallen asleep than the bier
and its sleeping burden began sliding towards the door.
Sims awoke with a start and let out some piercing yells
before the funeral movement stopped in front of the
locked door.   Our elder did not sleep on the bier after
that; but he never referred to his weird experience although many attempts were made to draw him.

His marriage was a romance; two articles comprised
his courtship creed,—there was to be no courting on
Sundays, and no time was to be wasted.   He was not
quite so precipitate as the Welsh preacher who turned
to a lady of his acquaintance, and nervously asked her to
marry him.   "But, Mr.——," replied the coy maiden,
"this is very, very sudden."

"It is to be now or never," was the uncompromising
answer.   They were married within a few weeks.

Sims was not so sudden as that, but he dreaded a
protracted courtship.   In fact, our puritan ancestors de-
plored the necessity of any courtship.

David Williams, a bachelor minister from Llanwnda,
was asked whether he would not like to get married some

day. Said he: "I would get married were it not for that silly business of courtship."

After his marriage, Sims gave up teaching, and opened a grocery store; but he spent more time in chapel than at the shop.

He was a great Bible reader, tense and definite at prayer, and usually pleaded for Jews and Gipsies; he could pray anywhere, under all circumstances, and had petitions suitable for every occasion, and an appropriate portion of Scripture. There was no trace of cant or sanctimoniousness about his piety; it was his life and atmosphere.

Irreligious men on street corners would remove their pipes when Sims approached, and oaths expired on their lips in his vicinity; it was an illustration of the persuasive power of natural piety.

He was responsible for arranging the "Wakes." On one occasion Sims was too precipitate. A report came to hand on a certain Sunday that one neighbour was unlikely to survive the night. Consequently, Sims announced, during the evening service, that a prayer meeting would be held at the dying neighbour's house on the following Tuesday night, and the funeral take place on Thursday. When we arrived at the house where mourning should be, we found that the presumed dead brother had taken a turn for the better, and was likely to live for many a day.

Sims strongly opposed picnics and Sunday School treats; his annual protest ended with the verse: "And the people rose up to play." Strange enough, however we altered the date for our treat, it usually rained, and children in their wet finery would be heard crying: "Old Evan Sims is praying!" Some of the elder scholars added: "Blast him!" Everybody believed that our puritan's prayers affected the weather.

Long before the Welsh Sunday Closing Act Sims canvassed public houses to advocate closing on the Lord's Day.

Three of us held a prayer meeting at 9 o'clock every Sunday morning for several years. Sims was leader, John Beavan came next, and I was like a child between them. Beavan had lost his memory as the result of a pit explosion, and could not remember anything for long, except his Bible and chapel; his name even slipped him at times; but he rarely missed a service at Cwm.

We would carry on a meeting for a full hour of reading, singing, and praying. The singing was not very harmonious; reading also must have been excusably faulty; the prayers were not insincere, long, or mere repetitions.

For over two years I had been allowed to read and to recite hymns; but one morning Sims said that I might engage in prayer also. After reading a long chapter and reciting a hymn, I knelt. But there were preliminaries to observe; my beautiful topee of hair, of which I was so proud, was pronounced unsuitable for approaching the Throne of Grace; so Sims drew his thick fingers through that, and left my thatch in the form of a donkey's crop. Again, white linen cuffs were pushed up the coat sleeves, and my silver watch-chain (newly bought) put out of sight. Then, with one hand of Sims on my left shoulder, and John Beavan pressing my right, I falteringly offered my first public prayer.

Many a time since, when leading in church worship, have I felt the gentle pressure of those two hands on my shoulders; neither do I feel the need of any other laying on of hands.

Sims would interrupt my discourse if he believed I was going astray. When catechising children once, I told a boy who had said "God made all things," that, since God gave all life we should never destroy any if we could help it. "Stop, James!" shouted my elder, "you are misleading the child. Do you mean to say that we are to kill nothing?" "Yes, Sims," said I, "if it can be avoided." "My dear man," he replied, "when I was this boy's age, I had lice in my head; I caught and

killed them. Was that wrong?" Then came the inevitable verse of scripture to crush me: "Brute beasts made
to be taken and destroyed."

When I left for college, Sims said to me: "Jonah
learnt more during a stay of three days in the belly of a
fish than you can learn at Trevecca in five years."

He disliked musical instruments in chapel. We
smuggled an American organ into church one night, and
when, at the following prayer meeting, Thomas Beddoe
asked Sims to take part, he pointed to our modest instrument and said, "Ask that!"

Years afterwards we had a wonderful choir led by a
young musician of great promise, Ben Hughes; we rendered the "Messiah," "Elijah," and several of the great
classics. Saturday night was the most convenient time
for this, and it was necessary to erect a stage which
covered the Big Pew. A concert would last until late;
consequently the stage was left over Sunday, and the elders were expected to sit on it. But Sims could not be
seen on this special Sunday morning, and everybody was
enquiring about him; towards the end of the service the
elder was espied in his usual chair, under the stage, and
bent in his double.

A new generation got tired of the overcrowded old
chapel, and began clamouring for a more commodious
and modern edifice. Our elders felt grieved, and one
need not wonder at their conservatism; everything great
in their lives related to the old chapel; there they were
christened, confirmed, married, and found their souls
and Saviour; and near the ancient building loved ones
had been laid to rest. Every stone was sacred to them;
there were traditions to all the pews, and the pulpit was
holy in their sight. Who could think of leaving West-
minster Abbey for a more modern edifice !

But our leaders were humble and pliable enough to
give way to a younger age; it was decided to erect a

new chapel at a cost of £7,000—no small undertaking for a congregation of colliers and their families.

Although Sims gracefully agreed it nearly broke his heart; he seemed to waste away as the building progressed. Soon his memory became faulty. The family knew where to find him if he were missing from home,— in the old chapel, either on his knees, or lost in meditation before the open Bible. On his last visit to the old chapel he was heard praying for me as "Thomas Davyth's Mary Morgan's James."

Evan Sims lived to see the new sanctuary completed; but his heart was not at home there. He died when the old chapel was left amidst its memories. It was all so appropriate and natural. Who could wish it otherwise? Not I.

He took to his bed about a week before passing on. " Are you afraid, father?" asked his devoted daughter.

"Of what, my dear?" queried the elder. "They are calling me—the friends of the Chapel-on-a-Hill! Do you not see them beckoning at the door?"

I sent the following letter to Mrs. Sims:

" My dear Mrs. Sims,

I have just heard of your great bereavement through the death of your saintly husband, and I greatly, and deeply, sympathise with you as a family. To me, *f'Ewyrth Evan* was a spiritual father; he taught me to pray in public at the *" Cwrdd naw"* on Sunday mornings; many an hour did I spend with him in the old Chapel on a Hill in sweet communion with the Unseen, which was always so very real to him!

How they are going—the old stalwarts of Cwm! I can imagine them now as I saw them when I first came into their midst over twenty years ago—so strong, and faithful, and true, and *f'Ewyrth Evan* was the life of the *" set fawr."* The old elders were a forest of giant oaks. But the resistless hurricane has swept over them, and left here and there a lonely trunk, despoiled of its verdure, shorn of its foliage, unshading and unshaded, to murmur in a few more gentle breezes, and to combat a few more rude storms, and then to sink from our gaze beyond the sea of gold!

If I ever met a man of God, *f'Ewyrth Evan* was one. Were I told that I had seen but one saint in the world my mind would naturally turn to your departed husband or to Mary Davies. What a privilege to have him a partner in life! What an honour to know such a father! and I will always thank God for him as a teacher in my youth. His character has grown upon me since I left the Cwm; his saintliness impresses me more the older I grow. We appreciate the greatness of a mountain better from a distance than at its base. His advice was always timely, his *"profiad"* inspiring, and his prayers ever made me long to be unselfish.

What will the ungodly of the place do now since this mighty interceder has been removed? He was the only one I ever remember in Cwm to pray for the Jews.

In fact, no man has ever impressed me so much by his force of character, conviction, and courage and devotion, as *f'Ewyrth Evan*. You knew him as husband, father and companion; and your loss must be great and lasting! Yet, he must have greeted death with a cheer; and his long-expected entrance through the pearly gates was surely a great event in the heavenly spheres!

My letter is already too long, and yet it is hard to stop writing of my beloved father in God. I feel towards him what Timothy must have felt when Paul passed beyond the veil—passionate grief, devotion and reverence.

You have my sympathy, my tears and my prayers, and my sincerest desire that you and the children may find in God what *f'Ewyrth Evan* found.

Unavoidable circumstances prevent me from attending the funeral; but, although absent in body, I shall be with you in spirit to shed a grateful tear over the open grave; and the light of hope and immortality shining through

the dewy drops will form a glorious rainbow which links
that grave to the throne of God.

'Why weepest thou! He is not here. He is arisen!'

> *' Gweddïwr mawr, gorchfygwr ydoedd ef.*
> *Nid ffurf, ond bywyd oedd ei weddi gref;*
> *A phan orffennodd ei ddaearol daith,*
> *Lle'r aethai'r weddi y gweddïwr aeth.'*

I remain, dear friend,

Yours in Christ,

J. H. HOWARD."

CHAPTER FIVE

HOW NOT TO PREPARE FOR THE MINISTRY

EARLY in 1898, I left the pit, and began to prepare for the Ministry. Preliminary stages are never easy in Welsh Nonconformity. My first hurdle was the Big Pew where elders decide upon the suitability of a candidate. Our leaders could not overlook the fact that I was an Englishman with a very elementary knowledge of the Welsh language; they were well aware also of my natural propensities for mischief; and this made them pause. Thomas Davies could not press my claims; he had neither the necessary ability nor confidence. Twice was my formal request refused. The authorities reminded me that I was young, English, and had been mischievous. When I told Evan Sims that I contemplated turning to the Episcopal Church he persuaded his fellow officers to give way; and then my case was placed before the church. I found no difficulty there, and soon permission was granted to visit the churches of the District Meeting and the Presbytery. This entailed preaching twice in each of twelve churches, being catechised publicly at the home church, and, then, after a year's probation, and another written examination, and an oral test before the Presbytery, a two years academic course to prepare for college.

I determined to preach my trial sermons in Welsh, although that was not compulsory. It was an ordeal for me, and worse for my audiences who listened to me distorting their beautiful language. Two sermons and two prayers learnt off by heart comprised my whole repertory. How people bore the infliction is still beyond my comprehension: " Here is the patience of the

saints." I cannot remember the substance of those prayers and sermons; but I know that my Welsh was atroci-
ous. Like French, Welsh has no neuter gender, and it
is almost impossible for an alien to master the problem;
there is no infallible rule; locality is, frequently, the de-
ciding factor. But the greatest difficulty is with mutations. D- becomes dd-; c- mutates into g- or ch-; t- goes
d- after a preposition or an adjective, etc. It is all
very confusing for a beginner. Proficiency comes with
long practice; absolute accuracy is rare even with
natives; and then one finds variations between dialects
of North and South Wales, and also in different
counties.

A faulty mutation may convey an erroneous mean-
ing; and it sounds most discordant to the musical ear.
That is why, at this distance, I can sympathise with the
reluctance of the elders to let me loose upon Welsh
congregations; it was a case of prevention of cruelty to
long-suffering saints. At a church in Cwmrhydyceirw
my mutations were so faulty that one elder lost his
temper, and said (in Welsh): "Boy, go home, and never
again attempt to preach until you know Welsh."

I had done my best,—evidently, a very poor best;
but it proved too painful for the old man, and, today, I
am not surprised.

I wept bitterly all the way home from that service,
and, for years, found it hard to forgive the old critic;
but both he and I laughed many a time, subsequently,
when recalling the episode.

By a casting vote I was accepted at the District
Meeting; but I found no difficulty in passing the Pres-
bytery examinations. Then I went to the Gwynfryn
Academy, Ammanford, to prepare for college.

There used to be several of those academies, or
grammar schools in Wales; and they performed a very
necessary service. Secondary schools were scarce, and,
if they had been plentiful, the huge majority of the men
who entered the Ministry at that time were too old to

benefit by the instruction imparted at those centres of higher education.

Nonconformist ministers of that period usually came from the pits and quarries, and the farms of the country; they were in their late twenties or older, and had spent years at manual or other labour. Today things are different; secondary schools supply most candidates for the pulpit. I am not sure that this is all to the good. Most of our people belong to the labouring classes, and earn their living by daily toil; a minister possessing personal experience of that life has an advantage over men who go straight from school to pulpit, and have only a theoretical knowledge of industry and the life of labour. But such men must make a new start in education; and that is where the old academies proved useful. My mind had lain practically fallow for about nine years; life was too full and laborious to find time or inclination for scholarship when working in the mines; and one easily forgot the lessons learnt at elementary schools.

Ammanford is an industrial centre in West Carmarthenshire. Gwynfryn Academy was run by a Congregational minister whose bardic name was Watcyn Wyn. His sole assistant, "Gwili," became renowned as Arch-druid, college professor, church historian, and theological writer.

I shall always wonder why Watcyn Wyn turned schoolmaster. His scholarship was very limited; he never got beyond irregular verbs in Latin and Greek; his knowledge of English would barely attain matriculation standard. But he was an authority on Welsh — until the advent of Professor J. Morris-Jones.

Everybody loved the old bard; and his witticisms became classics in Welsh circles. He could converse in rhyme; with less wit he would have been a great poet. But he trifled with the Muse and lost inspiration; people expected him to make a pun of everything, until he became a victim to his own wit. In this he was not alone; some of our best preachers are remembered because of their witticisms, and for very little else; that is their tragedy.   One could fill pages with the authentic and reputed witticisms of Watcyn Wyn; all are not humorous; some border on the uncouth, and were better forgotten.   But, at times, people were hilarious in the company of our old schoolmaster.

Once he heard his friend Valentine Evans read as a text: "And in hell he lifted up his eyes."

"Yes," whispered the bard to his neighbour, "Val is quite at home in that region."

I heard him preach when a colliery strike was on; he read every word from a large copybook, and poured ridicule upon masters and men as the ten virgins: "five were foolish and five more foolish still." But he did not apportion the folly.

Gwynfryn students went in batches of six or eight to preach in neighbouring churches, and collected money for the school.   Sometimes the Head accompanied us, and arranged the order of service.   He sat in the Big Pew, made the announcements, and appealed for subscriptions.   At one church he heard that, on the previous Sunday, a deacon had announced: "Watcyn Wyn and his sheep will visit us next Sabbath." When his turn to speak came, he turned to the official announcer, and said: "John Davies, feed my sheep"; and then to each of the deacons, in turn, "Feed my lambs," "feed my sheep."   . . . .   We had a record collection that day.

One sultry afternoon, the torrential Towyn Jones, later a Member of Parliament and a Junior Lord of the Treasury, had preached to a crowded church; preacher and audience suffered from the heat.   "Watcyn *bach* (Dear Watcyn,") said Towyn, "it was difficult to preach to-day."

"My dear fellow," replied Watcyn, "don't mention it; what if you had to listen"!

There was no venom in his wit. Like Charles Lamb, he was humorous even when dying. His devoted wife moistened his parched lips just a few minutes before he passed on; "That's it, Dear," gasped the whimsical bard, "keep spooning to the very end."

The greatest benefit we received at the old academy was a passion for preaching. Not many famous scholars passed through that school; but some of the best preachers of our generation sat at the feet of Watcyn Wyn.

It was at Gwynfryn that I first met my wife. But I would never have matriculated from there. In fact, I actually failed the examination. My mind was set upon preaching to the exclusion of every thing else in school; and, at that time, my greatest need was to prepare for college.

Consequently I left Ammanford, and went to the Newcastle Emlyn Academy which was kept by John Phillips, son of the renowned preacher, Evan Phillips. The first, and supreme consideration there was work. John Phillips was a glutton for home lessons and test examinations; he drove into me a love of Greek, and a strong liking for Latin. My mind awoke at Newcastle Emlyn just as Nature awakes after the dormant months of winter; I seemed to make up in alertness and receptivity for all the fallow years. It was the law of compensation at work. I easily headed the list in the entrance examination for a college course.

What a beautiful place is Newcastle Emlyn! Ruins of the old castle stand out like ghosts of the past, especially on moonlight nights; the river Teivy meanders around the little town as though loath to leave an enchanted isle; surrounding resorts—Henllan, Llandysul, Cilgerran, Aberporth, and Cardigan,—are redolent of myth, tradition and history. During my all-too-short stay there I got steeped in local lore; spirits of scholars and soldiers, poets and preachers, seemed to haunt the whole district which is a never ceasing wonder to artists,

writers and poets. I found it easy to believe in fairies at
Newcastle Emlyn. Some of the most beautiful faces in
Wales are found there; cosmetics could add nothing to
natural endowment in Cardiganshire.

The chief attraction for students was the veteran
preacher Evan Phillips, father of our Principal. His
home was an open house for us all. We entered without
knocking, and helped ourselves to the tobacco jar always
to be found on the table; and then we sat in a circle
about the sage, who would argue, scold, and bless us
according to the prevailing mood or need. If a boy was
in the throes of composing a new sermon, our old theologian would give him points, and perhaps preach them
himself on the following Sunday.

He summarised books for us, taught us to breathe
aright, how to stand before an audience, to produce and regulate the voice, and then brought us face
to face with eternal verities. Evan Phillips left his
stamp upon generations of students, and was revered
throughout Wales. His sermon seldom lasted longer
than twenty minutes; but not a word was wasted, and
each sentence carried weight. He had become a legend
long before his death. I listened to him nearly every
Sunday for four months, and always found him fresh
and impressive. One telling illustration adorned each
sermon, and the whole discourse worked up to that;
probably the text was chosen to suit an illustration. He
possessed a musical baritone voice of no great range;
unlike most preachers, he lowered the voice when deeply
moved, and never rose to a shout. His descriptive powers
were remarkable; so vividly did he once describe David
felling Goliath that one listener shouted "*Diawl dyna
fe lawr*" ("The devil! down he goes").

Underneath the saint there was a humorist in Evan
Phillips. One Sunday he was conveyed to an afternoon
service by a cabman who had another appointment
within the hour. "If you promise to be out in forty-
five minutes, I shall wait for you," said the anxious

driver. "Very well," replied Evan Phillips. Before his sermon, the preacher said that if he saw anybody falling asleep he would immediately close the service.

When he had been preaching for about fifteen minutes, a warning whistle was heard from outside the window, and, without more ado, the preacher closed the Bible, and said "Amen."

"I should like to know," exclaimed one listener, loud enough for all to hear, "who the devil went to sleep now!"

It was with considerable reluctance I left Newcastle Emlyn where I formed some life-long friendships. From there I went to Cardiff University College, and a new exciting world.

Cardiff city is the rival of Caernarvon as capital for Wales. So far as population, wealth, industry, and active citizenship are concerned, the City of Coal is undoubtedly the centre of Gwalia, and has no serious competitor. Today, its Municipal and University buildings are superb, and will compare favourably with those of any city of its size in Great Britain. But for history, tradition, and Welsh sentiment the claims of the Northern town are supreme. At Caernarvon Castle nearly every Prince of Wales has been invested ever since the first King Edward gave our people a Prince; the ancient town disdains its mushroom competitor in the South. Cleavage between North and South is more than geographical; hence the difficulty that confronts Welsh Home Rule. A united Wales will be as hard to secure as a united Ireland; it would require two Parliaments. Caernarvon is too proud to submit to Cardiff, and our city in the South has the conceit of wealth and numbers. More than that, autonomy might be too expensive for our nation, especially if we had to set up two Parliaments. A few examples might be instructive.

Ulster with six counties and a population of 1,293,000 has a Governor General, a Cabinet of seven members, and a Parliament of fifty-two, costing £33,600. There is

F

also a new Parliament House which cost £650,000 to build. Five High Court Judges are maintained at £20,000 per annum in all, and there is seldom work enough for one judge.

The Irish Free State, or Eire, has a population of 2,949,000. A Cabinet of 10, and 9 High Court judges, costing £25,000.

At present, England and Wales together with a population of nearly 40,000,000, maintain 39 judges of the High Court at a cost of £174,000.

Canada (population 8,788,483) has 150 judges. Each province has its own Parliament, its Lieutenant General, its Cabinet and Judicature.

Prince Edward Island, for instance, with a population equal to that of Wigan, has its own Lieutenant Governor, Executive Council, Legislative Assembly jand four judges. If London were governed like Canada, it would have ten Parliaments for itself.

Australia has seven Parliaments for 6,000,000 people.

South Africa maintains four Parliaments for 1,700,000 whites alone.

During my time, classes at Cardiff University College were housed in wooden huts; but, the then Principal, Viriamu Jones, had a wonderful Staff, many of whom achieved European fame. Conway, Burrows, Mackenzie, Arnold, Bruce and Campagnac belonged to the first rank of scholars. They gave us students glimpses into a wonderful world of beauty and knowledge unexplored by us before. How eager for education some of us became about that period! Can I ever forget my ecstasies over Euripides and Ovid, and even Caesar's Commentaries! It seems incredible now that I spent a whole night once learning Tennyson's " *In Memoriam* " off by heart. But all was so new and marvellous to my starved mind. When Professor Littledale opened my eyes to the charm of Wordsworth, the genius of Shelley, the wistfulness of Keats, and, above all, the power and glory of Carlyle, old things passed away, behold all the world was made new.

I had entered the City Beautiful of literature, and have not been satisfied for long outside its portals since.

I was first of my year in most of our classes at Cardiff; not because of cleverness or genius on my part, but owing to my insatiate thirst for knowledge; examinations were secondary considerations with me. I read all sorts of books, and ransacked second-hand bookstalls weekly. The "Penny Poets" series, which I collected then, will always be treasured by me. At Cardiff my passion for authorship began, and it has never left me for more than a few weeks at a time.

Scholarship for its own sake never appealed to me. I did not trouble even to complete my Arts degree at Cardiff, although I was more than half way through the course, and top of my classes. I wished to enjoy knowledge; sitting examinations in English literature seemed like sacrilege, just as I feel about Scripture tests. Who would discourse about geology beside his mother's grave? or dissect a body in sight of a baby's cot? or discuss finance on top of the Rigi? or quarrel in the reflections of a setting sun? That is what I felt when under the spell of the Masters at Cardiff. Like others, I compromised later on, and sat examinations, and took some degrees. But there is something more than an academic or commercial value in education for me. Culture is of the soul, and not to be judged by University diplomas.

I had some delightful fellow-students at Cardiff; several of them have since attained eminence in various spheres, and in different countries. Our debating society was a training ground for a few subsequent Members of Parliament. The man or woman who could sway that crowd was fit to face any audience; not many survived a maiden speech. It was a rough house always; but whenever a fresher attempted to take part in a discussion, the place was in an uproar. I got off with a soaking of ink and a torn coat. But I had my say and generous applause in the end; and spoke at nearly every

other meeting during that session.   Some of our
debates would be no discredit to the House of Commons.
Of course, we were dogmatic, intolerant, assertive and
abusive, and most of what we said was arrant nonsense.
But it was Spartan training for public speaking, and I
made full use of it.

The Christian Union also helped our devotional life,
and I rarely missed a service.   Some members of the
Union took to slumming in the lower parts of the city,
and I joined them.   We visited lodging houses, doss
houses, public houses, and Chinese opium dens, and
witnessed sights, then, that opened my eyes to the depths
of degradation a human being can experience.   We were
very amateurish and inefficient in our efforts to help the
victims of drink, drugs, and organised vice.   Occasionally, thieves robbed us of our watches and tram fare;
worse still, a few of our number succumbed to the very
evils we had set out to combat.   Some of my fellow-
students at Cardiff took to drink.   They were young lads
from the country having their first fling of freedom from
home restraints.   That usually occurred during the first
or second year of the Course.   The majority pulled themselves together by the third year, and warned freshers
" off the grass."

While slumming in Cardiff I came to realise not only
the ramifications of evil but also the enormous powers
for good at work in the haunts of sin.   John Pugh had
started the Forward Movement, and his missioners
were active.   The Salvation Army was a mighty force;
there were rescue homes, orphanages, ever-open doors of
refuge, and numerous charities ready to help the needy,
the lonely, and the lost.   I was convinced that the powers
of good are more numerous than the forces of evil; that
there are two angels for every devil; that a church is
mightier than a public house; that the saint out-lasts the
sinner.   Where sin abounds, grace doth much more
abound; God is the winning side.

At Cardiff I first heard the leading English preachers of our generation—Parker, Jowett, John MacNeill, Alexander Maclaren, Meyer, Gipsy Smith, Silvester Horne, Clifford and R. J. Campbell. Until then my great preachers belonged to the Welsh pulpit; at last I met a different type of preaching.

John Pugh made use of ministerial students in his work of the Forward Movement; he persuaded us to canvass neighbourhoods and to start new Causes. I was one of three to open a Branch at Heath Moor; we preached in a front room belonging to a converted negro, for a whole week, mostly to children and a few loafers; twice our meeting was rushed. But it was all very exhilarating, and we were sure of a good supper with the Pughs. What faith John Pugh and his first evangelists had! Seth Joshua and his brother Frank were real pioneers who discovered the romance of religion; and they stirred the whole of South Wales for a time.

The two years I spent at Cardiff were rich in experience, if not in academic distinction. My fellow-lodger, Richard Williams, and I used to conduct week-night missions in several of the little churches outside the city. All we got for our labour was our keep, unlimited kindness, and encouragement.

A favourite church with us was New Mill, Miskin. We collected sufficient money, one week, to buy an American organ for the little chapel, and persuaded Judge Gwilym Williams of Miskin Manor to attend the dedication service. That resulted in an invitation for us to spend a night at the Manor. We were only two raw students, and very nervous; but the judge soon put us at ease by relating stories about his favourite Aberdare where that very day he had been holding his Court. One story remains with me yet.

A collier named John Williams was accused of beating his wife, and of persistent cruelty. The judge knew this culprit, and addressed him by name, thus: "John Williams, I am sorry to see you in the dock, and more sorry still for the reason of your appearance. Have you never tried being kind to your wife? Remember the Old Book says that kindness is hot coals on an enemy's head."

"Did you say hot coals, judge?" asked the culprit.

"Yes, John Williams, hot coals," was the reply.

"Thank you, judge; I have already tried hot water," said John Williams.

Miskin Manor was a lovely home, and had a spacious picture gallery of which our host was justly proud. We enjoyed every minute of our brief visit.

One other incident stands out in my memory of New Mill. The kind farmer with whom we stayed invited us to accompany him shooting rabbits. So, for the first time, a hunting we did go; we would force the ferret down a rabbit hole, and then wait outside with our guns at full cock. The little rabbits were driven up, poked their heads out, and retreated back again and again, until, at last, the terror behind proved worse than the threat above. Then there would be a scamper, and a shot, and the little bundle of quivering fur passed into our bag. This went on for several hours, until time for the evening service.

It was my turn to preach that night, and Williams sang. In the Big Pew we had four deacons whose heads were unusually bald, and shining like full moons; whenever one of those heads moved, my hand immediately shot out at it—just as I had been doing all day at rabbits. I never went with a deacon shooting rabbits before service after that.

Another amusing episode of those days may be worth relating. Some ministerial students were very popular with the churches, and received numerous requests for their services. My invitations were few and far between, and I was thankful for any leavings from the rich students' table. A Congregationalist lucky one asked me, if, as usual, I was unbooked for a certain Sunday. He was the proud possessor of two appointments. He could only go to one, of course, but did not wish to lose the monetary value of the other.   So if I would go to the spare " publication " and preach, I could get my keep for the day, and hand over the fee to him, which I actually did.   He gracefully accepted the 5/-, and emphasised my good fortune in obtaining my keep for the Sabbath.   I wonder what became of that man! He ought to be a recruiter of Chinese labour.

From Cardiff I went to Trevecca Theological College, which is situated in the heart of Breconshire, about two miles from the village of Talgarth.   It was a great change from the city, and I did not relish the move.   Instead of four or five hundred students and a big teaching Staff, we were reduced to thirty or thirty-five students with four Professors.   There were no outside attractions, and few avenues for letting off steam.   We were a small community, self contained, and cut off from the world,—the nearest approach possible to a monastery, but lacking vows of chastity, obedience, and poverty.   Most of us were in a rebellious mood starting our theological course. Unfortunately, that temper remained with some all through, and caused no end of trouble to those concerned.   And yet, if we had possessed a historical sense, and reverence for the rock from which our Denomination was hewn, Trevecca would have been to us, as it really is, one of the most romantic spots in Wales, especially for Welsh   Presbyterians.   At   Talgarth   church   Howell Harris, the great revivalist, was converted ; and there he lies buried.   In the adjacent graveyard, William Williams, the sweet singer of the Revival, responded to the appeals of Harris, and dedicated his muse to the work of Christ.

Trevecca farm lies on the road to the college ; there Harris experimented in Christian communism.   The college itself was a gift from Lady Huntingdon, and, for a time, Whitefield was Acting President.   The whole district is a Mecca for Nonconformists.   But we were not in a mood to appreciate all this.   We felt rebellious, and I blush now to think of the way we teased and annoyed our tutors; it was unfair and foolish.

Principal Prys was a short, nervy, excitable man, very reserved and taciturn. I sometimes thought that he feared his students. To his sensitive soul we must have seemed a pack of irresponsible ruffians. Occasionally, he would invite a few of us to tea; but the work of entertaining was left to his wife; and we ourselves did most of the talking. The event was, evidently, a painful ordeal to our host, who seemed tongue-tied. The Principal was misunderstood because of his taciturnity. One exasperated youth asked him : " Are you a man or a gentleman?"

The learned preacher was expected at a home in Mid-Rhondda where was an only child nine years old, who had been sent to bed before the great man arrived on Saturday night. Early next morning the youth came down to see the Principal; but, when he entered the breakfast room the distinguished guest was reading some book. A gentle cough from the doorway failed to disturb the reader; neither did a noisy walk round the room draw attention; rubbing against the occupied armchair also proved futile. In sheer despair, the boy pushed his head between reader and book and exclaimed: "Well, you are a mug!"

In his early days, Principal Prys had been a teacher at an elementary school, and he carried the elementary school-teacher spirit with him through life; even when dealing with full-grown men he was unconsciously brusque, and could not understand why students felt aggrieved. Consequently, there was considerable friction at the college. For one whole week we cut lectures and declared a general strike; and it was all because of a trivial misunderstanding with the Principal, who had refused to grant the customary holiday on Ascension Day for the annual pilgrimage to Llanthony Abbey, where, for years, students had gone to hear the eloquent Father Ignatius preach. We went in spite of the prohibition, and defied the wrath of the authorities. It was a humiliating experience for our sensitive Principal, and, in fact, he threatened to resign.   I was able to pacify him that time, and, on behalf of the whole college, made him a handsome apology.   Later, I grew to admire the reserved Head of Trevecca.

I was guilty of cutting lectures.   Hebrew I never mastered; Church History could be " swotted " from text books.   Our Greek Professor was the most amiable of men, but his lectures were not so memorable as his poetry. He could rhyme in English, Welsh, Latin, and Greek, and frequently asked us to sing his compositions, which we readily did to enliven classes.

My success as first prize-man every year placated the ordinary Staff who never reported my delinquencies. But the Principal got to know somehow, and he reduced my prize money to half the usual amount.   Remonstrations on my part were of no avail, and, to-day, I regret my retort.   But I was really sore, and needed the money.

I possessed a retentive memory whilst at college. One external examiner asked if I had cribbed an answer to a question.   My reply was a request that he should read any paragraph from the textbook, and I would give him its page and section,—which I did.

Trevecca was not a residential college; we were housed in a terrace close by, four students to each cottage.   Those abodes had no baths, and sanitary arrangements were truly primitive; the wonder was that our health did not suffer.   Not until after an outbreak of typhoid fever were improvements effected.

Our landlady was a kindly, pious, and motherly old widow whom all students petted. The simple soul never believed in the kinship of godliness and cleanliness; she rarely washed her hands, and her neck clamoured for soap.   One often wished to spray her with scent; her fingernails were in perpetual mourning and always long. An unappetising sight was the ancient carrying a basin of gravy to the table whilst her fingers were half covered in the greasy liquid.   A boiled cabbage was more than a vegetable; it usually contained several grubs.

But no student would dare offend the old lady by seeking lodgings elsewhere; we stayed on right to the end of our course. To us she was "Old Mother," and we helped her with the heavy work. Each man gave her an extra five shillings at the end of every term, until we discovered that it all went for foreign missions. She contributed every spare penny to "the little blacks in India," and frequently deprived herself of necessities in order to help the Cause. When she grew too old to wait upon students, Principal Prys, at his own expense, pensioned her, and gave her a cottage rent free until she died over a hundred years old. Deeds like that endeared the Principal to men who frequently disagreed with him.

In such a lonely place students had to make their own fun, and create diversion. Surrounding farms were much appreciated as outlets for our superfluous energies, and we found scope for budding talent in the local chapels as well as at Talgarth mental hospital. We organised an annual concert at a remote hamlet called Pengenffordd; our singing left much to be desired, and the recitations were worse. But we provided endless pleasure for the people; especially for the shepherds who trooped down from surrounding hills to give us a tumultuous welcome and a rousing encore for every item until we had exhausted our repertory and our voices. Then came a jolly supper and dance; such dancing was not to be seen elsewhere. But our rustics enjoyed every moment as they whirled rosy-cheeked girls to the accompaniment of a thousand discords banged out of the cracked piano.

Perhaps the most memorable musical event ever organised by Trevecca students was a certain competitive meeting where the test piece for a quartet was the Halleluiah Chorus! Five quartets competed.

Nearly every Sunday a student preached at the Mental Home. Nobody liked the ordeal, but it was funny sometimes. "Do come again, sir," said an inmate to our most serious preacher, "you are so like one of us."

One suspects that many of the men were more interested in the nurses than in the inmates. Not infrequently, a young lady found herself on the wrong side of locked gates after curfew had rung; and then porters had to be bribed for admittance.

The little Bethels were excellent places to practise English; and strange was the Saxon language that fell from the lips of monoglot Welshmen experimenting with their first English sermon. No wonder one church secretary wrote to the Principal : " Please, sir, do you come to preach to we next time. Us can understand you, sir, but the students are too larned for we."

One Welshman found it difficult to draw his public prayer to an appropriate close. After repeated attempts, he ended with a curt, " Yours truly, Amen."

Of my fellow students at Trevecca, the one who subsequently rendered most service outside the pulpit was Edward Evans, now of Towyn, confidant of Dr. Puleston Jones, and familiar friend of Sir Owen Edwards, the historian. Evans became educationalist, politician, journalist, and a member of numerous Public Bodies where he had considerable influence. He always was a fighter, and could not give in. A voracious reader, keen student, and a loyal friend was Evans. He has had more than his share of sorrow; but his spirit remains sweet, and his faith firm, and he retains a childlike simplicity. It was worth spending two years in college to know a man who can extract joy out of pain, and convert sorrow into a sacrament.

At this college I met John Green, Twrgwyn, the fearless critic and opponent of compromise, who can be as tender as a mother towards a sinner in the throes of remorse, and as brave as an old-time prophet in the presence of oppressors. He delivered a knockout blow to one deacon who had cast an aspersion upon the pulpit; and then he helped his victim home and prayed with him. Green has before now frightened a magisterial bench into refusing a Public House licence, taught law to lawyers, and compelled a General Assembly to revoke decisions.   His sermons are denunciatory as a rule.   I remonstrated with him once.

"My dear Howard," said he, "you don't know the sinners this way.   You must either kill or save them." And yet, I have heard him use the wooing note with effect.

Richard Williams and I shared the same rooms for two years, and remained firm friends until his untimely and sudden death. He breakfasted with his family and supped with God.   There always was a tear in his eye; towards the end one heard a sob in his voice. His smile was a benediction, and his friendship proved precious to those who were admitted into the holy places of his life.

J. E. Davies, so unassuming and reserved, was our best batter, and the most formidable goal-keeper ever known at the college.   His Welsh mutations were as faulty as mine.   But how powerful he could be at prayer! He would not hurt a fly, and always pleaded for the failure.   There was a measure of nobility in the man that grew with the years, and made him a tower of strength to people in distress.   J.E. was a fine character.

Teivy Davies has the most musical voice I ever heard in the pulpit, or outside.   He could have made a fortune at opera.   To hear him read a hymn will bring tears to the eyes of the most matter of fact listener.   There is a gospel in his "How are you, Howard?", and I count his friendship amongst the sanctities of my life.   He is not a great reader of books, but he understands men; people do not consider him a deep thinker, but Teivy is in living touch with the things that abide.   He is a man to trust and to love, and would make a wonderful Father Confessor; eternity only will reveal the secrets entrusted by saints and sinners to that sympathetic soul.   Even Dr. Cynddylan Jones turned to Teivy for help when about to pass on to the great Beyond.   I could hope for no greater comfort in an hour of distress than to feel the pressure of my friend's hand.

I can still see Grey Davies—the impulsive, but true and trustworthy supporter of every losing cause. He lost many a battle, but never a friend. Grey hated humbug, and would always help a lame dog. I heard him preach once,—it was a torrent of words laden with thought. In England he would have rivalled Ossian Davies, only that Grey Davies is more persuasive.

Derry Morgan always beamed goodwill and the practice of optimism. However dark the sky he saw some star, and rarely trod the slough of despond. His was not a superficial optimism, but confidence born of deep conviction that the best is yet to be. Derry has an endless capacity for reverence and appreciation. Many a time has this Onesiphorus revived my faith; his name should be Barnabas the Consoler.

What a sweet soul was David Jones, Blaenannerch! Simple like a child and as lovable; naturally pious, with a keen sense of humour; in him is no guile, and people never could quarrel with such a gentle soul. He came from the hills of Cardiganshire, and his heart has remained on the heights where it is eternal calm.

John Edwards, Llanfynydd, was our bard, with the far away gaze as though he saw realms unknown to us ordinary mortals. He could speak in rhyme, and lived with the spirit of hills, rippling brooks, wayside flowers, sailing clouds, and birds on the wing. Edwards often tempted me to sit under the trees and feel pure.

There were others of my year whom I admired: R. R. Davies, so musical; David Evans with an infectious laugh; impressive Daniel Davies; Richard Harris the provocative; Moses Davies, a half-blind seer; studious R. D. Edwards; J. N. Jones, a most congenial soul; Philip Evans, blunt, loud and loyal; T. C. Lewis, my double in features, and friendly rival for prizes; Evan Lewis, so modest and sincere, and the mild-mannered E. J. Herbert. They were a fine set of men. However much one criticised Trevecca, we left its sheltered life with some regrets, though not many. I liked Llangors lake with its legend of the buried town and ghostly bell-chimes heard when the moon is at full. The farmers were friendly, and gave students good suppers and home-brewed cider, and related hair-raising stories about ghosts. Not without some pang did we leave the orchards whose purloined fruit had frequently enriched our tables, and made us trouble the doctor. Going out to the great world after six or seven years of school and college life is a mighty adventure, and however light-hearted a man appeared, there would be an uncontrollable tremor in his voice as he bade good-bye to fellow students.

What had Trevecca done to fit us for the new life? Who can assess an atmosphere, or an influence, or an attitude? They are absorbed unconsciously, and affect the inner being. We can recognise an Oxford accent, a Cambridge emphasis, an Eton tie, a Harrow style, a Bala stoop; so there was something like a Trevecca stamp on a man. But, apart from friendships formed, the college did very little to fit one for the practical work of the Ministry.

We had been cut off from the world and its problems. Destined, as most of us were, for the Welsh pulpit, we had no Welsh class to study the language and the problems of Wales. We heard nothing about the difficulties of the Pastorate, the administration of the Sacraments, and the conduct of public worship. Economics was an unknown science to us. The teaching of the young, so important in the work of a minister, was not mentioned. Protestantism received slight attention; but Nonconformity and Welsh Presbyterianism might not have existed so far as our curriculum was concerned. Although we then lived in the very birthplace of the Welsh Methodist Revival, our tutors never referred to that momentous Movement in my hearing. A lay research student, Mr. Richard Bennett, of Caersws, first enthused me with the stirring history of my denomination and the romance of the Harris Diaries. Trevecca was a great disappoint-

ment.   Things have improved now that we have the
United Colleges at Aberystwyth and Bala.   Our ministerial students today receive a more practical training,
and are kept longer in the atmosphere of a university
town.   I believe that a Chair of Theology in the Welsh
University would be of incalculable benefit to the religious life of Wales.   It would remove many sectarian
divisions, and secure for us some of the best theologians
of Europe.   As things are we have to be satisfied with
less than the best.

Again, we should have apprentice appointments or
curacies.   Nonconformist ordinands are inducted to pas-
torates without any practical training.   This is unfair to
churches, and cruel to young ministers.   That is why
very few men remain in their first churches for more than
two or three years.   The deplorable fact brought home
to them is that they were inadequately trained for their
life-work.

I had realised that deficiency in our Trevecca curriculum from the very start, and therefore undertook a student pastorate during the long vacation of my first year.
It was at Newbridge, Mon., in the old Temple.   I also
helped with a Forward Movement van in the same district.   But that experiment nearly broke my heart; two
sermons a Sunday and three week-day addresses in the
open air sorely taxed my scant resources.   It was my
custom to rehearse my sermons aloud in a wood close to
the lodgings.   One morning I was overheard practising
something resembling a swear word. The listener spread
abroad a rumour that I was raving mad in the woods ;
next day was Sunday, and I had my first full house.

On the second Sunday Lord George Sanger brought
his circus to Newbridge.   I visited the veteran showman,
and invited him and his workers to our evening service.

"Young man," exclaimed the proprietor, "why not
bring your congregation along to my show?"

"Certainly," said I, "we'll be here at six p.m.
prompt."

For once I preached the Gospel to many creatures. Lions, tigers, camels and elephants heard our singing, and some of them roared their protest or applause. We had a crowd of 1,500 people at the show, free of charge. The Bohemian Lord George stood by my side as we yelled " Tell mother I'll be there."

After the service I spoke to some " hands," and found amongst them one Welshman. It was no small joy to write on his behalf seeking reconciliation with the family he had deserted.

When I started my ministry, Nonconformity was at its zenith in England and Wales. It was the epoch of mighty preaching when Parker, Spurgeon, Stopford Brooke, John Clifford, and Silvester Horne preached to packed churches; and when Hugh Price-Hughes was a bright and shining light in the National Free Church Council. The Nonconformist conscience was a terror to evil doers and reactionary politicians. In Wales also we had our great leaders and eloquent preachers in every denomination; no wonder I felt badly equipped for the times.

The motor car was in its experimental stage; flying was a remote possibility; Sunday golf was unknown, and political demonstrations were not attempted on Sundays. Nonconformity could compel the Government of the day to ban a fight between a white and a coloured boxer in London. But what a change has taken place since! Dissent is no longer the mighty force it once was in the life of our nation. We are more concerned with funds than with Causes; commemoration not consecration is the chief theme discussed at Assemblies; graves lure more than altars; ancestor-worship is not confined to Asia. Toleration, as practised by us, is camouflaged indifference; superficiality we call broad-mindedness. Where does the fault for all this spiritual lassitude lie?

The national life of Wales was aggressive and virile at that time, and a minister had to be well informed and active to justify his calling and leadership. Our people were becoming politically-minded even in the churches. Disestablishment and Welsh autonomy were practical politics, owing, chiefly, to the influence of Tom Ellis, O. M. Edwards, Viriamu Jones and D. Lloyd George. The new Nationalism was not merely literary and cultural; it was aggressively political.

"So far back as August 23rd, 1882, Alderman W. J. Parry of Bethesda advocated the establishment of five provincial authorities, the latter divided as follows:—

One for Scotland to meet at Edinburgh; one for Ireland to sit at Dublin; one for Northern England to meet at York; one for Southern England to meet at Oxford, and one for Wales and Monmouthshire to meet at Aberystwyth." — (*Ellis Davies*).

Welshmen were gradually breaking away from the old English Liberalism of the Gladstone school, and talking about a General Council for Wales on which Welsh members of the English parliament also should sit. I heard Gladstone speak once, at Swansea, and, with the conceit of youth, I proclaimed to all within hearing that a statesman who could talk for a whole hour without revealing his plans for Wales was a "*Grand Old Humbug.*"

My extravagant outburst was indicative of the Welsh awakening from the Gladstone stupor. Of course, that period also was a false dawn; for the Tom Ellis ebullition of Welsh Nationalism expired on the doorstep of a Junior Liberal Whip's office. Wales had to await the Lleyn arson for our next national awakening; and one wonders whether the Knights of the Round Table will remain awake this time.

Our Nationalism at the time I entered the Ministry was more moral than economic, more religious than patriotic. Lord Howard de Walden's description fits our then mood and spirit:

G

"The true Nationalist, though he may talk politics
and economics, is really a prophet, a moral prophet, like the old prophets of Israel. He is fiercely
discontented with the ways of his people; he
longs and longs that his people save its soul, and
calls it to that duty. ' Rise up ' he says, ' quit your
low aims ; remember the Land that gave you birth;
serve it and turn away from self and the vision of
self-advancement.' That is a noble cry, a cry for
social self-regeneration, a cry for cultural nationalism, lifted to the highest where it becomes more
than cultural and is touched to great spiritual
issues.

Though the stars fall, and States and Empires
fade away, a people must be free to save its soul."
(Quoted by W. Hughes-Jones, " What is happen-
ing in Wales," p. 33).

Immediately preceding the 1904-5 religious Revival
there was a passion for service and for the social gospel
abroad in our churches. Those years resembled the end
of the 18th, and the beginning of the 19th centuries when
Wilberforce, Romilly, Brougham, Francis Place and the
early Christian Socialists were at their reforms. We
eagerly read disclosures of social abuses, and investigated
them for ourselves. Our favourite writers were W. T.
Stead, G. R. Sims, Rowntree, Booth, and the reporters of
the Anti-Sweating League. Most young preachers were
aflame with zeal for social reform, and our pulpits re-
sounded with the humanitarian note. Strange to say, the
Welsh religious Revival associated with the name of
Evan Roberts lessened and curtailed the social emphasis of the Gospel in our churches, and gave in its
stead what is called the Keswick stress upon personal
perfection.

But the rise and phenomenal growth of the new
Labour Party influenced the industrial, the social, and,
to a large extent, the religious outlook of our generation.

CHAPTER SIX

SWANSEA SIDELIGHTS

My first church pastorate was Terrace Road English Presbyterian Church, Swansea. The call was extended two years before I was due to leave college; and my release within one year came in response to an urgent appeal from the church to the college authorities.

There was something fatalistic in an invitation to a Swansea church situated so near the home of my youth, and almost within sight of Cockett. The coincidence was more remarkable still when Sir J. T. D. Llewelyn, the patron of my boyhood, presided at the induction service. The Squire of Penllergaer remained my friend so long as he lived, and, several times, he pressed me to return to the Episcopal Church where I had been confirmed, and in which he held patronage. He was a fine gentleman, a good friend, and a staunch Tory. I still treasure several of his letters in which he forcibly expressed himself on education, Nonconformity, and his pet aversion, Radicalism. The old sportsman seldom minced his words, and he commanded a copious vocabulary.

Terrace Road was a comparatively young church of 120 members belonging to the middle and labouring classes. We had three elders, two of whom were fairly rich and generous; the third was poor, pious, and very helpful at week-night services.

John Hopkins, our church secretary, was near my own age; he was enthusiastic, and had much initiative. His house was my second home, where I frequently led his boys in their bed-time devotions. We have remained friends ever since.

My stipend was £110 a year, and our worthy treasurer saw to it that the sum total did not exceed that amount.

If the two requisites of a successful pastor are grace and poverty, then that church officer was determined that I should acquire the second virtue. But he was a good soul, and his family were exceedingly kind.

We were a lively church, and always ready for enterprise. The 1904-5 Revival was at fever heat when I began my pastorate; services were held each night of the week, and they rarely closed without conversions. I had great times at open air work. A note appeared in one local evening paper to the effect that "Rev. J. H. Howard and his band of revivalists were seen outside the 'Mountain Dew' last night singing.

'May I come in, May I come in?'"

Another day, somebody reported that I sang in front of the Y.W.C.A. building,

"What must it be to be there?"

The Welsh Revival was a wonderful experience, inexplicable in origin, scope and sudden collapse. But who can explain the working of the Spirit?

I knew Evan Roberts, the foremost human agent in the Movement. He was a young collier from Loughor, near Swansea, who had entered the Newcastle Emlyn Academy to prepare for the Ministry, and was a student there when, like John Wesley, he received the baptism of fire.

New Quay was the starting place of the Revival which soon spread throughout Wales; the most unlikely people and places were stirred. Singing, not preaching, predominated; people would burst into song almost everywhere, and the hills and valleys of Glamorganshire echoed to the hymns of Pantycelyn and Ann Griffiths, day and night. Chapels were filled daily; colliers went straight from the pit to services without so much as bathing, and would remain for hours singing, and praying, and weeping. Some ministers collapsed under the strain, and nervous casualties were numerous.

Thousands were admitted into the churches; many remained steadfast; but a great number backslided after the excitement had passed. The daily Press did much to spread the Revival; this was not altogether beneficial, because conversions became "copy"; religious excitement was news when an emotional cyclone swept the whole country. Then some of our leaders courted publicity, and were eager to be interviewed. Journalists came to see and report; foreign observers made fantastic assertions for home consumption; services were exploited, and people sought sensations.

Much lasting good was accomplished; but some regrettable phases followed the Revival. Inexperienced youths adversely criticised tried leaders in the churches; old members mistrusted, and, often, obstructed the newly converted; censoriousness was not the monopoly of either young or old. Many a church was divided; some people became insane, and one saw examples of what is called demon-possession.

The Revival lasted nearly twelve months, and collapsed when the Movement became organised and scheduled. So long as the young leaders went about from place to place just as the Spirit moved them, the fire spread. I believed then that it would be better for the workers to remain in South Wales much longer than they did, and I said so to Evan Roberts the night before he departed for Liverpool where a committee had arranged an itinerary for him. He himself expressed some doubts about the advisability of going; but to Merseyside, and to North Wales he went, and in a very short time, the Revival was one of the wonders of the past.

Mrs. Penn Lewis then enlisted the revivalist for her work in the " *Life of Faith* " campaign. But the Loughor man was a nervous wreck, and for well over thirty years Evan Roberts has dwelt amongst the memories of one of the most remarkable religious upheavals in the history of our land.

Unfortunately, the Welsh Revival inaugurated no definite social awakening as did other spiritual stirrings known in history. The Sankey and Moody revival, for example, brought about the religious reformation of the American and British Universities, University Settlements, temperance reform, and a new social vision as preached by men like Henry Drummond. The Methodist Revival of the 18th century inspired prison reform, factory legislation, and, to some extent, the abolition of slavery. Social salvation usually follows spiritual awakening. But the Welsh Revival recalls no names of social reformers like Hannah More, Zachary Macaulay, and Shaftesbury. Religious revivals suffer early collapse when they produce no practical emphasis and social application. If we neglect to launch a Cause on the rising tide of spiritual flow, our ecclesiastical barques get stranded during a time of ebb.

I witnessed some stirring scenes during the Revival; but my phlegmatic Saxon temperament rendered me immune from hysteria. The Movement was a study as well as an experience for me. I could not get excited even when huge crowds went beyond control and my fellow ministers were groaning and shouting in agony or with joy. It was a psychological study at close quarters. I accompanied the chief revivalists to scores of services. Evan Roberts was a mystery; he would groan and perspire, and, sometimes, writhe in agony owing to the terrible strain. Was it a case of vicarious suffering? In some churches he remained silent throughout a whole service as though the Spirit had deserted him. Sometimes, he was clairvoyant, and would call attention to people who were in the throes of conviction, and that unknown to those nearest them. He could say, beforehand, the number of conversions that would take place at a service, and where the converted sat. We are told that David Morgan, of Ysbyty, and Richard Owen, two earlier Welsh revivalists, possessed this "second sight" for a time. Old Testament prophets were called "seers."

Great was the disappointment of religious Wales when Evan Roberts passed into obscurity, and the Loughor voice was silenced. Attempts have been made to stage a come back; but no human being could stand that strain a second time. Organised revivals can do more harm than good; repetition and imitation are poor substitutes for the uprisings of new life.

Church work was difficult during, and especially, immediately after the Revival. Whilst the agitation lasted one lived at high tension and nervous strain. There was an inevitable clash between the newly converted and those who knew of no recent crisis in their religious experience; and then came the reaction. One-time enthusiasts backslided; we witnessed a landslide in church membership for several years in succession. Once more, drinking dens were full and chapels deserted; we saw apostacy, hostility, and, worse still, growing indifference.

It was then I again took an active interest in social problems. Near my church were stark poverty, children half-starved, homeless women, men unemployed, homes wrecked by sensuality, drink and gambling,—and the majority of my people seemed callous or ignorant of the facts staring them in the face.

If my conscience awoke at Capel-y-Cwm, and my intellectual re-birth took place at Cardiff, Swansea was the scene of my dedication to the social gospel of Christ.

On my fortieth birthday the editor of a Sunday newspaper, whose circulation runs into the third million, made his third request for a sketch of my life and career. The answer that finally brought me peace from that quarter was,—" There is nothing in my very ordinary life worth recording except my Conversion and my marriage to the most wonderful woman in the world." On March 1st, 1905, I married Annie Mathilda Davies of The Park, Ammanford. My friends know why I am so attached to our home; I owe much to my patient wife.

The horror of social vice at seaports was brought to my notice very forcibly at Swansea, and that in a

way I am not likely to forget. One remarkable man
of that town lived near me at Mount Pleasant; he was a
prosperous draper, had a beautiful home, and was a loyal
church-worker. With the hearty approval of his family,
this gentleman devoted his spare time and superfluous
cash to the task of rescuing fallen women. Some Swansea folk were unwise enough to criticise that unselfish
man in his heart-breaking mission, and to insinuate unworthy motives. No one finds fault with a physician who
visits sick-rooms, hospitals, or plague-ridden districts;
and yet, respectable religionists look askance at would-
be saviours of souls from the deepest hell of destruction.
W. T. Stead, Josephine Butler, and Mr. Gladstone found
that to their cost. Did not the Saviour of the world suffer
from similar carping critics?

One Saturday night I accompanied my friend on his
usual round of mercy. Watch and money were left at
home, and we were not clad in our Sunday best. Before
midnight, six public houses had been visited (there was no
early closing). Mr. R. was well known in each, and
nobody molested us. The publicans were friendly, and
one informed me that my companion was better than
four policemen for keeping the peace. Several girls, in
various stages of drunkenness, spoke to Mr. R. about
their troubles; one begged his help to find her "man"
who had gone off with some female; another was hiding
from her infuriated husband, and would drown her fear
in drink; a sailor was enticing a very young woman away
from home. . . . . Then we did the arches where
harpies watch for passers by. Some approached us,
but when they recognised my friend they poured out their
tales of woe.

"Why not give it up, Susie? You know how it must
end!" asked the would-be rescuer.

"I have gone too far, sir! The sooner it ends the
better," was the typical reply.

Susie was well educated, and had been deceived and
deserted by a man who was then in the public eye, and on

his way to wealth and position. Another weeping girl was the daughter of a clergyman. One half-doped woman offered my friend money to help his mission of rescue. She herself was sent home twice and had drifted back. Not one in ten, Mr. R. said, is ultimately saved.

We visited the cheap lodging houses to which misery creeps in the early hours of morning. The sight was indescribable and nauseating; and by 2 a.m., I was violently sick. We had spoken to 35 martyrs of hell's highway within a radius of one mile. I felt helpless and dumb in the presence of that morass of filth and sin, and am not ashamed to confess that I wept on the way home. Why did God tolerate it all?

But there was one ray of light even in that realm of infamy; a Salvation Army Captain, who ran an all night coffee stall, called to us, "Come into our cathedral for a rest." It was a bare shed where casualties could be taken in an emergency. After all, " cathedral " suggests God's presence; there must be room for hope where He is.

It was difficult to preach next morning; but I wrote an account of the Saturday night's experience to an evening paper. That article created much talk and a spate of criticism amongst people who lived in a fool's paradise. I received several encouraging letters from friends and strangers; some from so far away as Australia; the letter-card that thrilled me ran: —

" God bless and keep you, Reverend Howard!

From

A Rescued Fallen Woman."

Since those days I have met many social workers like Mr. R. who carry the torch of faith and hope into the shadows where lurk misery, sin and despair. How thankful we should be for The National Vigilant

Society, The Josephine Butler Homes, and the League
of Nations' fight against social vice! But the work is
difficult and disheartening because of the wilful ignorance and prejudice of a huge majority of our people.
Few citizens seem to realise that the "fallen woman"
is both a curse and the safety valve of our seaports
under the present social system.

> "That unhappy being whose very name is shame to
> speak; who counterfeits with a cold heart the
> transport of affection, and submits herself as a
> passive instrument of lust, who is scorned and
> insulted as the vilest of her sex, and doomed for
> the most part to disease and abject wretchedness
> and an early death, appears in every age as a
> perpetual symbol of the degradation and sin-
> fulness of man. Herself the supreme type of
> vice, she is ultimately the most efficient guardian
> of virtue. But for her, the unchallenged purity
> of countless happy homes would be polluted,
> and not a few who in the pride of their intrepid
> chastity, think of her with indignant shudder,
> would have known the agony of remorse and
> despair. On that one degraded and ignoble
> form are concentrated the passions that might
> have filled the world with shame. She remains
> while creeds and civilisations rise and fall the
> eternal priestess of humanity, blasted for the sins
> of the people." (Lecky Hist: Eur: Morals.
> Vol 2. p. 283).

However much we try to ignore the problem, prosti-
tution exists on a gigantic scale in Britain. And let us
remember that the economic factor, not moral perver-
sity is the main cause of the evil.

One of the most celebrated criminal advocates of
our century, perhaps of any century, Sir Marshall Hall,
concluded a passionate defence of one unfortunate

woman who had confessed to the murder of her para-
mour thus:—

> "There she stands, friendless, homeless, nameless;
> born in poverty; reared amidst sordiness, strife
> and sin; a victim of man's cruelty, greed and
> lust. *God never gave her a chance, Gentlemen
> of the Jury, will you?*"

It may sound unorthodox for me to so much as
mention the "controlled house," and I am well aware of
the arguments adduced against State control of the
evil. State purchase and State control of alcohol and
pernicious drugs come under a similar category. Evils
should be abolished not controlled, or exploited, by the
community. True that "prohibition" in America convinced us of the unwisdom of legislating in advance of
public opinion, and before the real awakening of a
social conscience; that experiment became the occasion of gangsterdom and a long list of new crimes.
Nevertheless, the Hidden Plague must be combated in a
rational manner, or the whole nation will, in time,
suffer from its ravages in some form or other.

I once asked a French statesman why the house of
the red lamp was tolerated in his country; the reply
he gave was: "We can locate the evil, and control it;
but your raiding police scatter the carriers of disease,
and therefore cannot trace the source of contagion."

Swansea was a fine town, and could, then, as now,
boast of some excellent social leaders, preachers, and
civic servants. One of my best friends there was J. D.
Williams, then editor of the old *Cambria Daily Leader*.
Another was Dr. Rawlings, a medico beloved by the
poor of the town. Neither can I forget Mr. Rose
Richards, a colliery proprietor, who publicly thanked
me once for my persistence in bringing necessitous
cases to his notice.

Yes, there were more angels than devils at work in
Swansea.

CHAPTER SEVEN

CWMAVON IN THE MOUNTAINS

Towards the end of 1905, I accepted a call to the pastor-ate of " Tabernacl," a Welsh church of 450 members, at Cwmavon, Glamorgan. My immediate predecessor was Thomas Edwards, an original and popular preacher.

There are strange coincidences in every life, and this was one in mine. Thomas Edwards was examiner at the Denominational Examination the year I was sole candi-date for the whole of Llansamlet. My proctor on that occasion was William Jones, the well-known preacher from Morriston.

I succeeded Thomas Edwards at Tabernacl; and wrote the biography of William Jones.

Cwmavon seemed a replica of Llansamlet; it was a little world of its own, surrounded by hills, above which towered the huge stack of the " Voel " emitting yellow smoke from the local Rio Tinto copper works. The place was a hive of industry; employment was plentiful, and wages high. Nearly every family owned a cottage and vegetable garden. Houses, there, were in long, monotonous rows containing four rooms each. They had no stone pavements in front, and no bathrooms within; sanitary conditions proved primitive. The rows had been erected without any attempt at town planning, and were really plain outside. But every house was spotlessly clean within; the women are houseproud; kitchen stoves glisten; hearths are bright; the mantle-piece displays its dozen brass candlesticks with a copper kettle in the middle. Then, a shining brass sheet adorns the whole front above the fireplace, and to this is suspended a long brass rod; every home has at least one heavy brass stand aside the fender. The stone

floor of the kitchen is sprinkled with clean sand twice a
week, and a kettle is usually on the boil for the inevitable cup of tea that awaits a visitor.

The staple diet is tinned salmon and strong tea. But
colliers are fond of broth and stew, and, on Saturday
nights, laver bread and bacon. Laver bread is a green,
almost black sea weed that grows on rocks. It is plucked
leaf by leaf, washed several times, and then simmered in
a cauldron for hours; the dish has considerable medicinal
value.

Centre of our social life was the chapel, and
Tabernacl is the mother church of that village. It is a
large edifice, with seating accommodation for 800
people. On ordinary Sundays the church was comfort-
ably full. But, during special services, our congregation would over-flow, and we had to open windows for
people outside to share in the worship. Loud speakers
were unknown at that time, and we had not heard of the
microphone.

The "preaching festival" remains a prominent
feature in Welsh Nonconformity. It must be a relic of
the times when preachers were few and itinerant, travelling in couples, and preaching one after the other at each
service. A double sermon service can still draw the
crowds at any time in rural Wales; but town churches
are satisfied with one sermon at a service to-day; older
folks regard this as a sign of spiritual declension.

I preached one of three in the same service once during my young days; the other two were William Jones,
Morriston, and Moses Thomas, Port Talbot. They both
preached Welsh, and my English sermon was wedged in
between. Ten sermons over a week-end was nothing exceptional at Tabernacl church anniversaries.

It is difficult for English people to appreciate the
significance of preaching festivals in Wales; and one
must admit that much of their utility has vanished by
now; they are kept up in some places from mere sentiment. Nevertheless, these functions do develop and

sustain the passion for preaching amongst our people. Of course one gets repeats of old sermons at these "big meetings." But the patience of Welsh audiences is proverbial; they expect well-worn sermons, and will listen, uncomplainingly, again and again, to the same discourse that may have done service for years.

"I heard that sermon from you fifteen years ago, Mr. P——," said one elder to the great man.

"Indeed, sir," replied the preacher, unblushingly, "it keeps well, does it not?"

Welsh preachers are often remembered by their pet sermons, which one hears, sometimes, recited by young and old people at concerts and competitive meetings; they are popular items even at convivial gatherings.

A fine set of elders occupied our Big Pew when first I went to Tabernacl. They were strong, solemn, and reliable. To them as a whole one could apply words written about Earl Grey of Fallodon:

"Swinging to the high tides of life, his soul was always at anchor. The man had a central calm in the heart of ceaseless agitation."

They were men to trust; I was follower more than leader among them, and they fathered me like the wayward man I was.

The congregation of Tabernacl was a mixture of colliers, tin-workers, and people engaged at the copper works. They blended well together, and we had very little friction, in spite of the backwash of the Revival.

Some of the women were wonderful, especially at public prayers. At my last service in the chapel, Charlotte Griffiths exclaimed: "Lord, we are losing our pastor; we thank Thee that the elders remain with us; they are sober men at any rate."

A Mrs. Hopkins lived in perpetual revival; she would interrupt my sermon with a shout of "Glory, Haleluiah," and then stand with arms uplifted in praise or prayer. It was difficult to close a service as she kept on repeating the last verse of the final hymn. But we rarely complained, because all of us knew of the double tragedy in her life. Her religion kept the woman sane.

An interesting character was Rees David, the cattle-dealer. He was not a church member, but seldom missed a service when I occupied the pulpit. A rare treat was to listen to the drover haggling over a bargain at Neath Fair. He could be heard all over the field arguing and swearing; his voice rose with the increasing crowd. I loved to see him swishing his cudgel, clapping fist in hand, prodding a vendor in chest or rib, leaving the place in apparent disgust, and then returning to make a modified offer. This went on for fully half an hour amidst the amusement of the crowd. When the contestants had arrived to within a difference of ten or twenty pounds, they adjourned to an adjoining public house for rest and refreshment. Not a word about the sale was uttered whilst they drank two glasses of beer apiece. They then returned to the pen and resumed their interrupted argument with increased vigour and noise. Everybody knew that this second battle of wits would end in a fifty-fifty settlement; but the tug of wordy war was part of the ritual in a recognised procedure.

At last, a neighbouring farmer, or drover, would be invited to arbitrate, and he, with an air of innocence and importance, then gave the award everyone expected—split the difference. Buyer and seller shook hands, and there was a final visit to the public house, and mutual congratulations. Without a verbal tussle, offer and counter-offer, quarrel and compromise, Rees David feared some snag in a bargain.

He was asked once to value a litter of piglets at Brecon. "Fifteen shillings a head, and not one penny more," said our drover.

"Very well, Rees David," replied the farmer, "they are yours at that price."

My old friend was too much of a gentleman to withdraw; but, actually, he was dumb with surprise, and all the way back to Cwmavon could be heard mumbling, "D—— those pigs! D—— those pigs!" He felt that something was wrong.

Rees David was known to estimate the weight of two hundred live sheep to within ten pounds. Vale of Glamorgan farmers used to forward animals to our drover without taking the trouble to weigh them; such was their faith in the Cwmavon man.

He delighted in teasing me with offers of whisky whenever I paid him a visit. I know that he would have been horrified if I so much as touched the liquor.

When preaching within ten or twelve miles of home, and being desirous of returning after an evening service, I seldom hesitated to ask David to fetch me in his gig. On such occasions he combined business with pleasure.

I remember him awaiting me outside the chapel at Porthcawl. When I emerged, he was surrounded by local farmers trying to sell him their sheep. The spirited horse was prancing, and Rees David in his element shouting at the animal, swearing about preachers, and bargaining for sheep. It was an amusing sight, and the crowd were convulsed with laughter.

On the way home that night I had an insight into a noble soul under that rough exterior.

"See that farm on the left, Parson? That man owes me a hundred pounds, and I shall not be paid; he was an elder in a church known to you."

"See that house over to the right? That poor fellow died leaving a widow and three children. He owed me seventy pounds; the widow shall not be told."

Half a dozen similar instances within a radius of twelve miles could he have cited; but the man was too modest to mention them. Rees David swearing like a trooper was fitter for Heaven than some men I have heard praying like saints. He never refused any request of mine for aid in helping the weak.

Another remarkable character was William MacNeil, A mixture of Irish and Welsh was sure to produce something extraordinary. MacNeil sold lamp oil, and always smelt of paraffin even in chapel; his sarcasm was scathing, and was frequently exercised upon his pet aversion, David Williams, the butcher. Occasionally, both warriors would forget their Biblical language, and revert to old-Adam phraseology, and then we were treated to a real competition in the art of swearing. Repentance, but not reconciliation, invariably followed those outbursts.

The oil-king had lapses of inebriety as well; he would be on the spree for three or four weeks at a time, and his place in chapel knew him not. It was useless reasoning with him until the bout was over, and his money spent. When in his cups, MacNeil was violent and maudlin in turns, sang hymns, and wanted to preach. But no grocer's bill and no rent did he pay, and selling paraffin was beneath his dignity. He would be drunk morning, noon, and night, and the church was compelled to excommunicate him. Then, on a Sunday evening, the old character would turn up as fresh as ever, and beg to be re-instated. Pardon, accompanied with a stated period of probation, would then be granted, and MacNeil again became the life and soul of our church meetings,—until the next bout.

At prayer, MacNeil was irrepressible. We laughed and wept, shouted and groaned in sympathy with the old sinner. Even David Williams, the butcher, would surrender sometimes, but not often.

"Lord, the Cuckoo has come again to Cwmavon. She has the same song as last year—'cuck-oo!' The identical notes as our fathers heard—'cuck-oo!' It is just what the first sinner, Adam, listened to —cuck-oo! cuck-oo! cuck-oo!' (in ascending notes). And here is this old sinner, Will

H

MacNeil, Lord, with the same prayer as six
months ago—Pardon! Forgive! Pardon! 'Cuck-
oo! Cuck-oo! Cuck-oo!'" (with the final note in
double C.)

Then followed a long pause, during which we sobbed, or
laughed. I caught Will opening his eyes for a peep to see
how things were going.

Again the wag took up his tale before the Throne of
Grace!

"Yes, Lord, I know Thou wilt pardon; I know Jesus
can save or take away the demon of drink from
my soul. Thou art a pardoning God—Cuck-oo!
Thou art a loving God—Cuck-oo. Thou art a
true Friend — Cuck-oo! But Lord, David Williams, the butcher, will not forgive—Cuck-oo!
The elders are hard — Cuck-oo! The pastor is
not much better—Cuck-oo! Cuck-oo! Cuck-oo!"

Who could withstand that herald of Spring, whose
cry echoed throughout Cwmavon for months, and made a
hero of the oil vendor!

Outside Tabernacl my greatest friends were John
Phillips, pastor of Sion Congregational Chapel, and S. M.
Morris, the Baptist minister. The former was more of
my own age, and we had much in common. The latter
was amongst the most spiritual of men and a powerful
preacher.

Phillips and I went together on long walking and cycl-
ing tours. We would compare notes often on Saturday
nights, and listen to each other's sermons for the following day. My friend helped me considerably with a
Welsh translation of John MacNeil's book, "*The Spirit-
filled Life,*" which I published whilst in Cwmavon. Our
respective families were on visiting terms, and we frequently exchanged pulpits. John Phillips was a keen
politician, and an ardent follower of Mr. Lloyd
George. We were together (as students) in Brecon,

when the distinguished Welshman made his remarkable speech against the Balfour Education Bill, and when a Vicar Beaven distinguished himself through heckling.

Again we were at Wood Street Chapel, Cardiff, in 1907, when the Rev. Evan Jones, Caernarvon, won a definite undertaking from Mr. Lloyd George to introduce the Disestablishment Bill for Wales. That was a remarkable meeting. I seldom, if ever, witnessed such an oratorical triumph as was then won by the great man of Wales. D. A. Thomas (Lord Rhondda), S. T. Evans, Mabon, and nearly all the Welsh Members of Parliament were on the platform, and admittedly hostile to Lloyd George, who was then President of the Board of Trade. Evan Jones had made a bitter onslaught upon the Liberal Government for their supposed betrayal of Wales. In a dead silence Mr. Lloyd George was called upon to speak. I was told afterwards that some members of the Executive Committee wished to ignore his presence, and that it was the insistence of Evan Jones and Ellis Davies which secured a hearing for the Welsh Cabinet Minister. Not one cheer greeted his appearance, and he began his speech in a palpably hostile atmosphere. The orator tried every trick and all sorts of appeal to win over his audience. But he was faced with stony silence until he referred to his own record and his labours on behalf of the Boers, when he had risked his living, his career, his health, yes, his life for a small nation. "Is it likely that I could betray the land of my birth? Can you not be fair to your friends? Would I remain in a Government that ignored my own country?" These sentences were hurled at us with terrific force; and then, in a hush that brought us to our feet, Evan Jones came to the front of the platform, and placed his hand on the shoulder of the speaker.

"Mr. Lloyd George," said he, "do we understand that you will leave the Cabinet unless they bring forward a Bill for Disestablishment?" It was an electric moment, and we held our breath as the statesman, after a few moments' hesitation, nodded—"Yes!"

Then pandemonium broke loose, and we shouted for fully five minutes; following which we had half an hour of bewitching eloquence from a real master of assemblies. That was the first time I heard the oft-repeated peroration of dawn breaking over the Welsh hills.

Phillips owns a powerful voice. It always is a treat to hear him recite Welsh poetry, especially the works of Eifion Wyn and Goronwy Owen. He is a good mimic, and has a wonderful memory. He persuaded me to stand with him for a Parish Council election. We were both returned at the wrong end of the poll.

During my stay at Cwmavon the young Independent Labour Party was very active all over South Wales. That was the time most of its Welsh Branches were formed, and the Party came in for much hostile criticism from the churches, and especially amongst old Liberals. There was fault on both sides. Liberals dominated Nonconformist churches, and they bitterly attacked the Independent Labour Party on the score of atheism, supposed or real. Naturally, members of the Party became anti-church, if not anti-God. Agnostic and infidel literature was on sale at the Branches, and pressed upon people. "The Clarion," "God and my Neighbour" and the Secularist Press publications were displayed in windows; young I.L.P.'ites left the churches, and became bitter opponents of ministers; they held political meetings on Sundays, and challenged the clergy to public debates. A spirit of persecution was abroad, and it was not the monopoly of one side.

Yet the original founders of the I.L.P. were deeply religious men. Reference has already been made to Keir Hardie. Ramsay MacDonald remained throughout a staunch Presbyterian; Phillip Snowden was a humble believer; one of my literary treasures is Snowden's "The Christ that is to Be." The same can be said about J. W. Jowett, Anderson, and other pioneers. The Party was born in a religious atmosphere, enshrined a religious motive, and marched towards a moral goal. Leaders realised the dangers of secularism capturing the Party. A crisis was reached when Bruce-Glasier refused to open the new Landore Branch until all agnostic literature had been removed from the window.

In 1908, Phillip Snowden formed a Nonconformist Socialist League during the Swansea annual conference of the National Free Church Council. Snowden was ablaze then with zeal for Christian Socialism. Nothing came of that League; but the Methodist Socialist League is still flourishing, and so is the Socialist League of the Episcopal Church.

I engaged in public debate with a Mr. Black from Leicester. At this distance the subject discussed has escaped my memory; but I well remember the excited crowd and the cat-calls of partizans in the crowded hall. My opponent was a good debater, well informed, and a gentleman. The honours went easily to him.

Our chairman was the best speaker in the hall. He was leader of the local Branch of the I.L.P., clerk to the Parish Council, County Councillor, and a professed atheist. I expected him to go far in public life; but he disappointed his friends.

In time, the I.L.P. shed its secularism and anti-church spirit. The Party then became the real brain of Labour and a mighty power in the life of Britain; it was the only political party to exclude alcohol from its premises. Uncompromising pacifism appealed to us young ministers, and we found that true Socialism had much in common with Christianity. Both teach rebellion against evil; both believe in a possible better world; both are animated with the spirit of altruism. And these were the principles inculcated by the early Christian Socialists— Frederick Denison Maurice in his sermons; Charles Kingsley through his novels; Thomas Hughes with his speeches. Then we were introduced to the " Song of the Shirt" (Tom Hood), "The Cry of the Children" (Mrs. Browning) and the works of Robert Owen, Francis

Place, Brougham, Hume, and the Chartists. People who studied these things found something approaching New Testament ideals in the work of socialists at home and abroad. Before I left Cwmavon I had become dissatisfied with Liberalism, but hesitated to accept the full socialist creed and philosophy.

Our Member of Parliament was Sir D. Brynmor-Jones, brother of my old Principal at Cardiff, and son of the poet-preacher, Thomas Jones. He was a good committee man, a safe Liberal, and worshipper of the name of Gladstone. His speeches were of the sort that give offence to nobody, and do neither good nor evil.

His neighbour, S. T. Evans, Member for Mid-Glamorgan, and, later, a famous judge, was a different type, —witty, sarcastic and aggressive. He had a long nose which he fondled before answering a question. Our colliers loved to tease and threaten him; but he was sure of their votes.

"You rarely visit us unless there is an election on," said Thomas Thomas, Pontrhydyfen, at one meeting.

"No, Thomas Thomas," replied Evans, "you do not invite me to have tea at your house, and I should love it. More than that, I know that Pontrhydyfen is safe so long as Thomas Thomas is here! How pleasant it is when brethren dwell together in unity."

A verse of Scripture always placated us in those days.

The first Labour onslaught upon S. T. Evans in that Liberal stronghold came from Vernon Hartshorn, a native of Maesteg. That was something new to Wales, and the work of the I.L.P., whose leaders entered the fray. One night, at Cymer, I was last speaker for S. T. Evans, and, just fifteen minutes before the end of my speech, I noticed a stubby man pushing his way through the crowd. The stranger came to congratulate me after my people had dispersed. That was my first meeting with Arthur Henderson, who sponsored Hartshorn. We became friends, and when Henderson was Foreign Secretary in the second Labour Government he reminded me of our first encounter at Cymer. Little did I, or anybody else, dream that the slow, stodgy speaker who followed me on that Cymer platform was destined to play such a wonderful part in world politics as did Arthur Henderson.

In 1910, I accepted a call to Willmer Road Church, Birkenhead. It was a great surprise to all my friends, because I was happy and successful at Cwmavon, and had refused a call to Newport two years previously.

The Birkenhead church was in a very low condition at the time, practically bankrupt. Several of the wealthiest and most influential members had left the church, and there was talk of closing the doors and selling the edifice. A small denominational committee of three gave me a challenge to tackle the place. Dr. John Williams, formerly of Princes Road, Liverpool, and Mr. John Owens, of Chester, were most insistent; and I accepted.

Another fact that weighed with me was my dissatisfaction with the itinerant system of the Welsh pulpit. I felt that preaching in my own pulpit just once a month was not only ridiculous, but demoralising to pastor and people. A man becomes lazy and afraid of new sermons; he loses self-confidence and strives to please those upon whom he depends for preaching engagements; his livelihood is in their hands. The elder who has charge of the pulpit diary can be a little tyrant, and, not infrequently, is. Then the churches become filled with sermon tasters, and one discovers unhealthy criticism amongst congregations. They contrast visiting ministers with each other and with their own pastor. W. E. Prytherch occupied his own pulpit but three times one year, four times another year, and not once during a whole twelve months.

I realised that if I was to save my own, or any other soul, I should have to secure a more settled ministry; at that time, this was not available in the Welsh pulpit.

Both my children were born at Cwmavon, and I still love the place and the people. Perhaps the greatest good I got there was a conviction of the necessity for economic emancipation in the life that is life indeed. I trace that to the indirect influence of my critics in the I.L.P.

CHAPTER EIGHT

BIRKENHEAD . . . . A GREY SPOT ON THE MERSEY

FROM Cwmavon to Birkenhead was a great change.
I left a prosperous church for one facing bankruptcy;
from a village of about 2,000 souls I went to a great industrial centre of over 200,000 inhabitants. But I
never regretted the change. Birkenhead folk were
kind, industrious, and anxious to help. We had some
excellent church workers, especially amongst the women
members. They organised sales of work, concerts, and
parties which brought in large sums of money. There
are times when I detest church bazaars; but they are a
wonderful means of bringing people together, and their
social value is not negligible. On such occasions we
can appeal to outsiders for donations, and many readily
respond.

I wish it was unnecessary to solicit subscriptions
for religious work. Nevertheless, even begging can be
made sacramental, as witness Francis of Assisi, Bar-
nardo and Spurgeon; spirit, motive, method count in
everything. I am not a good beggar; but large sums
of money for charities have passed through my hands,
and I feel that some service is being rendered a donor
by giving him an opportunity of helping a good cause.
The collection plate is a means of grace, not a regrettable
adjunct to a religious service.

Willmer Road church used to be controlled by a
committee, elected annually; but I expressed a desire
to have elders. Frequent elections disturb a church,
and imperil continuity of policy; when the best qualified
people are not returned there is disappointment and real
loss. I am fully aware of the arguments against life

eldership. Sometimes office is retained long after use-
fulness has ended. The personnel of a city church
changes in about five or ten years, and people who
voted a man to office can leave; then their successors
may have no use for those who were elected long ago.
Elders cannot be removed even when they prove ob-
structive in a church. But, speaking generally, life
eldership has worked well with the Presbyterian
Churches in the past. Amongst the Scotch, Irish, and
English sections, elder and deacon are two distinct
orders, the former nominated for life, and the latter
elected for a term of years to care for the finances of
a church. But in the Welsh Presbyterian Church there
is only one order, and office is for life, or until resignation through removal from a Presbytery.

I got my elders at Birkenhead, and they were a fine
set of men who co-operated with me loyally right
through. Our secretary was George Burroughs, a lame
philatelist, quick-tempered, an ardent Tory who hated
Socialism. But he loved his pastor, and delighted in
doing good by stealth; he saved several of his friends
from bankruptcy during one industrial slump.

Our treasurer was Deputy-judge Granville Morris,
a cultured, patient and most considerate soul whose
humility always surprised me. His is a greatness that can
stoop, a culture that captivates, a wisdom bringing
offerings to the helpless who can promise nothing in
return. Were my friend more ambitious and assertive
he would amass wealth in the profession he adorns. But,
whilst ever ready to press the claims of others, O. G.
Morris seeks but little for himself.

I started a Brotherhood at the church, one of the
earliest in the Denomination, and it became a power in
Birkenhead. We had a band of twelve enthusiasts who
helped me to canvass the neighbourhood. It was very
amusing work, since people wished to know what we
were getting out of the business. Progress proved slow
because the average Merseysider is argumentative, and

loves teasing parsons. In time we collected a crowd of
nearly 100 men to meet on Sunday afternoons. By
the second year we numbered over two hundred, and,
before I left there was a membership of four hundred
subscribing members. The work was not all of the
usual "pleasant Sunday afternoon" type. Lapses were
frequent, and often I had to bail a Brother out of court
because of some unbrotherly conduct; or visit members
of the fraternity during compulsory retirement in Wal-
ton gaol.

Our Labour Bureau was a full-time job for more
than one man. Old lags gave as much trouble as the
shirkers. Building contractors used to disappear when
I approached; they were afraid that I would coax a job
for some bounder,—which was often the case. I placed
125 men in work during two years. We concentrated
upon one street at a time for intensive evangelism. A
magic lantern was helpful in the open-air work, and loafers and children had a glorious time with it; whilst the
show was on, the whole street would be out of doors,
and every lamp-post supported sight-seers. We sang
ourselves hoarse, and frequently suffered from sore or
relaxed throats. I knew each urchin in the district by
name, and could be sure of a welcome at every house.
Not infrequently, I attended Catholic wakes, and stayed
until the wakers started seeing things. It was time to
leave then.

One Saturday night, about 11 o'clock, I felt an irrepressible urge to visit a house in the mission district.
My wife accompanied me. When we arrived at the
door, shuffling and shouting could be heard from within.
A second loud and prolonged knock on my part
brought a dishevelled, blood-shot-eyed man to the door.
He held a razor in one hand, and, in a frenzy, was going
to attack me, until I shouted his name. He then recognised us, and blubbered out: "Thank God you came,
sir, I was trying to kill my wife; you have saved us
both." I believe that we were Divinely led to that
house.

Our chief mission street swarmed with children. In fact, the increase of population in Britain is almost confined to the slums; child-birth is nearly an annual event with poor families. Somebody has said that Britain will soon be depending upon Irish Catholics for her population. And what chance has a child born in the slums? He is not so much born as damned into a world of dirt, depravity and disease.

Overcrowding is chronic in our slums; grown-up boys and girls are put to sleep together, and, sometimes, have to share the bed of their parents. Sodomy and incest are more than mere hearsay in such surroundings. People there become over-sexed; that is emphatically so with the feeble-minded. Several times I have seen a man return home from some mental institution, and remain until his wife became pregnant; then a relapse necessitated his removal for another spell; and this goes on repeatedly until the wretched woman prays for her husband's permanent detention or his death. Yet church folk have opposed divorce on the ground of incurable insanity!

The problem of traffic in women was brought home to the leaders of my church on one occasion. For a long time I had missed a girl from our Sunday services; her friends declared that she had gone on an extended holiday; but they refused me her address. After about two years the girl herself came to the Manse and asked to see me. I always insist upon my wife being present, if at all possible, when interviewing a woman, and did so on this occasion. When the trembling sister was fully convinced that her confidence would be kept secret, she poured out a startling story of being entrapped in a house of shame, and how she had been sent into the country twice for the purpose of abortion. We discovered that den of iniquity, and persuaded the police to raid the premises. But news must have leaked out, because the birds of night had flown, and never returned even to claim the furniture. I was informed that my life was in danger for a time afterwards, and that a detective, who had been sent to shadow me, saved me from a knife-thrust twice.

In fact, the White Slave traffic was brisk in Birkenhead about that time. Our Vigilance Society performed wonders. The secretary, a solicitor, became a terror to evil-doers; within one year he was the means of stopping thirty girls being shipped out of the country. Our representatives searched trains, boarded ships, met aliens arriving from abroad, and frustrated devilish plots of demons in the forms of men. But ramifications of the traffic are awful, and exploiters of innocence prove unscrupulous. Voluntary efforts seem insufficient to cope with this international evil.

I enjoyed more than one temperance crusade. Birkenhead " Haymarket " on Saturday nights resembled Hyde Park on Sundays. It was a fine place to get accustomed to heckling and repartee, and I benefitted by the experience.

At one meeting I concluded my address with a strong appeal to my male listeners to leave the drink for the sake of their wives and sweethearts. " It is no good, Parson Howard," shouted one who was well under way, " my ruddy wife drinks much more than me." That heckler spoiled a fine peroration which I had diligently rehearsed during the day.

Ruffians, sometimes, rushed our platform; one red nosed brother caused considerable concern through his repeated attempts to " punch your b—— nose off." He kept turning up at successive meetings. Once I lost patience with him, and tried to get at the son of mischief; but four young men closed round and escorted me home. That group, I found afterwards, had formed themselves into a self-elected body-guard who stood near me at every meeting, and were always ready for a row.

My open-air work won me many friends and some enemies. One tub-thumper made a series of slashing attacks upon my work and sincerity. At last I challenged him to the test of an election. He accepted, and, inasmuch as there was a vacancy then for the Board of Guardians, six of us got nominated for the by-election. For some reason I received more votes than the other five candidates put together; my detractor was the bottom name on that poll.

My Brotherhood ran the election for me on an independent ticket. Two years afterwards, the Board of Guardians' general election took place. Again I fought as an independent, easily headed the poll, and was made Chairman of the Tranmere Infirmary. I revelled in the work of the Board; not only did I get an insight to Poor Law administration, but found opportunities of helping people outside my own circle.

One man I came to know was a consumptive, a pronounced atheist, and hated parsons. He determined to meet the inevitable end with a stiff lip; but two days before passing on, he begged me to look after his two children soon to be made orphans, and wished them to be reared in the Protestant faith.

"But, friend," I asked, "why this of me, a parson?" I shall always remember his reply:

"I can trust the followers of the Nazarene, although I do not accept the Christ."

My colleagues on the Board regarded me as a stormy petrel, and on several occasions, saw me at variance with officials. In retrospect, my attitude seems excessively combative; but I had a consuming desire to ease the lot of the poor, and the mere suspicion of harshness towards the necessitous made me see red. My fellow members were very patient, and I grew to respect our considerate officials.

The most impressive personality on that Board was Dr. Guy Warman, then Principal of St. Aidan's College, —a ripe scholar, an excellent preacher, and wise administrator, who, subsequently, became Vicar of Bradford, Bishop of Truro, and, at the time of writing, is the esteemed Bishop of Manchester. We took long walks together between meetings, and discussed all manner of things of interest to Church and State. I learnt much from that erudite ecclesiastic. We frequently crossed swords in debate, and voted on opposite sides; but our friendship and mutual esteem remained unimpaired.

There was one unhappy disagreement at the Workhouse, and certain officials were dismissed after a Local Government Board inquiry had been held. I interviewed John Burns to plead for one man; but the President was adamant. I always find that socialists in office are rather conservative.

When the elderly clerk to the Guardians retired, he received a pension of nearly £1,000 a year. About a week or so previously some of us had proposed an increase of one shilling a week all round for outdoor relief, and that had been turned down. Consequently, we held meetings of protest all over the town, and were reported even in "John Bull." But it was useless; the retiring official was entitled to his full pension, and got it. That gentleman bore me no grudge for my criticisms; and when he moved to Colwyn Bay he and his family frequently attended my church. In fact, we enjoyed many a good laugh over our reminiscences.

During July, 1914, I published a Welsh book, "Cristionogaeth a Chymdeithas" (Christianity and Society), dealing with poverty, labour, and the Christian conception of an ideal society. Mr. Lloyd George, then Chancellor of the Exchequer, wrote an appreciative preface. According to reviewers, mine was the first Welsh book to deal with those subjects from the purely Christian standpoint, and it received a flattering reception throughout Wales, and amongst compatriots elsewhere.

About that time the new Welsh orthography was all the rage in our educational circles. The double n, and the double r became obsessions with the new School. One

of the reviewers, Gwili, my old tutor at Gwynfryn, had
been badly bitten by the grammatical bug. He ignored
the substance and theme of my book, and treated his
readers to three columns of examples where the new
spelling conflicted with the old. (I had left the matter
to my experienced printers.) I wrote my friend the
following on a postcard:—

> "Formerly I knew Gwili to be a mighty hunter
> before the Lord; I see now that he is merely a
> catcher of verbal fleas" (*chwilotwr chwain*).

Months afterwards we met at a public dinner, and the
affable critic said: "Howard, you hurt me terribly
with that P.C.; but you were quite right, my review was
childish."

My membership on the Board of Guardians gave me
wonderful opportunities to study poverty at first hand.
For one whole winter I specialised in the casual wards,
and interviewed hundreds of tramps, male and female.
I spent one night in a cell on my own, but shied at
the morning task allotted to knights of the road. The
ordinary tramp is a special creation, not of God, but of
an acquisitive society inspired by greed and callous-
ness, which offers no second chance to the failure. I
met barristers, doctors, clergymen, in casual wards, and
it was only by persistent persuasion one could elicit
their story, much of which, in all probability, was imaginary. Once a man takes to the life of a tramp he
seldom returns to decent society. Yet we can cite some
brilliant exceptions like the poets W. H. Davies, Francis
Thompson, and Orwell, etc.

John Burns did much to alleviate the lot of the homeless; and the casual ward has been improved since the
days of his administration. But what a seething mass of
misery and potential danger are the 10,000 tramps of
Britain! (There has been a marked decrease during
1936-1937.)

I also studied casual labour at close quarters whilst at Birkenhead, and published the results of my investigations. For over thirty years now I have preached that the root cause of pauperism is in our economic system.

The year 1937 is regarded as a year of revived prosperity and industrial boom consequent upon re-armament. But Mr. Graham White, M.P. (no alarmist) said in the House of Commons (29/7/37) that 4,500,000 Britons spend only 4/- a week on food; 9,000,000 spend only 6/- a week on food; and a further 9,000,000 can spare only 8/- a week for eatables, whilst the Nutriment Committee of the British Medical Association has fixed 8/- a week as a minimum.

We received hundreds of wounded soldiers into Tranmere Infirmary, and, as Chairman, I spent many hours in their midst. They were an interesting set, very cheerful, and glad to be out of the shambles at the Front. Their patience with inquisitive visitors was remarkable; but they often drew the long bow over their "adventures." Irish lads were screamingly funny and popular with elderly ladies avid for thrills; no tale was too extravagant for them, and the more gruesome it was the better the females liked it. One lady paid £5 for the "lobe of a German's ear." The vendor laughingly admitted to me that it was a snip off his rubber tobacco pouch.

Another credulous visitor parted with three pounds for a German officer's tooth. (Ludendorff's at that!). There was a suspicious dental gap in the mouth of the lad who effected that deal, and I heard that the dentist had paid him a recent visit.

One man, whose accent belonged to Anglesey, stoutly maintained that he had saved the life of Lord French. This story proved very remunerative to the Welshman, and it was regarded by all as a monopoly and copyright of the son of " Sir Fôn."

I

But who could blame the men? It was all in the game, and helped them to forget much.

There was some trouble with nurses, especially the young and inexperienced girls. But our Matron was a good disciplinarian; times were exceptional, and nobody was living the normal life.

Another problem came with the Belgian refugees who were housed together at Bebington Hall. They were difficult to manage owing to their customs, language and religion. The Protestants among them attended my church, and I felt responsible for their welfare. They quarrelled incessantly, and could not be satisfied with their food; as for discipline, it did not enter into their calculations.

We entertained the exiles in chapel and at home, and got to know them well. When I left Birkenhead, the church presented me with a fine set of book-shelves made by the refugees, and inscribed with their names.

I well remember the riots that broke out in Birkenhead after the sinking of the *Lusitania*. We were quite accustomed to riots in the town; there was an epidemic of colour-clashes, just before and immediately after the war in most British seaports. But on that occasion a dead set was made against German stores. Opposite one pork shop women were seen skipping with ropes of sausages. A female looter carried two hams to a window sill, and went for a further supply. During her absence somebody else discovered how patriotism agreed with ham; because, when the avaricious lady returned with her extra spoils, the original pieces of pig had disappeared. In consternation she shouted, "There are some d—— thieves about here to-night."

The police were helpless or indifferent at the time, and feelings ran high. One member of my church sank with the *Lusitania*, and it was difficult to console his people, and harder still to preach Christian fortitude and forgiveness. The whole nation seemed fired with hatred and the spirit of revenge; men were out for blood and ready to believe any evil story. It was treason to insinuate that the *Lusitania* carried munitions,—which has been proved, since, to be true. "Revenge the *Lusitania*" was the cry that roused our country; and when it became known that medals were struck in Germany to commemorate the atrocity, a fit of righteous indignation seized nations. Probably that was a turning point in the war for us; recruiting was brisk afterwards. The Derby scheme boomed. Our local M.P., Mr. Bigland, recruited a Bantam Brigade; clergymen took the platform as recruiters for the Army; but comparatively few ministers entered the ranks.

Personally, I could not advise others to join up, because, although of military age, I was not ready to go myself. When I heard men like Gautry and F. B. Meyer urging men to fight, I asked why they themselves did not enlist. Their answers were not complimentary to me, neither did they reveal heroism on the part of our ministerial recruiters.

There is a story concerning one recruiting meeting held at a village chapel in Wales about that time. A retired colonel, and one well known clergyman, were the speakers. Our old warrior opened with a fiery appeal to the patriotism of his audience. Then the preacher delivered a rousing peroration; but the call for volunteers achieved no result. Again the clergyman spoke in pleading tones; still there was no response. The cleric then changed his tactics, and taunted his hearers with cowardice. There was a long silence afterwards, until the colonel, almost choking with wrath, exploded. "What can we do, Reverend? The devils will not come?"

I volunteered to go to France as interpreter or ambulance bearer, without pay. But the authorities would not entertain the idea. Everybody had to be part of the military machine, and subject to discipline. That was the trouble between Kitchener and independent journalists.

About Lusitania week I again became interested in
the I.L.P. Uncompromising pacifism seemed to me the
nearest approach to Christianity. I met some of the
leaders of the Party, and was captivated by their readi-
ness to suffer for their principles. I cared little for their
economics, and their literature, then, left me quite cold.
But the contrast between their outlook and the jingoism
of the churches was challenging. Prominent pulpiteers
were militarists, and church organisations were publicly
offered for the work of recruiting. The religious Press
was sad reading, and, for three years I ceased perusing
it, owing to what I considered its blasphemy.

I seriously contemplated resigning from the Ministry
at that time, and spent two months in spiritual agony.
Preaching became a torture, and I felt at variance with
nearly all my former friends. What kept me in the
Church was the influence of certain Quakers, and the
Fellowship of Reconciliation which had recently been
formed. In the Fellowship I found a real mission and
inspiration; and it was in that mood I accepted a call to
Colwyn Bay.

I learnt much in Birkenhead. Church work was
strenuous, but happy. Sunday was a full day: Adult
class at 10 a.m.; Service, 11; Brotherhood at 3 p.m.; Service, 6.30, and, in summer months, an open-air meeting
afterwards.

Mission work convinced me that poor and rich will
not blend for long even in church. When the destitute
attended service, better dressed folk stayed away; and
then the mission people sulked and drifted back to their
old ways. The pride of poverty is as stubborn as the
conceit of wealth. Lazarus may feel more at home with
the dogs under the table than when sitting near purple
and fine linen; I wonder whether he would care to be
clothed like Dives! At any rate, I had to hold two
separate services.

Before the end of my stay at Willmer Road my
economic studies had driven me to accept the Socialist

creed and philosophy; and rabid militarism compelled
me to face up to the fact that Christ and War are in-
compatibles. I became known as that contradiction-in-
terms, a pugnacious pacifist.

Whilst at Birkenhead I enjoyed much of the company
of E. D. Morel, the one-time Liverpool shipping clerk
who defied a king, and, through his disclosures of the
Congo atrocities that accompanied the production of
rubber, created a social revolution. He was a remarkable man—poet and politician, mystic and merchant.
He came frequently to spend the evening at our home,
and spoke several times from my pulpit. One of the
many tragedies of the world war on the home front was
the imprisonment of that cultured soul, and the ruin of
his health because of his advocacy of peace.

Late in 1914 I interviewed John Burns, who along
with Morley, and Trevelyan, had resigned office after
the declaration of war. The old lion was peeved; but
as full of himself as ever. Before introducing me to his
wife, he took me round to his library. In one room
was arranged everything written about Sir Thomas
More. "Hold that book for a moment, boy, it is valued
at £2,000. The only other copy is in the British Museum." I suitably expressed my awe as the little volume
was reverently replaced.

In another room was the Milton collection; and here
again I was allowed to handle a book valued at £1,500.

There was one room dedicated to books dealing with
London alone.

Then with a sweeping gesture worthy of Henry Irving,
he said: "This room, Sir, contains a little of what
is written about your humble servant, the Right Honourable John Burns, former President of the Local
Government Board."

I might have uttered three sentences during that afternoon, scarcely more, until I spoke to Mrs. Burns. John
then whisked me off to the House of Commons. His
bowler hat was in constant requisition acknowledging

salutations as we crossed the Common. In the tramcar a Church dignitary sat next to my host, and diffident-
ly broke in upon our conversation with: "Have I the
privilege of speaking to Mr. John Burns?"

"John Burns is my name, and at your service, reverend sir," said J.B., loud enough for all the passengers
to hear, and so explosively that our cleric nearly jumped
from the seat. The excited dignitary then jerkingly
added: "I am pleased to meet you, sir; but like many
of your admirers, I feel grieved at your anti-war attitude."

"War! War!" shouted Burns, "you wearing that
collar dare to support war!"

Even the tramcar slowed down as we all listened to
the most violent tirade I ever heard against jingoism,
parsons and politicians. Then, taking my arm, he said,
"Howard, we get off here." I was speechless; but
Burns was thoroughly enjoying himself. His parting
word to me was: "When you go home, write in your
diary that you listened to John Burns teaching a Dean of
the Episcopal Church to respect the Sermon on the
Mount."

In 1924 I went specially to ask John Burns to accept
nomination for a Parliamentary Election. His uncompromising reply was: "Never, so long as your distinguished fellow-countryman, Lloyd George, is in public
life."

The Right Hon. LORD COLWYN

CHAPTER NINE

COLWYN BAY—A GARDEN WITH FEW WEEDS

TOWARDS the end of 1915, I accepted a call to the English Presbyterian Church of Colwyn Bay. Here again I faced an entirely different sphere of labour, another class of people, and some new problems. It was a definite break.

Colwyn Bay is called the Garden City of the North. The town as seen from Penmaen-head is a semi-circular gem of beauty. Pwllycrochan wood forms a wonderful background of undulating green; the two promontories of Rhos and Old Colwyn stand out like sentries of the sea; the blend of variegated colours is a challenge to an artist by day, and the scene, when lit up at night, resembles an enchanted isle of one's dreams. At Colwyn Bay I really awoke to the appeal and lure of natural beauty. Apart from the brief interludes at Newcastle Emlyn and Trevecca, I had spent all my life, previously, within industrial centres; coal tips, grimy docks, tall chimneys belching smoke day and night, monotonous streets, and noisy tramcars were the sights I usually gazed upon. Street smells, not the scent of mown hay, honeysuckle, and ozone, filled the air I breathed. Flowers occupied too much space where vegetables were scarce; a geranium box on the window sill was our substitute for meadows, orchards, and fields of ripe corn; sparrow chirp, or the brave trill of a caged canary gave us the music of the spheres; our horizon ended in walls across the road; and, if, sometimes, a patch of blue glimpsed between drifting banks of cloud, or sunrays on the pavement did awaken yearnings for the countryside and dancing waves on the shingle, we were fairly satisfied to live in towns.

Holidays have not made me dissatisfied with my lot.
Candidly, I dislike vacations, and cannot decide where
to go until the last minute, and then I feel it was a mistake. The best part of a holiday to me is the day for
returning home. Why should we leave comfortable
homes for noisy hotels or dreary boarding houses, and
pay exorbitant prices for being made uncomfortable?
Perhaps natural distaste for change and a double dose
of temperamental indolence account for my disinclina-
tion to leave home. I object to being disturbed, having
to pack trunks, and to leave familiar things.

One day I met a kindred soul on the Great Orme;
that was subsequent to what I call my awakening to
Nature. It was the hour of sunset; I had climbed the
mountain in the company of a parish priest on holiday
from the East End of London. As we stood in awe
and breathless silence watching the sun sink in a tremul-
ous sea of glory beyond the waves, I felt like kneeling
in worship. Turning to my companion, I found him in
tears. "Howard," said he, "thirty years in slumdom
has robbed me of the capacity to enjoy a sunset; I long
to get back to my drab streets, and more drab parishioners." My removal to Colwyn Bay saved me from
that numbness of soul. But the awakening did not come
at once; it took me two years and a half to really settle
down in the Garden City of the North. The temptation to accept a call back to Birkenhead was almost
irresistible until this change took place.

The season of bluebells and hawthorn had arrived. I
was travelling by train along the Lledr Valley. Being
alone in the compartment, I relaxed, and let my mind
drift with the passing scenery visible from the train. On
our left, the sluggish Conway river reflected Moel
Siabod and Snowdonian peaks glistening amidst drifts
of lingering snow. Towards the right were several
groves of trees set in broad patches of bluebells, framed
with white hawthorn, and divided by fields of butter-
cups and daisies in rich pastures where sheep and kine

browsed at peace. Songs of birds blended with the rhythm of the moving train; and white cloudlets hovered like benedictions above our world. For a brief moment time seemed to stop. It was as though a thick veil had been turned aside and one was given a glimpse into some Holy of Holies; breathing was an ecstasy of pain; the world spoke in pulsations, and thought could not keep pace with sensation, "Day unto day uttereth speech." Are these the words that cannot be uttered? Poets and mystics feel at home in a world I glimpsed that day. All too soon the veil rolled back, and life resumed its ordinary tale. But the world about me has not seemed quite the same since. Trees now have thoughts; rivers yield more than trout. "Turn a stone and stir a wing"; I cannot wantonly step on a daisy, and a bluebell rings for me the chimes of heaven; a bird on the wing is a perpetual wonder; clouds are chariots of the King; scent from a wayside violet is incense of some hidden shrine; every streamlet flows through the City of bliss; the sough of wind is part of harmony divine. If God should create something more beautiful than a wild rose entwined with honeysuckle I would love to see it.

> "I have felt
> A presence that disturbs me with the joy
> Of elevated thoughts; a sense sublime
> Of something far more deeply interfused,
> Whose dwelling is the light of setting suns,
> And the round ocean, and the living air,
> And the blue sky, and in the mind of man:
> A motion and a spirit, that impels
> All thinking things, all objects of all thought,
> And rolls through all things. Therefore am I still
> A lover of the meadows and the woods,
> And mountains; and of all that we behold
> From this green earth."
> —*Wordsworth.*

What glorious hours I spent on the seashore at Colwyn Bay! Not when visitors thronged the beach; not listening to brave pierrot troups amusing holiday crowds; not only amidst joyous children and their sand-castles awaiting the incoming tide, but on the deserted sands bathed in moonlight witchery, when spirits were abroad, in the shrieking wind, or with the moan of distant waves, or when the inrushing tide sprayed one's brow whilst serried clouds raced across the horizon. Again, the dawn after a night of storm; roars of a baffled tempest in retreat, romance of the debris, sea-walls dented, promenade forms awry, the heaving main beyond like emotion under strain, and circling seagulls bemoaning the forgotten dead! Secrets of the sea! mystery of waters never at rest, ominous and sublime! "He that would learn to pray, let him go to sea."

> "The sea-wind and the sea
> Made all my soul in me
> A song for ever."

Mountains also began to speak to my soul. When in the neighbourhood of Betws-y-Coed I frequently lost my way through trying to follow the paths of Winnie Wyn and Sinfi Lovell from the pages of "Aylwin" (Watts-Dunton).

We spent several holidays at Dolwyddelan, and did much climbing, fishing, and dreaming in that romantic spot. One day, five of us climbed over Moel Siabod, and went down to a farm in Nant Gwynant in time for supper and a short rest before starting for Snowdon where we hoped to see a sunrise. It was full moon that night, and, in view of each lake, we rested whilst one of our company related some lake legend; we stood on the summit at 3 a.m. in a thick and clammy mist. We saw no sunrise; but it had been a glorious climb, and the descent through one cloud after another was a wonderful experience.

There is a Snowdon of the prospector in search of material wealth; see the wounded sides of our premier mountain to mark the desecration.

We saw the Snowdon of the artist that morning,— the elusive beauty of light and shade, and symmetry of the universe.

But to the mystic, Snowdon is the vision of the eternal, the inexhaustible, the Divine amidst perpetual change in an ephemeral world. Storms and tumults expire beneath the mount; and a man who has learnt the secret of Snowdon can meet events without one tremor. Snowdon must remain a memory henceforth. The thrill of vision is rarely re-captured.

> "A mountain, by virtue of its height, remoteness and aloofness from familiar things, is a medium whereby beauty is interpreted and revealed. It quickens the perception and fires the imagination; it is a visible and tremendous expression of power and beauty; it touches notes potentially vibrant with the etheric rhythm of the universe. This music of hills bears man gently upwards on waves of pure harmony, and brings him an immeasurable joy." (*F. S. Smythe*).

W. H. Davies describes "*A Great Time*" for him:

> "Sweet Chance, that led my steps abroad,
> Beyond the town, where wild flowers grow—
> A rainbow and a cuckoo, Lord,
> How rich and great the times are now!
>   Know, all ye sheep
>   And cows, that keep
> On staring that I stand so long
> In grass that's wet from heavy rain—
> A rainbow and a cuckoo's song
> May never come together again;
>   May never come
>   This side the tomb."

Yet, the cuckoo's song is ephemeral like the rainbow itself; both are temporary, evanescent and soon mere memories in the course of the seasons. But I have heard the cuckoo's song on the slopes of Snowdon; it was the glory of contrast—the temporal and the eternal, the evanescent and that which abides, a momentarily vocal and the age-long silence of Nature. The highest mountain of Wales survives all stages in the drama of history.

I grew to love Nant Gwynant, Capel Curig, Beddgelert and Llanberis. Whenever I feel stale, and in need of special clarity of mind, I endeavour to spend a day or two in those surroundings, and can always return home refreshed in body and soul. The up-reaches of earth to heaven give solace and strength to me; they are so solid and dignified, and peaceful even when empires are tottering, and nations drift to their doom!

Pageantry soon palls on me; children playing marbles can detain me much longer than a Lord Mayor's procession ever did. But I have motored seventy miles, back and fore, with the purpose of watching cloud shadows play along the slopes of Snowdon, and always felt amply repaid for the journey.

Another name for Colwyn Bay is "Manchester by the Sea," because so many of its residents hail from the Metropolis of Cotton. Manchester people differ from Merseyside folk in many things. "Liverpool gentlemen and Manchester merchants" is an old saying. But with well over twenty years' experience, I maintain that one is as good as the other, if not better. Manchester folks are kind and generous, and will never let their pastor down.

We had several big employers of labour in our congregation, and they were wonderful supporters of the church. Although the majority of them voted Tory, they seemed to trust their socialist minister, and poured kindness upon my head even when I preached practical communism.

A friend followed in the wake of two workmen after one Sunday evening service, and overheard them talk:

"Tell me, Bill," asked one of his partner, "how do you explain it? The sermon we listened to this evening from Howard was undiluted socialism; and there was C——, a big Tory, and P——, a bloated capitalist, and several of his ilk all enjoying it; and they seldom miss a service if that blighter occupies the pulpit. How is one to explain it, man?"

After a brief silence, Bill replied :—"I don't know, unless they know that Howard is telling the truth."

When I took over the church it had been, from its very inception, in receipt of a heavy grant-in-aid. We voluntarily relinquished that within eighteen months. Every sitting was let and occupied, and we had a list of families applying for pews. Nobody was sure of a seat on ordinary Sunday evenings if late.

The liberality of that congregation was wonderful. We contributed large sums annually to outside causes, and although my stipend was doubled, we always had a surplus in hand at the end of each financial year.

Our church membership trebled during the war years, and that notwithstanding the fact that I was the only anti-war minister in Colwyn Bay.

The war period was a difficult time for preachers of pacifist convictions. At our seaside resort we had many retired people who fought battles from the security of armchairs, or on the golf course. Elderly ladies were the most bellicose of all, especially members of the White Feather Brigade, who were very active in the town. By handing a white feather to a man in mufti they endeavoured to shame youths into the Army.

One friend of mine, convalescing after a serious wound, and allowed out in mufti, was going by tram to Old Colwyn. A lady of uncertain age stood holding on to the strap; so the lad got up and politely offered her his place. Said she: "No, I cannot accept the place of a coward: where is your war badge?"

"Madam," replied the disgusted lad, loud enough for all the passengers to hear, "where is your war-baby?"

My pulpit utterances were challenged very often during 1916-1917 when war fever was at its height, and spy mania an obsession with some people. Listeners would sometimes rise to protest, and walk out in the middle of a service. One elderly worshipper created a scene when I read for a text, "Love your enemies." Our local Pressmen interviewed the amiable ancient after that service, and got some good "copy." But the old man sent me a basketful of eggs and two pounds of grapes as a peace-offering next morning. A few of my elders begged me to modify my pacifism for a time; they were hesitant and kind, and I was equally courteous in my answer: "Gentlemen, if you can show that I am not preaching the Gospel, I shall desist. I can change my church but not the Christ." No further attempt was made to interfere with my preaching in Colwyn Bay. But my sermons were taken down in short hand, and many friends feared that I would be arrested for sedition. The police were friendly, though; and, once, I put them on the track of a foreign gentleman who had visited me in a suspicious manner.

Soldiers on leave came in large numbers to our church, and we rarely sat down to supper at home without gladly sharing it with a lad or lads in khaki.

Conscientious objectors provided a problem to all of us, and took up much of my time. I maintain that the exemption of clergy from conscription was unfair, except on the grounds of conscience like ordinary conscientious objectors. In fact, the Government made one attempt to conscript them, in April 1918; but withdrew the clause in face of the commotion aroused in the country. Hansard is well worth consulting. (Vols. 104 and 105 (1918)).

Mr. Whitehouse, Mr. Pringle, Sir Thomas Esmonde and Mr. Tim Healy attacked the proposal to conscript the clergy; but the person who carried greatest weight with the Government was Mr. Ellis Davies.

9th April, 1918.

The Prime Minister (Mr. Lloyd George):

There is shortage of fit men, very largely, for the service of the sick and wounded, and I am perfectly certain that ministers of religion would not care to feel that they are exempted from the obligations to serve, and especially to render service of this kind on the battle field. We have consulted several authorities on the subject, and some of them with whom it has been my privilege to communicate seem to feel that ministers of religion would be the last men in the world to claim exemption from an obligation of that kind. It is obvious if this change be made, care must be taken not to put an end to religious ministration in the country, and it has been arranged for this purpose that the Minister of National Service shall endeavour to act in concert with the authorities of the different denominations, so that in every denomination an adequate staff shall be reserved (Vol. 104/1356).

10th April 1918.

The Secretary of State for the Home Department (Sir George Cave):

As regards the proposal for taking ministers of religion, I do not think I need add anything to what the Prime Minister said yesterday, but I desire just to say this: I know that many ministers of religion will be willing, and indeed are anxious to take their place in the combatant forces. This is not confined to ministers of my church (Vol. 104/1478).

10th April 1918.

Mr. Ellis Davies :

I regret I cannot see my way to support this Bill. . . . There is another thing to which I strongly object, and that is the provision by which it is intended to bring ministers of religion under military law. I do not profess to agree with those who say that it is against their convictions as ministers of religion to take part in the maintenance and protection of the State. . . . I cannot understand under what circumstances the present Prime Minister has come down to this House to propose that Ministers of religion shall, whether they agree or not, whatever their conscientious convictions may be, be compelled to place their services at the disposal of the Military Authorities. . . . What is going to happen under this Bill? Ministers of religion, we are told, are not in future to be exempted, but will be subject to Military Law, although they may not be compelled to give combatant service. But let me take the position of Nonconformist Ministers in Wales. With regard to the clergyman of the Established Church, as he is in charge of a parish and responsible for the cure of the souls of the parishioners, I have not the slightest doubt that in ninety-nine cases out of a hundred he will be regarded as indispensable to the parish. But will that protection apply to the Nonconformist Minister, to the man in charge of a small church, who possibly adds to that duty the work of a farmer, or grocer, so as to eke out a living? . . . I have no doubt that if the Bill is carried in the form in which it now stands the people who will really suffer will be the Nonconformist Ministers of the country, and particularly those who have no settled Ministry and no wealthy congregation. Under these circumstances it is impossible for me to vote for the Bill. . . . (Vol 104 / 1547-8).

On the Second Reading, the late Mr. Llewelyn Williams, of Carmarthen, joined Mr. Ellis Davies in voting against the Bill.

During the Committee stage, on April 15th, Mr. Ellis Davies again raised the question of the position of Non-conformist Ministers under conscription. Several members supported him then, especially the Irish, who were concerned about the prospects of their priests and monks (Vol. 105/125-6).

Sir G. Cave:

I should like to be allowed to say a few words on the question which has just been put by the Hon. Gentleman (Mr. Ellis Davies), because I pressed the Committee of a previous stage to allow us to reserve until the Report Stage the question of the manner in which we should deal with the Ministers of religion. I am now prepared to present to the Committee a reply to the Hon. Gentleman's question. We were influenced in proposing to abolish the exemption of Ministers of religion by a number of representations we had received from Authorities and Ministers of certain Churches who felt it somewhat of a grievance that they were not put in the same position as the rest of the manhood of the country. . . . On the other hand, Members of this House and others, elsewhere, have used arguments which, no doubt, must have force with all of us. I believe that it is necessary to keep alive the religious ministrations of this country. . . . I have had one object and one object only throughout, the increase of man-power, and therefore we have asked ourselves how far the abolition of this exception would increase the man-power of the country. I have made enquiries, and I do not think the amount of man-power would be large. I think, after you had allowed enough for the religious needs of the country, you would not obtain a large increase

J

of military man-power from the remainder of the
Ministers of religion. On the whole, we have come
to the conclusion that we will not press this element
of the Bill (Vol. 105 / 126-7).

15th April 1918.

Discussion on Conscription of Priests in Ireland:

Sir George Cave:

The point as to the Ministers of religion was raised by
one of the Hon. Gentlemen below the Gangway,
and my answer was to the speech of his.

Mr. Healy:

I recognise the great courtesy of the Right Hon. Gentle-
man. He was answering a Welsh Member. Twenty
Irish Members got up, and one Welsh Member, Mr.
Ellis Davies, was able to persuade him.

The exemption of the clergy from military service
proved an astute move on the part of the authorities in
the end, because many ministers of religion became ardent defenders of the war and militarism, and they used
their pulpits to urge men on in the work of slaughter.
The New Testament was unpopular, and on one occasion
at least, was pronounced seditious by an official, who
confiscated a copy. "*A War Museum* 1914—1918," is
sad reading today. The Mosaic law of revenge dis-
placed the forgiving love of Christ; a Christian's duty
was to kill Germans; a man who fell in battle was sure
of salvation; heroism on the field of blood atoned for all
misdeeds; our theology was accommodated to military
necessity. What a tragedy it all was! and the aftermath
has been more tragic still. I feel sure that no "re-call"
to religion will be effective until the Church as a body
pronounces emphatically against war. Some of our pro-
fessional soldiers seem to be more ripe for this than do
many religious leaders. The late Brig.-General Crozier

and Sir Ian Hamilton have attested that "there is a fundamental rejection of the method of war in the Christian ethic." Stanley Jones quotes General John F. O. Ryan as saying:

> "I was a soldier for many years preparing for war. So when the world war came I had reason to believe the division I commanded was efficiently ready to kill enemy soldiers on a wholesale scale, employing bayonet, bullet, bomb and poison gas for the purpose. I felt the killing we were engaged in was contrary to Christian principles. I still think so. If we had another war in my time I should offer my services to the War Department, but, again, I should not try to reconcile my part in the war with my conception of Christian principles."

> "When Field-Marshal Haig said to a group of Ministers, 'It is your business to make my business impossible,' adds the same author, 'he put his finger on fact.'"

> Again: "In the first three centuries no Christian ever entered the army, or continued there after he became a Christian. After the third century no one could get into the army unless he were a Christian."

Many statesmen also seemed to be more conscious of the incompatibility of Christianity and war than did some ministers of religion. There is the well authenticated story of Mr. Lloyd George, then Prime Minister, sending his patronage secretary to hear one Church dignitary preach, and that with a view of offering the cleric high preferment. The report given was that the preacher would be good enough even for a Welsh Association: "But I ought to add, sir, that he is an ardent pacifist," said the secretary. "That is what all ministers should be; it is my business, not theirs, to wage war. Offer him the appointment," replied the greatest War Minister in the history of Britain,—not excepting William Pitt.

I became "Visitor" to conscientious objectors
at Kinmel Park camp. Brig.-General Owen Thomas
signed my permit which authorised me to visit
the guard rooms at any reasonable time. The first
man to be registered as a C.O. there was Percy
Ogwen Jones, a fine journalist, who subsequently became
assistant editor of the " *Cymro.*" There were as many
as seventy men in those rooms for a time, and I got to
know them all by name. But answering their volumi-
nous letters, and corresponding with their families was
work for more than one man. It was my custom to have
a personal talk with each, and then invite all to join in
a short prayer, ending with the Lord's Prayer. Never
can I forget opening my eyes once to see a young Jew,
with tears streaming down his cheeks, standing by my
side. "Friend Howard," said he, " if this is true Christianity, I must get to know more about it."

Several of those men became Members of Parliament,
and a few have been Ministers of the Crown.

From North Wales a well known C.O. was W. D.
Davies, who had such a brilliant career at Oxford ; he
became preacher, then professor at Aberystwyth Theological College, and a prolific author and journalist.

Another was George M. Ll. Davies whose life story
reads like a romance from the Middle Ages, when men
risked their all for Christ and the Church. This grandson of John Jones, Talysarn, one of the great preachers of his generation, has been bank manager, government official, Territorial officer, and several other things.
From the outbreak of war he was a most remarkable
out-and-out pacifist, who would accept no favouritism,
but insisted upon going through with his protest against
militarism. Nobody wished to send him to prison ; yet
to gaol he went, and became a problem to the authorities there. He won over governors, warders, and ordinary prisoners by his sincerity and forgiving love. When
sent to labour on farms, he converted Lleyn agricultural-
ists to his way of thinking. The man seems to despise
material wealth.

One evening, a servant of the late Sir Thomas
Roberts, Plasybryn, near Caernarvon, informed her
master that a very unusual sort of tramp was begging
food and permission to sleep in the barn. The worthy
knight went out to see for himself, and saw G.Ll.D.
"Come in, man, you can have whatever you need, and
the best room in the house," said Sir Thomas.

"No thanks, Sir Thomas," replied my friend, "a
basin of milk and a bed of hay is all I need," and nothing
more would he accept.

There could be no sleep for the anxious master that
night; his mind was in the barn with his relative. He
was up with the dawn, and found Davies helping servants
at the stables, and insisting upon breakfasting with them
in the kitchen. Sir Thomas did his utmost to persuade
the C.O. to return to "decent society," but it was a waste
of breath. On parting, the good man pressed a five
pound note upon Davies. "It is of no use to me,"
said the C.O., "I would only give it to the first tramp I
met on the road, and that would be unkind to the tramp."
Such is the man all through.

He was commissioned to supervise a reformatory for
criminals on parole. By sheer kindness and refusal to
punish or despair of any man or boy however refractory
there was created a moral revolution in scores of lives.
Judges, Cabinet Ministers, and society leaders of all
creeds, and many with no creed of their own, went to
observe and report upon the work.

The British people do not yet realise the part Davies
played in the partial pacification of Ireland. He did much
to bring the British Prime Minister and Mr. De Valera
together. When the Irish leader was "on the run,"
Davies could usually find him.

After the war G.Ll.D. represented the Welsh University in the House of Commons, but soon tired of
that. He then accepted ordination with the Presbyterian
Church of Wales, and a pastorate at Towyn. When his
friend, the Rev. Tom Nefyn Williams was suspended for

doctrinal reasons, Davies resigned from the active Ministry. Since then he has lived amongst, and for, the unemployed. I doubt whether Wales ever produced a more baffling personality than G.Ll.D. His autobiography would be a study in soul-making.

A group of Welsh pacifists met for consultation at Barmouth, and spent three days in conference. There we heard John Morgan Jones, Merthyr; Principal Thomas Rees, Bangor; Prof. Gwynn Jones, etc. Later on Peter Hughes-Griffiths and Richard Roberts met us at Wrexham. We made use of the daily Press as much as possible, and frequently engaged in public debate.

I was invited often to lecture upon "*Christ and War*," and, sometimes, with amusing results. At Gerlan, Bethesda, the chairman of the local military tribunal presided, and proposed a vote of thanks to the lecturer—much to the disgust of two police constables prepared to arrest me as a disturber of the peace. That crowd of quarrymen became hilarious.

In Cefn Eithin I was forewarned that a London vicar had brought a crowd of tough guys to cause disturbance. I saw the reverend gentleman seated in the very front of the gallery, and surrounded by his gang. When the chairman called upon me to speak, I opened by proposing a bargain with the packed audience; if they allowed me to deliver my lecture I was prepared to extend the same peaceful hearing to anybody who disagreed with me, and to answer questions, written or oral. A shout of approval greeted this, and I spoke for an hour and three quarters in an atmosphere which became more and more friendly as time went on. After my address, the chairman invited questions; none were forthcoming. Then he asked anybody who disagreed with the speaker to come forward and take the platform. Amidst a silence which could be felt the worthy vicar rose and said in a voice charged with deep emotion:

"I came here to break up this meeting and to discredit the lecturer. Ladies and gentlemen, as a Christian minister I confess my mistake. I go from this service a confirmed pacifist. God bless you, Mr. Howard!" He was a brave man, that vicar. Many people wept with joy, and so did I.

Things did not always end so peaceably as that, especially with some pacifists like Puleston Jones and J. M. Jones, Merthyr. But I, personally, received no rough treatment even when hostility was obvious and vocal.

Occasionally, elderly ministers were very difficult to understand. At a Presbytery held in Moriah (Vale of Conway) some time during 1917, the subject discussed at the afternoon session was "The Spirit of Adoption." That keen and brilliant theologian, the Rev. Evan Davies, Trefriw, opened with a remarkable discourse; he was followed by the persuasive Rev. William Thomas, Llanrwst, who lured us to the heights; then came versatile Rev. H. Barrow Williams, searching, witty, and telling as ever. Unfortunately for the peace of the brethren, our chairman insisted upon my drawing the discussion to a close; and I was in mischievous mood. After thanking the previous speakers for their contributions to the theory and history of Adoption, I endeavoured to apply it to practical life in its corollary of human brotherhood. If men are sons of one Father, then all are brothers in God, and members of the same family through Christ; how therefore could we countenance war? The Germans were our brothers; Austrians belonged to God; Turks have been bought with the blood of Christ. . . . That meeting ended in disorder. Some of the Fathers would not shake hands, and refused to speak to me for months; yet, I believe they were sincere, though war-blind.

My neighbour in Colwyn Bay was S. T. Jones, a well-known preacher of that period. With his two sons on active service, he felt bitter towards me for my anti-war activities.

One day the youngest daughter, Nancy, asked me to
see her father; a telegram from the War Office had arrived conveying the shattering news that the son Tom
had gone down with the *Monmouth* in the battle of Jut-
land.

When I entered the study there was my old friend
groaning in agony.

"Father, Mr. Howard is here," said Nancy. Sweat
was pouring down the face raised to look at me.

"Howard," cried he, "you are right! War is hell!
They have killed Tom! Pray for me, man, I cannot
pray for myself; my faith will not hold."

I had one brief glimpse of a tragic Gethsemane as I
tried to pray with the man who had swept scores into
the Kingdom through his preaching.

When the submarine menace threatened our food
supply at home, members of the Cabinet, notably Mr.
Lloyd George, advocated sowing wheat and planting
potatoes everywhere possible. They maintained
that it was justifiable even on Sundays. There
was a great outcry against this "desecration of the Sabbath," and protests were sent from all sorts of religious
societies. At the Free Church Council in Colwyn Bay,
one of our elderly ministers delivered an impassioned
speech against spending the Sabbath on a potato patch;
he worked up the meeting to a state of excitement and
real anger against those who would betray the sanctities
of religion. Before a resolution was put to the meeting I
asked permission to say a few words. I heartily agreed
with everything our friend had said in support of the protest against Sunday gardening; but why not object to
fighting and making munitions on the Sunday? That resolution was not pressed. Colwyn Bay was saved one
farce; common sense prevailed.

Something very similar happened when a deputation
from the local Urban District Council urged me to launch
a movement amongst our churches in aid of a war-savings
campaign. The appointed spokesmen were considerate

and courteous, and offered every help in the way of publicity. My answer must have been a disappointment to them: "Why not ask the churches to start a poison-gas campaign? or a bombing school? Is there any real difference between a silver bullet and an ordinary one?" We parted quite amicably; but I heard no more about that business.

At a preaching festival held in Bethesda, over Whitsun, in 1917, Dr. John Williams and I were put to preach in the same service, at Gerlan. My ideal preacher appeared in khaki, and the chapel was packed with a crowd prepared for some excitement. Whilst a hymn was being sung, I asked the Doctor what his text was to be."Moses," replied he. That was his great recruiting sermon at the time, and a real masterpiece.

I preached first, and spoke about Pharaoh's daughter as an example of suffering motherhood when loved ones respond to the call of a nation, a country, or a Cause. War is the calvary of the mother, and must be stopped by women who are the greatest sufferers in the end. Abraham has no right to sacrifice Isaac without the consent of Sarah. . . .

Dr. John Williams changed his text that night, and we were up arguing until 2 o'clock next morning. Neither of us minced matters; but we remained friends.

Whilst General Owen Thomas remained at Kinmel Park, I was not hindered in my work for conscientious objectors. In fact, the general placed his car and driver at my service several times. But when he was removed, an officer in temporary authority adopted a hostile attitude, and informed me that my permit would not operate at the camp any longer. I respectfully asked him to confirm, or renew permission; but he curtly refused. Consequently, I appealed to the War Office, and in a very short time secured a new permit signed by General Cuthbertson who had succeeded the Welsh commander.

Headquarters.

14th Res. Inf. Brigade.

Dear Mr. Howard.

Many thanks for your letter.

I enclose you a general permit to visit the conscientious objectors in my Brigade. Please visit them whenever you care to do so.

I hope some time to have the pleasure of making your acquaintance personally.

Yours sincerely,

F. B. CUTHBERTSON, Colonel.

Commanding 14th Res. Inf. Brigade.

Kinmel Park,
    Rhyl,
14/7/16.

I received a similar permit and covering letter from Col. R. H. Dunn of the 13th Reserve Infantry Brigade.

Probably, I unduly exasperated the officer who had tried to exclude me from the camp when I insisted upon showing him my permits and correspondence. But it was very necessary to watch things at the guard rooms. The first batches of C.O.'s were shamefully maltreated by some men in the Army; sufferers refused to report their torturers.

There was very little sympathy with conscientious objectors even in ecclestiastic circles. A few of us determined to extract a pronouncement from our Denomination. The General Assembly was held at Colwyn Bay in March 23—25, 1916. I was one of the local secretaries, and got to know something about the inner workings of our Higher Court. The Rev. Howell Harris Hughes, of Llandudno, and I, with the help of some sympathisers, framed a resolution expressing the sympathy of the Assembly with those who stood for freedom of conscience in time of war, whatever their creed. This was handed to the general secretaries, the Revs. John Thickens and

E. P. Jones, both of whom were sympathetic. But the
Executive turned it down, and refused permission to
place the matter before the Assembly. When Thickens
reported this, we held a hurried meeting, and arranged
a new method of approach.

Dr. John Williams was going to propose a protest
against the removal of General Owen Thomas from
the command at Kinmel camp. We, conscientious objectors, were in perfect agreement with that, because our
men had most to lose; but we threatened to divide the
Assembly on that resolution unless our proposal was accepted. The junta knew that this was no idle threat. In
fact, we had enlisted sufficient support to imperil the
Big Pew proposal. Three leaders were commissioned to
treat with the "rebels." Rev. John Williams, Rev. T. C.
Williams, and Principal J. H. Davies met H. H. Hughes
and myself during the luncheon hour. After a heated
discussion we arrived at a compromise. Great was the
surprise of the Assembly when Dr. John Williams proposed and Dr. T. C. Williams seconded our proposal;
both resolutions then went through with complete un-
animity and amidst applause (See *Goleuad*, June 2nd,
1916).

A similar reserve regarding C.O.'s was noticeable in
other religious circles. The evangelical Dr. Chavasse,
then Bishop of Liverpool, wrote:

"I have decided opinions indeed about conscientious
objectors to military service. I think that if they
decline to fight for their country and are content to
let other people do it for them, then their duty is to
leave their own shores and take up their residence in
some other land where they will not be called upon
to take up arms. Freedom of conscience does not
mean believing anything you like even though it is
to the detriment of your neighbour, and declining to
perform your duties as Christian men and citizens."
"Liverpool Post and Mercury," May 22nd, 1916.

A committee of the National Free Church Council held one special meeting in London on May 25th, 1916, to call the attention of the Government to harsh treatment meted out to conscientious objectors. But the end of the resolution reads strange from such a source:

"We cannot admit that the individual has a moral right to decline his part in the task and burden of the community, to expect advantages conferred by the State while refusing to share in its responsibilities. Nor can we view without concern the claims alleged by some on conscientious ground to be relieved from every kind of service to the Nation."

My work in Kinmel camp brought me into touch with some notable Quakers, especially, Sir John and Lady Barlow, who helped me with funds and contacts; but it was a distressing and disheartening business. I know that more courage and endurance are necessary to be a C.O. than to follow the crowd; many officers admitted to me that they lacked the courage to take a stand against war. That is why I have not pressed young students to sign the anti-war pledge so popular to-day with many who were among our greatest jingoes in 1914 —18. Would the churches really support C.O.'s in another war? I wonder!

At the begining of 1917 I published a book entitled, "Life beyond the Veil." Scores of letters I received convinced me that many mourners and sufferers found comfort through that little volume. Paper was scarce at the time; so, unfortunately, the publishers (Swarthmore Press) printed but one edition, and then distributed the type. The whole edition was sold out in two months, and people were offering three times the published price for a copy. The author did not escape criticism, especially over his expressed liking for Fellowship with the Dead, and the doctrine of Eternal Hope.

For years I have doubted the doctrine of a hell of burning fire for those who do not hear the gospel. When I think of followers of Muhammad, Buddha, and Confucius, and the human Race throughout the corridors of time, I cannot believe that they are all damned by a loving God because of their deficient knowledge of the whole Truth. Then remember the ignorant, the undeveloped, the misled, even in an age and country called Christian. Are all these fuel for hell fire? If the penal theology taught me when I was young is true the number of the redeemed must be a very small minority of mankind. I, at any rate, dare not admit that. Only one out of the hundred went astray; and the Shepherd seeks until He finds the last lost sheep.

About that time I began my thesis for the degree of Master of Arts at the Liverpool University. The subject was, *"Phases of Poor Law Policy and Administration, 1760—1834, with special reference to Denbighshire and Caernarvonshire Vestries."* I took four years over the work, and found pleasure in studying the old records of 32 vestries in different parts of the country so far apart as Cardiff and Llangefni. Sometimes I was disappointed; an incumbent would inform me, by letter, that he possessed a pile of old vestry minutes; but, after a long and expensive journey, I frequently found that only baptismal records had been kept. I grew to like the musty smell of ancient manuscripts, and could read them at a fair speed however scrawly the script.

I enjoyed perusing county records in the different centres. They throw a wonderful light upon those times. Mr. and Mrs. Sidney Webb and the Hammonds were helpful, and kind. Then I spent considerable time in the Public Records Office, London, as well as at various libraries.

The real social history of Wales has yet to be written. Sir J. E. Lloyd, Robert Richards, W. J. Gruffydd, Timothy Lewis and R. T. Jenkins are giving us history at last,based upon authentic and documentary evidence;

for too long Wales was satisfied with legend and romance instead of history. Another fact that impressed me was the haphazard way in which parish and county records were then being kept. I found some informative MSS. in a rubbish dump at the old court of Beaumaris. Not too soon the Welsh National Library authorities and the Church in Wales are heartily co-operating in a laudable endeavour to preserve parish registers and cognate records.

The Senate awarded me the degree of M.A. with congratulations. Prof. Firth, the well known Oxford historian, was very appreciative, and advised me to extend the study with a view to publication.

I published another book, *"Which Jesus?"* in 1919. It is based upon Pilate's question to the populace of Jerusalem: "Which Jesus will ye have? Choose either Barrabbas or Jesus called the Christ." The choice before after-war Europe is "Which Jesus?" brute force or sacrificial love, self or God.

This book has gone through seven impressions, and is still in demand. During 1937 over two hundred copies went to India.

My pen was rather active about that time. I was writing two articles a week for the Press, reviewing an average of three books weekly, editing a monthly magazine, publishing two sermons a month, and contributing to periodicals in America. Other avenues of service opened. We formed a branch of the Independent Labour Party at Colwyn Bay, and branches in several other parts of Denbighshire. We also secured the first Labour magistrates for our town.

I found great joy in my several missions at various colleges during those years. In 1923, Canon Raven, Dr. Maltby, George Davies and I had a great week with the students of Aberystwyth Colleges. The following year Miss Maud Royden and I conducted a mission amongst Bangor students.

In 1916, the Executive of the I.L.P. met at Conway, and I spent three days in the company of Ramsay Mac-Donald, Philip and Mrs. Snowden, F. W. Jowett, Norman Angell, Anderson, Bruce-Glasier, etc. I had a great uplift of soul. Snowden was wonderful; Angell captivated us all; the women members were vivacious, and the whole atmosphere proved exhilarating.

I felt strangely drawn to Ramsay MacDonald. He seemed lonely and detached even in the midst of jovial friends who evidently loved him. He and I took several long walks together, and I caught glimpses of a mighty Presbyterian faith and courage. The Welsh Premier had launched two bitter attacks upon our Scotchman near that time. I asked the pacifist if he felt sore over being driven out of Parliament and public life. Well do I remember the moment and the spot he placed a hand on my shoulder, saying: "Howard, I can afford to wait; my day will come."

He had said something similar in the House of Commons at the very outbreak of the War when answering Sir Edward Grey:

"The Right Honourable Gentleman's speech has been very impressive, and we have not been able to resist the moving character of his appeal. But I think he is wrong. . . . We shall see. What is the use of talking about coming to the aid of Belgium, when, as a matter of fact, you are engaging in a whole European war which is not going to leave the map of Europe in the position it is in now.

The feeling of the House is against us. I have been through this before, and 1906 came as part recompense. It will come again."

How truly prophetic were those words in the history of the man, who, subsequently, became three times British Prime Minister! Ramsay MacDonald survived many changes of public opinion. In turn he was hated and

flattered by Labourites, Liberals and Conservatives; but
through all he retained faith in his own destiny.

We are too near 1931 to appraise, dispassionately, the
Great Divide when MacDonald severed life-long friendships, and, seemingly, repudiated all that he had striven
and fought for during the previous forty years. It still
remains a mystery to most of his former admirers. His
sudden death at sea, when " in search of that most elusive
form of happiness, rest," was a shock to friend and foe
alike. Wonderful tributes were paid to his memory by
kings and peasants, in cathedrals and cottages. He
has taken a not insignificant place in history.

But what irony of Fate ordained that a British war-
ship should bring home the body of our erstwhile leading pacifist for burial? Did the coffin of the man from
Lossiemouth contain the dust of an ideal disdained by
arrogant militarism?

With the Armistice came the Coupon Election. I
was asked to contest a seat, and refused. But we wished
to take a stand for peace and reconciliation. Ultimately,
we persuaded E. T. John, a former Welsh Liberal M.P.
for Wrexham, to stand for West Denbighshire. He was
made a member of the Labour Party by telegram, and
paid all his own expenses.

E. T. John was a delightful person, and a man of
strong convictions, especially on peace, which was our
main concern. He knew that we were fighting a forlorn
hope, but was prepared to spend a few thousand pounds
to lodge his protest against militarism.

John was about the least inspiring orator who ever
took to a political platform. His long beard was a *cul-de-
sac* to involved sentences that refused to come forth.
He insisted upon my accompanying him to every
village, and the burden of meetings fell upon me. I addressed three meetings a day during that campaign.
Some critics spread the tale that I was receiving
fabulous fees from the millionaire. Little did they know
that I would not accept my out-of-pocket expenses, and

that I have not been paid one penny for work undertaken on behalf of the Labour Party. Democracy is a cause for which men are expected to sacrifice without hope of material rewards.

The Coalition nominee was Sir D. S. Davies. But that election was fought and won everywhere in the magical name of Lloyd George. Anybody holding the "Coupon" would have been elected. Politicians who had criticised or opposed the great man of Criccieth at any time were ruthlessly driven out of public life; it was the most remarkable personal triumph ever known in British politics.

Sir D. S. Davies requested me to withdraw the candidature of E. T. John; and when I refused, he actually threatened reprisals through the churches. I am afraid that I needlessly hurt my old friend when I submitted that such an attitude was unworthy of a Parish Council. It was unkind on my part; but I had had a most hostile meeting at Denbigh Town Hall the previous night, when some of Sir David's partisans endeavoured for 15 minutes to howl me down and to break up our meeting. That was an amusing experience. After E. T. John had mumbled a speech into his beard, and the Rev. Dr. Peter Price had shouted for ten minutes before sitting down, and the Rev. E. K. Jones, through sheer doggedness, secured a hearing, the chairman called upon me to speak. But, evidently, the organised opposition were waiting for that moment, because the storm broke, and our crowd sang for fully ten minutes something like this:

"We'll hang Jimmy Howard
On a sour apple tree,
And we'll go marching home."

I waited and laughed with my audience. When the noise abated a little, I resorted to an old platform trick of wildly gesticulating and pretending to shout, without saying one word. The singing went on again for ever so long; at last the quiet of exhaustion gave me a chance,

K

and I began with a pet peroration which had done long service. Amidst an increasing silence I carried on, and spoke for thirty minutes. The man who had been my most insistent interrupter was first to congratulate me at the end.

"I don't know what it is," said one listener to a sympathiser near the door of the packed hall, "but that b—— Howard always gets me when he refers to poverty and peace."

Of course we lost that election; but it was no mean feat to poll over 2,000 votes for peace at the Coupon Election in that part of Wales.

Sir D. S. Davies and I resumed our friendship after that. He helped me greatly when I was collecting for our new hospital. At one meeting Sir David introduced me by saying that at last the lion and the lamb lay down together. I began my speech by cordially thanking the worthy chairman for calling me a lamb.

During 1920—1921 the committee of the Cottage Hospital, of which I was a member, decided to erect a more commodious hospital to serve the whole of West Denbighshire. As one bilinguist on the committee I was commissioned to tour the county in search of funds. The tireless secretary, Mr. T. E. Purdy, a retired Manchester merchant who has devoted half a life-time to public work, accompanied me to most places, and I got to know him well. He brings to Wales the broad outlook, wide sympathy, and progressive note so characteristic of Lancashire men. Mr. Purdy is a wonderful collector for charities; £100,000 have passed through his hands for the numerous organisations that claim his support. He has served on the Urban District Council, and on the Denbighshire County Council for many years : is a Justice of the Peace, Chairman of the Public Assistance Committee, and of the Police Committee. His work on behalf of the Welsh League of Nations Union, and the King Edward VII. Memorial has made his name known throughout Wales. With his help scores of Welsh lads have been placed in good situations, not only in their own country but so far away as India and America. T. E. Purdy and his gracious wife seem to have identified themselves with Wales.

The local medical men also came with us in turn, and lent their cars for our use.

We had wonderful times in Welsh chapels and school rooms, in cottages and farms, and especially at auction marts where we commandeered the services of auctioneers, and ourselves delivered orations to the farmers. One lamb, presented by a shepherd, was auctioned twenty times, until, at last, Mr. Purdy and I were sick of the sight and smell of the creature; her bleat followed us everywhere; but she brought in £80 for the hospital. Between collections and bazaars, etc., about £20,000 were collected, and the new building was opened free of debt, or practically so.

The interesting work on behalf of that hospital brought me into touch with some remarkable people outside my usual circle, and I was agreeably surprised at the kindness and generosity of folk whom I had always regarded as aloof, and unacquainted with the needs and aspirations of the sons of toil. How little we understand each other! Those wealthy Tories welcomed me to their homes and tables, to their platforms and churches. And they gave freely of their money and encouragement.

I suppose that, ultimately, British hospitals will become a State responsibility, just like education and public relief; that seems to be the trend of things. But a wonderful social solvent will disappear when we lose the voluntary element in the upkeep of institutions for healing. At the Temples of Pain class distinctions must vanish; more than that, it is a case of the strong helping the weak, the healthy supporting the sick, and the rich taking over burdens of the poor. The people who contributed the bulk of the money for that charity are not likely to need the hospital for themselves.

One name which will always be associated with the new hospital is that of Lord Colwyn, who frequently invited me to Queen's Lodge, especially when some notability was being entertained there. In this way I first met Lord Robert Cecil, who had recently resigned his Government Office so as to devote his whole time to building up the League of Nations Union. There is something ecclesiastic about Lord Robert.   He has a penetrating and rather metallic voice, and looks a listener straight in the eye as though reading his very soul. He can ask awkward questions, and avoid answering them. Somebody called him a High Church mystic who strayed into politics. His sincerity is obvious; he is great enough to stoop to reason with men like me, and is fair in argument. , Jack Jones the genial Member for Silvertown was a puzzle to Lord Robert at the time. " Do you, Howard, agree with Jones?"

My reply was that Jack Jones represented Silvertown, and spoke the language of his constituents, who have as much right to find expression as has Oxford or Cambridge.

"Probably you are right," mused the meditative statesman, " but I never thought of it in that light."

Lord Emmott, another visitor at Queen's Lodge, was of a different type. I never asked if he was a Quaker; but that was the impression I received. I heard afterwards that he was a Congregationalist of Quaker ancestry. Rather heavy and sparing of speech, he yet impressed one as being alert and penetrating; whenever he did intervene in a discussion it was to reveal an angle forgotten by disputants; a strong conscientious man seemed Lord Emmott.

A week or so after the Armistice I was invited to dine at Queen's Lodge with Lords Colwyn and Emmott. There was one other visitor present, but I cannot recall his name. Naturally our talk was about the Armistice. My host and his friends were quite aware of my

aggresive pacifism and socialism, and seemed very play-
ful about it.

"And now, Howard," asked Lord Colwyn, "what do
you and your Party think of affairs?"

"With all deference, Lord Colwyn," was my reply,
"if you are a friend of the Prime Minister, and I know
you are, do your best to persuade him to resign and retire
from public life for at least three years." This was
greeted with something approaching genteel derision by
my listeners.

"Impossible," exclaimed Lord Emmott.

"Ridiculous," said Lord Colwyn, "Mr. Lloyd George
is the only man for the time. He won the war and must
make the peace."

"Well, gentlemen," I modestly added, "you may be
right. But I have read of another David who won wars;
yet he did not build the temple of peace. I believe that
history will be repeated here."

I have a note in my diary relating to another incident
at Queen's Lodge when Lord Emmott was present. It
was a few days before the Genoa Conference, April 15th
—May 19th, 1922. Lord Colwyn was keenly interested,
and very hopeful.

"How do your people regard the prospects, Howard?"
asked Lord Emmott.

"We do not expect Poincaré to attend," was my
reply. Sure enough, the French Premier absented himself from that Conference, although the great Dailies
predicted that, like the other Prime Ministers of the different nations represented, he was sure to attend. The following Sunday I was called to the Lodge. My host wished
to know the source of my information. Of course I had
only followed the Socialist Press which reported Poincaré's
protest against the Cannes conclave that preceded the
Conference. And, in addition, every reader of the foreign
Press knew that the then French Premier hated the new
Russia, and was no admirer of Mr. Lloyd George at the
time. Many European statesmen who met the great

Welshman in conference, had been discredited at home immediately afterwards. Poincaré was too astute to risk power and prestige so soon after Briand had lost the premiership over a game of golf.

On another occasion my fellow guests at the Lodge were T. E. Purdy, Sir William Vincent, and J. H. Thomas. Our conversation turned towards Christian missionaries, a subject upon which Thomas held strong views expressed with characteristic plainness of speech. Lord Colwyn endeavoured to steer us into a less controversial channel; and an awkward situation was saved by Sir William Vincent quietly remarking that he himself believed, after a very long experience in India, that the influence and work of Christian missionaries were our ultimate security against an Indian relapse into the anarchy and barbarism of centuries ago.

I have great regard for the Labour leader, who, for decades, faithfully served the railwaymen, and won for them many privileges which they now enjoy. He was treated ungenerously by old comrades in the end, and in a manner unworthy of the Labour Movement. J.H.T. may not be ranked as a great man; but he proved one of the ablest of negotiators in Trade Union matters; he is a kind soul, always ready to do a good turn, and is sure of a special niche in the history of the emancipation of Labour. I, for one, regret his temporary political eclipse.

In 1927, I accepted a call to Catharine Street Church, Liverpool. Four years previously I had refused this church, but felt that I dared not avoid the challenge a second time. It was with great reluctance that I left Colwyn Bay, and strong pressure was exerted to keep me in the church and town. I doubt, though, whether a minister in the prime of life is justified in staying long at a holiday centre. One can easily get out of touch with the realities of every day life; and, in such places a man misses youth from his congregation.

I thankfully remember some of our visitors, who, at intervals, joined us in worship at Colwyn Bay. For many months A. G. Hales, author of the M'Glusky series of stories, was a frequent listener; and so was William le Queux, the novelist. Prof. Anderson Scott came into my vestry once to thank me for quoting him in the course of a sermon. Dr. George Steven attended our services for weeks at a stretch, and, during nearly five years Dr. David Eaton, formerly of Glasgow, and his wife were communicants at our church. That choice soul preached for me two days before his sudden death. I loved the man and always felt better for his company. Amongst our pew-holders were two retired Anglican vicars, two Unitarian ministers, and one Swedenborgian.

Although loyal Wesleyan Methodists, the parents of Lord Hewart, the Lord Chief Justice, were pew-holders at our church. Mrs. Hewart was of Welsh parentage; but very rarely heard or spoke Welsh throughout her long married life. Yet, during her last illness she reverted to the language of her youth, and I went often to translate for the family. At my last visit I heard that saint repeat part of a Welsh Hymn:

" *Cyfaill yw yn afon angau,*   " In the cold and mortal river
    Ddeil fy mhen i uwch y don,   He will hold my head above ;
    Golwg arno wna i mi ganu,   I shall through the waves go singing
    Yn yr afon ddofon hon."   For one look of Him I love."
                                            Trans. ELVET LEWIS.

I made hosts of friends in Colwyn Bay. There were problems and difficulties, critics and opponents, and things were not always easy. The Garden of the North grew some weeds. But my life was amply blessed during those twelve years.

I must close this chapter with a brief reference to two unique souls.

Betty Champness is the only child of Harry and Ethel Champness, and was a never-ceasing wonder to me. Owing to an accident at birth, Betty has never walked, talks only with difficulty, does not feed herself,

and, in fact, is entirely dependant on the ministration of
others.   Yet she can enjoy books although unable to turn
over pages; thus friends find pleasure in reading to her.
She has a wonderful soul in that frail body, and we could
commune without ordinary words, because Betty is at-
tuned to the Infinite and associates with what is invisible
to most of us.   Birds crowd upon her spinal carriage;
dogs cross the road to look on; horses seem to recognise
her.   I used to fancy that flowers bloomed better in her
vicinity.   God is very real to Betty; Christ is her constant Companion; she is a stranger to fear because her
parents are gentle folk in a home of piety and peace.   I
was always humbled, and longed to be holy after a visit
to Betty's home "Avoca."

When going on a fishing holiday once, I called to say
goodbye to Betty, and promised her the first fish I caught.
That very evening I fished at Llyn-y-Foel, on the side of
Siabod.   Within about ten minutes of the first cast I
landed a beautiful trout which weighed three quarters of
a pound.   Betty Champness got that fish; but although I
spent hours during the week fishing in the same lake, not
one more bite did I get there.

Another remarkable personality was Judge Caradoc
Rees, who was a member of the church, and frequently
brought legal luminaries to the services, and saw that
each of them contributed liberally to the collection plate.
One of his guests, a High Court Judge, had not been to
church for a long time, and tried to shirk the ordeal; but
my friend brought him along and made him pay five
pound notes as back payment for services neglected.

The early death of Caradoc Rees was a heavy blow
to all who were privileged to call him friend.   Friday
evening was a standing engagement of mine with him
at his bachelor quarters.   Whilst his strong-willed mother
ruled I was a privileged guest; and after she passed on I
dared not miss a Friday visit.

I had the sad duty of burying mother and son.

The judge was intimate with F. E. Smith (Lord Birkenhead). They were playmates and school chums as boys, and had much in common; charm of personality, wit, dash, and the spirit of adventure were found in both.

Caradoc Rees was journalist, solicitor, barrister, member of Parliament, and County Court judge in succession. Many of his admirers were disappointed when he left politics and accepted a county court judgeship. But he had suffered, for years, from an incurable complaint, and knew, to within a few months, how long he was to live. I stood at his side a short time before the end. Both of us realised that it was to be "farewell"; so, with a wan smile and one final slight pressure of the hand, we parted until there shall be no more pain, no more parting, and no more death.

CHAPTER TEN

BEYOND OFFA'S DYKE

I ALWAYS wished to see the other side of a hill, and never believed that the world ended with our Welsh borders.

All my family were roamers, and the sea called to me when I was quite a youth. Twice I tried to stow-away.

Our first trip abroad was to Brittany in 1921. We chose the nearest and cheapest country whose language closely resembles Welsh. Literature about ancient Armorica, as it used to be called, is plentiful, and we eagerly read it. Then, on a lovely moonlight night we sailed from Southampton; sleeping on the open deck was no hardship during that eleven hours' sail.

A dawn at sea thrills me at all times, and I cannot forget my first glimpse of the " Azure Coast." The light green colour of sea and the verdure often reflected in its transparent waters form a harmony in its different shades of green, and make it a real emerald coast.

Our objective was St. Malo, called the "city jewel of architecture of the Middle Ages," labyrinth of tortu-ous streets enclosed within ramparts overlooking golden sands. We were in Brittany, home of intrepid warriors, renowned bards and illustrious saints!

The scene on the quay was amusing; there were about a hundred hotel touts begging, shouting and gesticula-ting, and each trying to grab a bag. We engaged the least villainous-looking to pilot us through the Customs, and to the Hotel Central Benoit.

The smells were awful until one got used to them; rotten eggs in a stagnant pool of eau-de-cologne and sea-weed flavoured with onions suggested themselves to me;

it was not smell but real stench which followed one
everywhere, and clung like a damp mist to our clothes.

The street of our temporary abode was narrow, cobbled, and winding. Externally, the inn was uninviting,
but proved comfortable within. Our bedroom was
musty and suggestive of ghosts or cut-throats lurking in
each corner. All the noises of Brittany seemed to congregate outside our window by night, and sleep was
difficult until the dawn, when a new series of discords
took up the tale.

Every house in St. Malo has a history. The town
was founded in the 11th century by a Welsh apostle,—
Mac-Law or Malo, and is called the city of great men.
The ramparts that overlook an open sea date from the
twelfth or thirteenth centuries; the remainder were erected by Garangean.

Notable spots are the Fort National and the Square,
which was formerly a large bastion built to provide
against an attack by the Dutch fleet, about 1674. In the
middle of the Square stands a statue of Jacques Cartier,
reputed discoverer of Canada. The grave of Chateaubri-
and is on a little island; and the Hotel la France where
he was born lies close to the ramparts. The Cathedral
built by Jean de Chatillon, in 1152, is a mixture of two
or more styles of architecture. Its pictures are tawdry,
and the effigies of saints revolting,—to my mind.

I attended High Mass once, and Low Mass twice;
there were four collections taken at one service, and
everybody was expected to pay for a chair. The singing
was led by a single violin.

I followed one funeral. It was very like a Welsh
country burial, except that however many had been in-
terred in a grave the father's corpse must be placed
lowest of all, even though it may be necessary to disinter
other bodies. Another noticeable feature was that the
family name alone was engraved on the tombstone.

Death plays a great part in the social life of Brittany.
Even at a wedding the Litany for all Souls is recited or

chanted.   I first heard about the Log of the Dead in St.
Malo.   One favourite practice is to spend a night in the
coffin of a saint; this is called "passing through the
grave."   The cemetery is a centre of activity—"we live
with our dead."   Yet life is bright at St. Malo; there are
open-air cinemas, a picturesque casino, and drinking
cafés by the dozen in the open.

We witnessed the great Festival of the Assumption;
and one Pardon.

Paramé, two miles away, is modern, and, when we
visited it, was *en fête*.   We saw wonderful dancing at the
casinos, and the dresses were fine creations.   Good surf
bathing is to be had at Paramé; and the tub of hot water
for washing one's feet put the last touch to the luxury
of sea bathing.

Dinard is called the Nice of the North, and Queen of
Breton watering places.   The house of the Black Prince
(XVIth century) is interesting, and there is also a unique
granite statue of Christ facing the sea.   The convent of
the Trinity reminds us of Oliver and Geoffrey de Mont-
fort, together with the Crusades.   When the church clock
of Dinard strikes twelve, it turns round a thousand times,
says a legend; but so quickly does it revolve that on-
lookers have an impression of the stationary.

A trip up the river Rance takes two hours; and we
pass through exquisite scenery, little villages, and townlets.

Here is Saint Guliac with its 13th century church and
tower.

Tongrolaz—the country of cherries.

Port Saint Jean, and Cheme Vert.

Then the remarkable river lock and the lake beyond.
At last we come to Dinan, the old city of the dukes of
Brittany, which stands eighty metres above sea level.   Its
church dates from the 11th century; in the marble
cenotaph lies the heart of Dregnesilin.

The castle dates from the 14th century, and is the
most remarkable military monument of those parts—and

the second largest in Brittany.   Two thousand British were imprisoned there once. For one day England owned Brittany.   The ancient weapons on show are interesting; and so is the chapel of the Duchess Ann.   We saw the dungeon where Bertram du Guesclin starved his brother Giles.

A small motor boat took us to La Cast which was rather modern, but small and noisy.   The church is not old; its altar was made out of a ship's wood.   There is a beautiful legend to the effect that the Christus refused to remain at rest until planks from a shipwreck formed the crucifix.

At Rothenuf we saw the carved rocks—result of 20 years' labour of a hermit; there is an ugly little church also.

Mont St. Michel is the castle island with a long history of battle and treachery, heroism and suffering; it is well named the wonder of the West.   The castle was founded by St. Aubert who was inspired through St. Michel.   We enter by the 16th century gate near which are the old guns captured from the English in 1400. King Arthur delivered Mt. St. Michel from a murderous giant. The tide is reported to come in as fast as a galloping horse at St. Michel.   Here also monks still make Benedictine wine.   The dungeons contain gruesome relics, and we were glad to return to the open air.

We went up country and stayed at Rennes and Vannes; then on to Quimper where we were entertained by the Welsh missionary, Jenkyn Jones and his French wife. From there our journey was to Pont-l'Abbé, where my friend the Rev. Gerlan Williams is stationed.   We attended several Protestant chapels—all very small and bare; Gerlan translated my brief talks.

At Les Consel we saw the sardine factories, and the dumps of fish-heads used as manure; the stench arising from those dumps, added to the exhalations of ripe and rotting flax, is enough to poison ordinary beings; for a long time afterwards I could not look at a sardine.

In Brittany I heard names of saints that were new to me,—Efflam, Enora, Cornely, Bienze and Nicodemus. An additional Arthurian legend also was very welcome.

The Breton peasantry work hard, and are very badly housed; it was there we first saw cupboard bedrooms. An ordinary workman's dwelling is void of furniture, except bare tables and forms; the only window is an upper part of a front door.

Women seemed to work harder than men in Brittany; they plough, break stones, and drive horses. We frequently saw a wife driving horse and trap home from market, whilst her lord and master slept peacefully, if sonorously, on the floor of the cart.

The peasant costume varies with almost every village, and is really picturesque.

Trade Unionism is practically unknown outside the industrial towns, and illiteracy is common. Protestantism makes very little headway in a country regarded as the last stronghold of Catholicism; but, evidently, the Romish Church has lost the male population, and secularism is on the increase. Our Protestant Bethels make weak appeal to a nation so fond of ritual and show. If our missions are to succeed they will have to spend money in erecting more attractive places of worship.

Brittany does not compare with Wales for scenery; it is too flat and monotonous. But there are some beautiful parts along the sea coast.

Our next holiday abroad was to Switzerland; the long train journey from Calais is very exhausting. I never was good at sleeping in trains, and when one finds a lady's foot embedded in his ribs at 2 a.m., slumber is impossible. As I gently removed the offending member, its owner awoke and sweetly apologised. But my fitful snooze was broken in like manner three times during the following two hours. When we arrived at Basle the lady was overwhelmed with remorse; but she tried to console me, and ease the pain with praise for my Christian forbearance. It then transpired that the repentant disturber of innocent slumber was —— a popular lady novelist. At that time she and her sister-in-law were on a walking tour in Switzerland.

I was disappointed in Lucerne; it is too trippy and commercialised; wherever one went we found officially conducted groups of tourists; and some of those guides told tall tales—which few people believed. We visited all the usual historical spots, and were glad to leave the town, and go on to a little village called Wessen at the entrance of the St. Gotthard tunnel—one of the mightiest engineering feats of history.

Wessen is glorious. The hotel was not luxurious, but modern and comfortable, and spotlessly clean.

We saw no great industries in Switzerland; smoke, except from burning peat or logs, is unknown in the parts we visited. Everything is done by electricity which is ridiculously cheap owing to the abundance of water power available.

The Furka Pass is one of the marvels of the world, and contains many historical spots. We went up the Rigi, where I lost patience with an American who insisted upon talking whilst the whole company were dumb with wonder as we gazed upon the world and its glory spread beneath us; talk, sound even, was sacrilege on that peak where soul merges into the infinite, and man can think great thoughts, and, perhaps, feel God's presence.

From there we went to the Stanzahorn, and arrived at the hotel about 1.30 a.m. to be welcomed by a Swiss lady who had been educated at Ruthin, and insisted upon cooking ham and eggs for us at that unearthly hour.

We went up the mountain by funicular, and enjoyed a day of sunshine whilst our more timid friends dwelt in mist and rain below.

Another mountain we ascended was Pilatus, and I tried to believe the legend of the wandering Procurator of Judea on those heights.

We stayed a day at Lugano, the emerald gem in a setting of azure; it was the most beautiful place we saw in Switzerland. The usual excursions to Milan, etc., followed. It was in the Land of the Swiss that I faintly understood the prayer of a psalm—"Let the beauty of the Lord our God be upon us."

The end of that holiday was an anti-climax—at Paris. Such a contrast from the pure snows and glorious nights to artificial streets, theatres, taxi-cabs, opera and cosmetics was too violent.

Switzerland is a League of Nations in small, a confederation of canton states, a commonwealth of peoples. It is a stronghold of Protestantism, democracy and freedom; we must return there.

Our people have much to learn from the hardy Swiss.

August 1923 we went to the West of France, along the banks of the river Loire, the chateau country where one can almost re-construct pre-revolution France amongst the castles, still intact.

In Wales we have allowed most of our castles to go to ruins; they are a disgrace to our nation and blots on the landscape. With them has gone much of interest.

I remember visiting Abergavenny castle ruins once. A caretaker took my entrace fee of threepence, but when I asked if he knew anything about the castle he shook his head. In answer to my enquiry if there was no published story of the castle he replied: "There is no history to this blooming pile."

Things are different in France. The old castles are national trusts, maintained by the Government and kept as they were when tenanted by their original owners; they are the centuries in wood and stone, and one felt in the main stream of history within those walls. It was almost a baptism for the dead.

Orleans was interesting after reading Bernard Shaw's "St. Joan."

When we returned to Paris I would not have been surprised if somebody had told us that the very sparrows were from the twelfth or fourteenth century. For two whole weeks we had been living with those centuries, and I was sick of the sight of chateaux.

But I carried with me a few letters of introduction to some prominent Frenchmen. Here is a copy of one:

17th July, 1923.

"Dear Monsieur Briand,

This letter will introduce to you the Rev. J. H. Howard, M.A., of Colwyn Bay, North Wales.

Mr. Howard is personally well known to me. He is a man of good repute, and a very able social investigator. He is now engaged upon some research work concerning the administration of the "dole" system in Wales, subsequent to the Napoleonic wars. He hopes to compare the then situation with the present position in Britain. Deeming it desirable to contrast British methods with those of France during that period he is paying a visit to your country, and if you could spare him just a few minutes of your busy time, I should be greatly obliged.

Ever sincerely,

D. LLOYD-GEORGE."

The same distinguished benefactor gave me similar introductions to M. M. Painlevé and Loucheur.

I visited prisons and State hospitals, the senate, and the House of Deputies, theatres and workshops, and interviewed prominent people engaged in public work.

Briand, " that legendary hero of peace " (Blüm), gave me a warm welcome. He spoke very little English himself, but had a capable secretary who furnished me with a "pass" that worked miracles wherever I went in France.

L

"And how is my friend, Lloyd George?" asked the vivacious Breton, after we got through our more serious business. "He is a great man, Monsieur Howard; but tell him that his golf is devastating."

I was much impressed with Poincaré—so cold, detached, and keen with incisive questions and curt replies.

"You have interviewed M. Briand I see," said he, in perfect English. "Our Briand is a fox like your Lloyd George."

French statesmen live in an atmosphere of suspicion, and are often seeking to supplant others; they lack team spirit.

I admired Loucheur and Herriot, but was puzzled by Painlevé. Clemenceau was a closed book to his friends, and quite impossible with strangers. He was aptly called "Tiger" because he growled like a man-eater. Frenchmen cannot understand the British attitude towards what they consider to be the private concerns of statesmen—religion, morals and home life.

I should like to live a year in Paris. Opera there is wonderful, theatres are palaces, and noted for comfort. I was informed that Parisians rarely frequent low cabaret or questionable shows; those places are kept going by British and American tourists.

Street traffic is a nightmare in Paris; crossing the road proves a risk. Paris, said one man, has only two classes, "the quick and the dead"; but taxi fares are so moderate that one hires a cab simply to cross the street!

How we lingered in Nôtre Dame, and then turned afresh to Victor Hugo!

One should spend a week at the Louvre.

The Latin quarter fascinates a student, and, in imagination, whilst at Fontainebleau, we could almost visualise Marie Antoinette and her tragedy.

My son Ieuan and I spent one holiday in Belgium. Through my letters of introduction I again had a wonderful time with statesmen in that country; especially with Dr. Waters, then Chief Secretary to the Belgian Minister of Labour.

Belgium is a small country and the cockpit of Europe; every inch of its soil is replete with history My government " pass " paved the way to battlefields, cemeteries, collieries, institutions and factories, where I learnt much.

Antwerp had not been rebuilt then, and its Cathedral was in ruins.

The Mole of Zeebrugge was still a wonder. We stayed at ancient Bruges, but soon tired of its smells and famous bells.

Blankenburg was better, but too modern. Brussels is a miniature Paris, though cleaner and brighter.

At that time the franc was so cheap that we could have a whole box at the Opera for 2/6 in English money, and "do" a cinema for three pence. A good dinner cost 1/6, and cigars were two for an English penny.

One touring Agency wanted 30/- to take us to the battlefield of Waterloo. A Belgian waiter showed us how to do it for ninepence.

It was a thrill to stand on the spot where Edith Cavell gave her life with a benediction on her lips for her executioners.

Ypres and Hill 60 left a deep impression on our minds, as did the great cemeteries where sleep so many of Britain's dead. A lump rises to one's throat on reading the plain stone crosses:

" HERE LIES A BRITISH SOLDIER WHOSE NAME IS KNOWN TO GOD."

Ostend is a delightful watering place; we had to pay four different tips before every bathe in the sea, and two more by the time we had dressed; but sea bathing there is exhilarating.

Our finances had run rather low by then, so we had to put up at a cheap hotel, and be satisfied with a dinner which cost sevenpence in English money. The soup was

passable, but horse meat proved too tough for two Welshmen who still had all their teeth.

It was a bad channel crossing; thus food was no
temptation to us or to others.

We had our return railway tickets to Colwyn Bay,
and an extra five shillings in English money. By travelling
overnight we could save the price of a bed; four shillings
was spent upon a decent meal, and the remaining shilling
went on a telegram to say that we would arrive with the
mail in the morning.   That booking clerk must have
been a humorist, because what they received in Colwyn
Bay was: " Arriving with the *maid* in the morning."

We spent three weeks in Northern Spain during 1923.
Our company consisted of my wife and daughter
(Mercia); a niece, our church organist, and myself. We
started from Liverpool in the Oroya, then the newest
boat belonging to the P. & S.N.C.   It was a glorious
voyage of 9,183 miles in all.

Our first stop was at La Rochelle which has changed
hands so many times between English and French;
formerly, it was an important maritime port. From there
Bathencort set out to conquer the Canaries; it was also
the French centre of the Reformation struggles, and became the refuge of Huguenots after the massacre of St.
Bartholomew; the town is still a Protestant stronghold.

Prominent is the monument of Eugene Fromentin—
poet and painter (1820—1896).   A visitor lingers beside
the Tower of the Lantern with its 172 spiral steps.   The
Gate of the Great Clock also is interesting. We witnessed
a beautiful regatta, which ended in tragedy that evening.

I interviewed the chairman of the local Socialist Party
who proved to be an incurable pessimist.

We were fortunate to see Santander before the latest
civil war; there was Spain in its pomp.   The king and
his family were in residence at the time, and armed
soldiers were plentiful, whilst a gunboat plied back and
fore within sight of the palace all day.

I never saw so many beggars displaying sores as at Santander. There also we first saw oxen as beasts of burden dragging carts on squeaking wooden wheels. I asked one driver why he did not oil the wheels; he replied that an ox would not work in silence; those wheel squeaks could be heard in multiples, and they seldom harmonized.

The ox is almost a domestic pet in Spain; his stable is under the same roof as the house of his peasant owner. Only the gentry and military own horses, and, of course, the Arena authorities.

We did not witness a bull-fight; one was due the day after we left—Sunday. But we went into the Arena and saw some bulls which were to fight. It must be a nauseating business, and I am thankful that we were spared the sight.

We met many priests at Santander, and noticed that they were well fed and groomed. There was a cleric in every hotel we visited; never, we were informed, was a priest expected to pay money for his keep. Priests were, then, civil servants, and paid by the State. According to what we were told there was one to every fifty of the population.

Santander's cathedral was nothing special to look at either within or without. But I wonder whether it stands today!

Drake once failed to enter Corunna; we were more fortunate. The first spot to visit was the tomb of Sir John Moore which was beautifully kept in the only open space in the town, and was donated in 1809. Exactly opposite is a tablet commemorating the wreck of S.S. Serpent, 10th November, 1890, when 172 officers and men were lost.

The Hercules monument was a notable sight; its inner tower was built by Phoenicians. One of the lights has been kept for centuries at the expense of Britain.

The church of St. Maria Del Campo was a small Gothic edifice with three naves, a Norman porch and pyramid tower; there were pictures of animals on the walls. I was allowed to peruse some Manuscripts dating from the 8th century.

We arrived in Vigo at midnight. It is the third greatest harbour in the world, and the view from sea can never be forgotten; a ship passes for miles and miles between coloured revolving lights on both sides. There assembled the ill-fated Armada, and from that harbour sailed the victims of Trafalgar. How many Spanish galleons lie at the bottom of that sea!

The Castel Del Castrio still kept up the pretence of guarding the harbour; it was like playing at soldiers.

My clerical collar secured for us an easy passage through the Customs. It usually does in foreign countries.

The Hotel Continental was a high building, containing nearly 300 bedrooms. I wanted sheets to sleep in, but could not get the three maids and porter to understand, because all my Spanish seemed to have vanished as soon as I set foot in Spain. It was no good pointing to the dictionary; alas, none of them could read. I threw myself down on the bed and spread a white handkerchief over my face. That enlightened them, and we were given something like linen sheets, not very clean; I almost think they were table-cloths unwashed. Water was scarce in the hotel; when I asked for a jugful we were given about three pints of tepid liquid. They could not appreciate our wish to bath every morning. "Those English people are either very dirty, or their ancestors were fish."

But the food was delicious even though meals were unpunctual; we dined at 8 p.m., which meant 8.30 or 8-45, and finished about 10 o'clock. Theatres and cinemas opened at eleven. Everybody takes a siesta in the heat of day; thus late hours were not so exhausting as in France where people seem to forget sleep. The heat at Vigo was intense, and mosquitos were fierce by day and poisonous at night; woe betide the man or woman left without a net during sleep!

The fish market was very interesting; bare-footed women outbid the men, and bore away their purchases in high baskets carried on their heads. The shrill cries of females selling fish were terrible to an ordinary listener. How these fishwives could quarrel! It was a titanic clash of tongue and wit when two of them glared at each other, and, with arms akimbo, released torrents of abuse amidst the applause of an interested crowd of excited women.

We met two Welshmen from Tonypandy one evening, and they (not we) got drunk to celebrate the event.

Our hotel manager had never heard of Wales, and to convince him that such a country did exist I produced a map. I asked him if he was ignorant of the name of Mr. Lloyd George. " Senor," replied he, " was he one of the saints?"

A motor car and guide were placed at our disposal for a week, and we went over the greater part of Northern Spain.

Bayona used to be a larger harbour than Vigo. Drake destroyed it twice, and the place never recovered its former glory and prosperity. On our way there we passed miles of maize fields, with maize huts, and acres of vines in terraces.

The castle of Montereal, built by Philip IV., belonged to the town of Bayona whose inhabitants used to live in its grounds during times of war; it had a wonderful armoury, and a church of its own. But when we visited the place the castle was for sale. In that tower a Spanish prince pined for years, and sang plaintive songs which still are popular with peasants.

There is a statue of the Holy Virgin overlooking the town,—one of seven in Spain.

Pontevedra is called the birthplace of Columbus; other towns made a similar claim! We visited the college of St. Francis, and saw the renowned convent. The church of Santa Maria la Major belonged to the Spanish renaissance period; but its interior was partly English

Gothic. It had a massive altar, and large statues out of harmony with the edifice.

We arrived in Tuy late at night. The most interesting place shown us was a pawnshop which was evidently used as a meeting place for revolutionaries, a few of whom made us welcome, and acted as our escort out of the town. They were well educated, mild mannered, and remarkably courteous — until I touched upon the political situation. Then trouble began, and I looked anxiously towards the door. Why do men get so excited over politics and religion?

Hotel de la Toja was the most luxurious hotel I ever saw; grandees of Spain patronized it at a tariff of £5 a day; the whole island upon which the building stood belonged to the hotel Company. There were mineral and medicinal springs, and baths for skin diseases. Impecunious patients were treated at the expense of the State. One Casino seemed to flourish ; a golf course was kept in good order, and the soap factory of la Toja was known all over Europe. The waiters at the hotel were German university students.

It was there we met and spoke to the then Spanish dictator, Primo de Rivera.

When we called for our bill, after an excellent dinner, the manager himself brought each of us a souvenir on a silver salver, "With the compliments of la Toja to the Britishers"; and he would accept no payment. Even the three waiters refused gratuities.

I was nervous during our two miles spiral ascent by motor to the top of La Guardia mountain where Roman legions fought Spaniards more than once. Yearly pilgrimages to the wayside shrines and crosses were very popular, and the view of Portugal seen from the top is well worth the climb. But I was thankful when we reached the bottom in safety.

Mondariz Hydro was another famous place we visited to see its mineral springs. Ten thousand bottles of water used to be despatched daily from these springs.

The then British Consul, Senor Duran, took us for a cruise in his yacht. We spent a wonderful day along the coast, and visited the Lazaretto St. Simon where emigrants used to be isolated. Mahon was the only other lazaretto in the Mediterranean area. From this island the seven churches of the seven Virgins were visible at the same time.

Santiago de Compostello was reached at 10 a.m., after a three hours run at an average of 60 miles an hour. There was no speed limit in Spain; we had a 40 horse-power American car and a driver who thought it a disgrace to be under 65 m.p.h. When someone asked him to slow down he accelerated; so we left him alone, and hoped for the best.

There were four Universities in Santiago during the 7th century.

One Catholic martyr canonised there was John Roberts, a Welshman from Trawsfynydd.

The Cathedral was the most important in Spain from the 10th to the 17th centuries. It was formerly endowed with £800,000 a year; following the 1830 Revolution its income was reduced to £4,000 a year. An average of 10,000 pilgrims visited the church annually. For once there was no collection at the service, only for chairs.

The cloisters were beautiful, and the vestments priceless, some belonging to the 7th century. One room was reserved for vestments and tapestries insured for over a million pounds. There is a copy of Maistre Mate's 10th century Portico de la Gloria in the British Museum. But to see the original made one forget himself.

St. James, Spain's Patron saint, is painted on horseback, to represent chivalry, maybe. In other countries the saint is a pilgrim carrying a staff. There is as much controversy over the burial place of St. James as about the birthplace of Columbus.

The Santiago Royal Hospital had four courtyards and a chain running along the roof,—to signify sanctuary.

We drove up to the old church of Sâr which has lean-
ing pillars (like Pisa); the foundations were visible.
Following the service we were treated to a display of
fireworks, and then the whole congregation danced on
the side green to the music of guitars; but there was a
female stampede when one black cat ran into the crowd.

We saw the Vigo Procession of the " Victory Christ,"
when a whole regiment of armed soldiers escorted the
Figure on a cross through the town crowded with spectators; people knelt as the crucifix passed them, and most
of them made the sign of the cross when bishops and
priests, carrying six-foot lit candles, blessed the crowd.
One felt sad and awed to see people crawling on bare
knees for two miles over cobbled streets, as penance for
their sins. Most of the wretches would be crippled for
life; such is the power of supersition!

Poor Spain, casual, courteous and cruel, lazy, leisurely
and laughter-loving! The rich were very wealthy; her
poor went in rags; but both classes would share their last
loaf with a pilgrim. The welcome given in palace and
hovel was, " Senor, this is my home, and yours."

One heard rumblings in 1923. Bankers were nervous,
statesmen anxious, policemen went fully armed, the
Army was restless, and all labour leaders were being
watched or arrested. Said one consul to me, when parting: "Senor, when next you come it will be a new Spain."
Will it be better? More courteous it cannot be.

We spent a happy month in Northern Ireland during
1925. I exchanged manse and pulpit with the Presbyterian minister of Port Rush. Deep sea fishing proved exciting, especially when our boat nearly got run down
after being driven far out to sea by a sudden squall.
How we came back safe is still a mystery to me, unless
it was a definite answer to the prayers of our Presbyterian boatman, who swore and prayed alternately.

Golf was delightful so long as my opponent won.
But the caddie we shared suffered if I came off victor;
that lad tried to bribe me to lose one game.

I was disappointed with Giant's Causeway. Of much more interest were the Irish cabins where fowls and children shared hearths with the natural occupant of the sty. Frequently was I told: "If your Reverence can wait, we will share the cabbage with you."

The Irish are a delightful folk, topsy-turvy, and ever doing the unexpected. But Protestantism is a serious business in Northern Ireland. The Presbyterians have some fine churches and eloquent preachers.

I was at Port Rush on August 12th when the Orange Lodges met for a demonstration. Each section was headed by a fife band playing a tune on its own. The noise was deafening; but we enjoyed that march past. Then came fiery orations to the accompaniment of thunderous applause; after which the public houses were emptied of liquor, and had to close their doors by six o'clock for want of supplies. Several heads were cracked on the way home.

I conducted a funeral one day, and was surprised to see mourners awaiting the grave to be refilled. The grave-digger explained that this was a precaution against body-snatching, which, he darkly hinted, was still practised by medical students for the purpose of dissection. A shilling opened the flood gates of that sexton's memory; he related story after story which increased in gruesomeness with my growing wonder. I give but one instance out of his list, but not in his inimitable dialect.

In this big vault lies the body of widow Macrath who was a very tall woman. John Turner, a short rascal, determined to secure that fine corpse for the hospital; and the night after the burial, he broke into the tomb, extracted the body, and carried it away on his left shoulder. Soon he got nervous, and quickened his pace; the long body then began bumping the snatcher in the rear. He tried to run, and the kicks became harder and more frequent. This proved too much for Turner; so with a loud shriek, which drew two policemen to the spot, he dropped the corpse, and fled for dear life. With that violent fall widow Macrath awoke. She had been buried whilst in a trance!

I met some Irish clergymen who were exceedingly kind, obliging and amusing. Their humour was most refreshing, because natural and unconscious. But it was dangerous to touch upon politics and Protestantism; they were as excitable as Spaniards then. Here is a story told me by an elderly Presbyterian minister.

A young boy lay dying of consumption. His mother stood weeping by the bedside. "Mam," asked the lad, "please bring me my sash." The sash was tenderly placed around his wasted shoulders, and it seemed to give him great satisfaction. After a while he called again, "Mam, please bring me my drum." The drum also was brought and two little sticks were placed into his hands. The boy beat a brief tattoo and then dropped them. "Two or three minutes afterwards," said the minister, "the lad called for his fife, and sounded a few notes on the noble reed before laying it aside. Then that wee lamb gathered all his strength, and, in a voice heard over the whole house, shouted: 'To hell with the Pope'! and turned round to die like the true Christian he was."

A few Labour leaders showed me around Belfast where even militant Protestantism has not cleared away the slums.

Not until 1937 did we visit Dublin and the South of Ireland. The area was over-run with priests. Ordinary Dublin folk are kind and hospitable, and much less cautious than the Scotch-Irish of the North. They can talk by the hour, are never in a hurry, and, sometimes, forget to present their bills. We stayed a few days at Bray the Beautiful; and spent a glorious time amidst the ruins of Glendoloch.

The birthplace of Parnell fascinated me, and I had to be forced away from the home and tree of Tom Moore.

But five days is not enough in that land of myth, romance and revolution. Every street and stone in Dublin itself embodies some stirring episode.

In my early days I heard John and Willie Redmond,
T. P. O'Connor and Tim Healy. But I would give much
to have known O'Connor, Davitt, Arthur Griffiths,
Michael Collin, Childers, Casement, and Jim Larkin, at
their prime.

In Phoenix Park we met a retired army surgeon who
had served in China, India, Africa and Mesopotamia.
He regaled us with wonderful reminiscences, half of
which, maybe, were imaginary, or at least romantic. He
ended up with a parting shot at my Welsh accent: "British statesmen are tricksters; the worst of all is a Welshman, and an Englishman comes a slow second."

We have had some good holidays in Scotland. One
year we roamed about the haunts of Burns; another time
the country of Prince Charlie fascinated us. Sir Walter
Scott was the magnet one summer, and we have toured
the places associated with the names of Carlyle, Ruther-
ford, Chalmers, R. L. Stevenson and Barrie.

Edinburgh is inexhaustible, and I never tire of
Glasgow.

In the Highlands one learns about the old Covenant-
ers; and there, religion is still man's chief concern in
life.

I love the metrical psalms sung without an organ,
and the long prayers and longer sermons never timed by
a clock. The dour Scotch are strong and sincere, and the
most maligned of men. Scots are cautious, but never
mean, and they contribute more to foreign missions than
any nation of their number.

I admire their writers (prose), politicians, statesmen,
and business men. In literature, in politics, in commerce, in philanthropy, Scotland is pre-eminent. Wales
owes a great deal to the Scotch Universities, and to the
Scotch pulpit.

I find that Irish immigration is lowering the standard
of living along the Clyde, and causes great concern to
Protestant churches north of the Tweed.

CHAPTER ELEVEN

GOD'S OWN COUNTRY . . . . IN PARTS

DURING the early Spring of 1936 I visited America.

The *Berengaria* was a wonder ship, and a small town in itself, with accommodation for 3,000 people, including crew and passengers. She had a displacement of 50,000 tons, and travelled an average of 570 miles a day. At first, the ship belonged to Germany. I travelled " tourist," but had the freedom of First and Third class. We were a mixed set on board ; so far as one could gather I was the only Welshman in the passenger list ; but there were two compatriots amongst the crew.

I spent much of the time with George Lansbury, Dr. Salter and Mrs. Postgate, daughter of G.L., all of whom were on a peace crusade. Lansbury had recently relinquished the leadership of official Labour owing to his attitude over sanctions against Italy. Naturally this was the chief theme of our discussions.

On board I met Principal Arthur Johnson of Stockholm and Prof. Alf Kindofferum, who were travelling to a conference to be held at Columbus, Ohio. They felt concerned over the same problems as troubled us in Britain — peace, re-union, the revolt of Youth, and diminishing church attendance. To them the Oxford Group Movement seemed our only hope. Buchman himself expects the next religious Revival to start from Norway.

Monarchism has a strong hold in the Northern countries where Socialism is in power. Finland is the exception, being a Republic. Communism is a pervasive influence in the whole Federation, especially in Norway.

There were many Jews aboard on that voyage, most of them German refugees who had lost everything but their hope of reaching the Land of the Free. Their experience, as told me, would cure Sir Oswald Mosley of fanatic Fascism. But the young Israelites were not shy by any means; they monopolised the dancing floor, much to the disgust of one American. We watched the whirling crowd.

"Padre," said my neighbour, "I have a grudge against one character in the Bible." "And who may that be?" I asked.

"Pharaoh," came the reply, "why did the fool not finish his job?"

One of the most interesting men I met during that trip was F. A. Osan-Pinanko, the blackest of Negroes. He was Principal of a mission college on the West Coast; his ideal was Booker Washington, the educated coloured man who did so much for his own Race. Pinanko had very advanced ideas, and claimed equality for Black and White. No longer does a Negro admit the divinity of imperialism, and accept a religion of being white. The rape of Abyssinia may yet prove the beginning of the end for white domination; an "All African Movement" is something to count with outside the realms of fiction and the boxing saloon.

The first sight of America provides a thrill. I cannot imagine a man who will look unmoved at the huge statue of Liberty; although one passenger pointed to the thorns crowning the head of that marble female as a symbol of freedom on the way to a cross.

"Chew Wrigley's Gum" is the first placarded greeting to God's Own Country, and I noticed that most Americans literally respond to this; their jaws are seldom at rest.

The main purpose of immigration officers is to keep people out of the Land of the Free; questions to be answered are endless and amusing; religion and politics even are taken into account.

Touring in the United States is becoming very complicated; it is difficult to land, and even then the trouble is not at an end. Various States on the lookout for revenue are making their frontiers as impassable as those on the continent of Europe.

California insists on a permit for more than a five days stay; Idaho after 48 hours; Oregon for 24 hours.

Several States have established "Ports of Entry" at which a toll is levied on caravan trailers entering the State; all cars are stopped at these ports of entry.

The Rev. Cynolwyn Pugh saved me a tedious wait at the Customs, and whisked me away to his flat where a crowd awaited the visitor from across the Pond. For those two days I had my first experience of American hustle. We attended a Peace Demonstration the first evening; Lansbury was chief speaker, and there was an immense audience. The crowd were treated to three lectures on pigeons before the chairman called our Britisher, at 9.50. Knowing that the Labour leader was tired, I complained of the tedious wait. "My dear sir," said a clergyman sitting next to me, "you will soon realize that Americans are deficient in humour—notwithstanding Will Rogers." I stayed long enough to hear Dr. Fosdick deliver a fine speech, and then had to leave for a public dinner at which I arrived an hour late after losing my way in the Underground where there are no indicators or porters.

A fine city is New York:

"Home of the strip-tease and of cocktail parties that last for days. New York where the murder of a glamorous artist's model is the signal for scores and scores of nearly nude pictures in the Tabloids and Yellow Press; New York, where the brightest of Broadway's million lights advertise chewing gum."

"New York where the Bowery barber specialises in disguising a customer's black eyes; New York where a self-service shop permits women to handle and try on umpteen dresses and walk out without buying any; New York where dogs have nursemaids, men who take them out for a daily airing at so much a week, and caterers who bring them choice meals; New York the crazy, the exciting, the amazing city where the air is electric, and all the citizens are young—or seem young." (*H. Butcher*).

It is said that Jews own New York, Irish control it, and Negroes enjoy it—with the permission of Father Divine.

The Dollar, the Latest, and the Newest are sought by New Yorkers at all times. There are more Jews in America than in Palestine; New York alone has 2,000,000 Israelites; Chicago is the home of 300,000; Philadelphia houses 270,000.

I spent three hours in China Town, and two hours in Harlem, the centre of 200,000 Negroes who are so fond of necromancy, music and revival religion.

The Italian quarter made me timid; Latins are so sensitive and suspicious; but I felt more at home with them on my second visit to New York.

I carried a letter of introduction (again from Mr. Lloyd George) to J. W. Davis, former Ambassador, Jeffersonian Liberal who nearly got the Presidency in 1926, opposed the New Deal and Roosevelt, distrusts the League of Nations, prefers Fascism to Communism, and dislikes Polish Jews. He was very courteous and answered my questions without reserve. Davis is evidently a man of strong likes and dislikes. But his printed speeches are poor reading.

Vladeck, the Jewish editor whom I interviewed the same day, was quite the opposite; brilliant, enthusiastic, and expressing his convictions with an abandon that gladdened the heart of one in search of "copy." His ideas of Hitlerism, Communism, Zionism and world Jewry were most refreshing. He invited me to stay at his home for a few days, and promised insight to the real New York.

M

I missed Norman Thomas, Socialist candidate for the White House, but arranged to meet him in the West where he was on a speaking tour.

Philadelphia, my next stop, is the fourth greatest city of America. My friend, the Rev. O. R. Williams, the resident Welsh minister, rushed me about the city even before attending the Presbytery meetings where I was billed to preach that night. Philadelphia is very partial to club life; there are over 200 social clubs in the City. The Union League was the pride of my fellow minister; it is the most exclusive club in the States, and was formed in memory of Lincoln and for the purpose of maintaining the Union.

The curator at Liberty Hall was a native of St. Helens. I thought he would present me with the Hall and its contents when he learnt of my connection with Liverpool.

Philadelphia is redolent with history; William Penn still keeps the city under his hat. According to a byelaw, no building shall reach higher than the head of the Penn monument.

One lingered long beneath Penn's Tree, and in Penn's house. Millions visit them yearly.

Everything relating to George Washington is sacred in that city, and Lincoln's influence is all over the place.

Of interest to me was the birthplace of Benjamin Franklin, and the cottage of Betty Ross who devised " Old Glory "—the Flag of the Republic that is almost worshipped. It must be displayed in every public building, even in places of worship, and always is saluted by teachers and pupils at school.

May 12th, 1936, Dan Keeler, a teacher, was ordered to salute the Flag every morning at the local police station for thirty days, as a penalty for wiping his hands on a flag at Battle Creek. Scholars must repeat the oath of allegiance also after prayers daily at school.

There were many Welshmen amongst the pioneer Quakers at Pennsylvania in 1684; they were granted

50,000 acres of land by Penn to form a Welsh Barony. That explains Welsh place-names to be found around Philadelphia—Brynmawr, Llanuwchllyn, Pencader, etc. How interesting to read that the Barony broke away from Penn's administration over questions of the Welsh language in courts of justice, and tithes!

I received much kindness from Dr. Lewis Jones and his wife in Slatington, a slate quarry district where Welsh, Germans, and Dutch live together in peace. But a strike fever was abroad at that time, and workmen were taking forcible possession of town halls and local government in various districts. The "sit-down" strike spread throughout the States during 1937; a gang of youths "sat-down" in a New York cabaret to protest against early closing; a Missouri Assembly-man "sat-down" until a resolution he introduced was accepted by his fellow legislators; one wife "sat-down" until her husband increased her allowance. Ordinary policemen found it impossible to deal with the thousands of men who barricaded themselves in factories and kept out other workers by using clubs and sticks against them; attempts to dislodge the down-sitters led to serious disturbance and bloodshed. The chief cause of the trouble in Slatington was rivalry between the two labour organisations, the American Federation of Labour and the Committee for Industrial Organisation. William Green and John L. Lewis are the respective rival leaders. Of Lewis more anon.

At Slatington I attended an American funeral. Undertakers flourish in the States; it is more expensive to die than to live in the Land of high prices; the first question asked a bereaved family is, "For how much was the departed insured?" Most of that money goes into the pockets of an undertaker. America has commercialised death; a funeral spells ruin to uninsured families. A corpse is bled dry, embalmed, dressed in a new suit of clothes, trimmed, and rouged. If a female, she is decked in finery and jewels, and then placed on view for two or three days when relatives visit the funeral parlour to

pay their respects and read the glaring advertisements.
Coffins are elaborate with cover half of glass, and the
grave is decorated within and without.

Speculation is rife even in cemeteries. At Detroit
a tout offered to sell me a large plot of land cheap; when
I told him that I lived in Wales he enlarged eloquently
upon my chance to re-sell at a tremendous profit.

I spent a delightful time with Judge W. J. Thomas at
Langsford. He was the only judge in the County, and I
watched him dispense justice at his Court; it was amusing, and instructive. Judges and lawyers chew gum in
Court, and the jaws of policemen, warders and prisoners
are in perpetual motion. Ordinary judges are in mufti;
members of the Supreme Court wear gowns, but not wigs.
Solicitor and barrister are one in America.

Judge Thomas had an original idea concerning the
use of the automobile. Formerly. famine. plague and
war kept down the population of the world. Science has
mastered the first two, and common sense will ultimately
abolish war. The motor car will perform the function
of the three in the future. In sixteen years 250,000 people
were killed in wars; during the same period motors ac-
counted for 300,000 deaths.

Granville, my next stopping place, has a colony of
Welsh people hailing from Pen-y-Groes, Llanllyfni, Festiniog, Bethesda and Llanberis, whose families emigrated
during the Penrhyn strike. The depression had hit Granville hard; machinery was rusting, quarries lay idle, and
hundreds of unemployed quarrymen were being absorbed into the W.P.A.

I visited " Great Meadows," a State penitentiary outside Granville; at that prison inmates are not dressed in
convict garb; there was very little of the penal element
in the administration: within the walls a prisoner was
practically free. The place was more like a great hotel
than a State prison; cells are luxuriously furnished, and
have radio sets. There were 1,150 convicts at Great
Meadows. Prisoners were paid from two to eight cents

a day for work done, and can spend their money at the well-stocked stores on the premises. On the expiration of his term, the prisoner received a new suit of clothes, about ten dollars in money (together with wages due) and a railway voucher to his home town.

A high wall was recently built around the prison; the object of this, I was informed, is to keep people out, and not to stop convicts making their escape. Prior to the erection of that formidable wall with its sentry boxes, escapes were never attempted; of late there have been many, and, strange to say, prisoners nearing the very end of their term usually make the dash for freedom. I saw one who had been exemplary for over fifteen years, and, when within forty eight hours of release, he felled a warder, scaled the wall, overpowered an armed sentry, and got away—for twenty hours.

I had a delightful day in Harrisburg, the Capital of Pennsylvania. Governor Earle was exceedinly kind; he was the first Republican to hold the office of Governor. Two of his Cabinet Ministers spent several hours explaining to me the working of the W.P.A. and the E.R.B.

The State of Pennsylvania consists of 37 counties, and is larger, I am told, than England and Wales together. Its population was ten millions.

I joined a procession of 1,500 unemployed as they entered the city that morning, and found them in angry mood. There were a few arrests, but no bloodshed; for a time things looked rather ugly. A baton, or some other weapon, grazed my shoulder, and I had visions of a cracked skull. Earle's men pacified the crowd by granting their demands, and then all was serene.

I sat alongside the first commissioner of the Works Progress Administration whilst he received deputations from various localities. He was able to improvise temporary work and wages for bricklayers, miners, musicians, tailors and actors. On the day of my visit the W.P.A. was employing 248,000 people in Pennsylvania alone.

I was an interested spectator of the methods employed by the Emergency Relief Board (E.R.B.). For three hours I watched Dr. Schwinitze, Dr. Solan Veysen and Dr. R. T. Bowman, the renowned economists, dispensing relief; the unit catered for was not a person, but a " case " or family.

It was said that 20,000,000 American citizens were in receipt of unemployment relief at that time; and this was apart from rate or parish relief. Employability and legal residence alone were taken into account; morals were not considered; a prostitute, or gangster, could claim relief, and, sometimes, did successfully. Naturally there was criticism, but not always well founded. In Pittsburg 1,500 anomymous complaints were investigated, and only 117 proved partially justified.

I visited the town jail at Newcastle, and found a shocking state of affairs. There was no yard to exercise prisoners; the steel cages were dark, dirty, and unfit to house human beings. Food was not bad, but the Sheriff apologised for those dilapidated buildings; he was quite helpless in the matter; the authorities refused to spend money on the place.

The Newcastle Workhouse, on the other hand, was a fine modern building in a pleasant meadow; two hundred inmates lived in ease and comparative comfort at the time. But administration, as I saw it, was slack and open to possible abuse.

At Pittsburg the " *Druid* " Office folk were very obliging, and I received gracious hospitality at the hands of Mr. and Mrs. W. E. Morgan of the firm C. A. Verner & Co.

From there I proceeded to Bangor where I was due to preach three times, and then went back to Philadelphia again.

O. R. Williams motored me to Princeton Theological Seminary degree day. At the banquet my speech had a most flattering reception, and there I heard some real American eloquence.. Prof. Erdman, Principal

Stevenson, and Prof. Mackenzie are orators of a new type to me,—scholarly, humourous and torrential.

In the Homeland a degree ceremony provides occasion for horse-play, fun, and ribald jests; not infrequently illustrious visitors leave the platform in disgust. But Americans make the conferment of degrees into a religious service with hymns, prayer and sermon. The Dr. Williams' choir is wonderful, and I shall not forget the stately march up that long aisle to the accompaniment of "O God, our help in ages past," played on the high organ.

The following day we visited Captain Evans on the *Clytotheus*. I wished to get the story of Nov. 5—11, 1932, when his then ship the *Phemeus* was caught in a typhoon on the Caribbean sea. For seven days and seven nights was that drama of the sea played out; the crew had no bread for five days, and one cup of water per day was their portion the whole of that terrible week. How they survived is a mystery. Several of the Asiatics went mad. Through a miracle the survivors found themselves ashore on a Sunday morning; the Captain had lost eighteen pounds weight in one week, and his remaining crew of 70 Chinese and 17 Europeans were like skeletons, and unable to walk upright for want of sleep and food. The funnel of the ship, 35 tons in weight, had been blown away in the storm. "There was only one place to go to that morning," mused the Captain. So, without saying a word to his officers, he crept into the English church. But whom should he see already in the pews but the entire lot of his mixed crew. They had gone under the same impulse, and were weeping like children.

The pulpit was occupied by a young curate that morning, and he informed the startled congregation, that, for some reason which he failed to understand, he could not preach his prepared sermon. A verger went up to inform the cleric of the presence of the *Phemeus* captain and crew. Since the radio had enabled the whole listening world to follow the fortunes of the ship during that momentous week the clergyman then understood.

All that the captain remembers about what followed was that he could not take his eyes from the Figure of Christ in the coloured window behind the altar, and that, ultimately, he found himself back in his own cabin, and on his knees.

On the day of our visit, the *Clytotheus* was being loaded with scrap-iron for Japan. Said one officer to me, "This may come back to America as bullets and bombs before long."

Out of 1,620,114 tons of scrap-iron exported from U.S.A. between January and May 1937, some 1,035,963 tons went to Japan (*New Times*, 14/8/37).

I visited Gerrard's college from which the clergy are excluded by trust deed; it is supposed to be the heaviest endowed school in the world.

We motored to Lakehurst to see the giant airship Hindenberg. At the entrance to the airport, armed sentries let us through in response to the magical word "Press." We were again challenged at the hangar; "Press" even failed us there. But, with characteristic bluff, my American friend called: "Officer of the British Navy."

"Pass, British Navy," exclaimed the surprised, if not suspicious, sentry at salute.

Thus did I inspect that ill-fated monster of the skies.

Atlantic City was our next call. The Blackpool of America is its apt description; the place is run by rich Jews who turn night into day, and make pleasure a fine and lucrative art.

I well remember the moonlight motor run back to Philadelphia that night,—fifty miles or more, through forests where Indians used to hunt wild beasts and human foes, and the Pilgrim Fathers prayed, and the old pioneers hewed a path for civilisation. The stars still look down with pity upon the puny efforts and tragedies of man.

I visited the great Penitentiary at Philadelphia. Charles Dickens criticised it in his *American Notes*. At that time the cells were dark, narrow, and absolutely silent; a prisoner's head was covered with a hideous cowl whenever he emerged into the light. Those cells are still to be seen, but are not in use at present. The prisoner population on the day of my visit was 1,313,—989 white and 324 coloured. One hundred and forty two of these white prisoners were lifers—murderers; and there were 94 Negroes in the same class.

Two most interesting cases were both lifers, who had been saved from the Chair; they became well known radiologists, and were consulted by members of medical schools from all over the country.

There had been a strike in the prison a week before my visit; the inmates demanded a radio set for every cell instead of the one central set for each corridor. They also wished to have an extension of light time from nine to ten o'clock. Both demands were conceded. Five prisoners escaped through the sewers, early in 1936; how they fought the big rats, poisonous gases, and floods will ever remain a marvel. All got through to freedom and were at large for three days. Four were captured; two of them went to the Chair, and two committed suicide; but the remaining man was never found.

I visited St. David's Church, outside Philadelphia. It is an exact replica of our Welsh Cathedral; the stones even were brought over from Wales.

Swarthmore College was interesting because of its Quaker associations and beautiful surroundings.

My friends motored me to Trenton, the home town of the Lindbergs, and where Hauptmann paid his last penalty.

I was a guest at the Canadian Empire Banquet in Philadelphia. Dr. Parkes Cadman delivered an eloquent speech on that occasion; he dropped dead a few weeks afterwards at a similar function.

Mr. and Mrs. Arthur Roberts were wonderful hosts; their kindness was embarrassing. Then that wonderful Welshman, Dr. A. C. Morgan, did much to make my stay pleasant and profitable.

My next objective was Washington, the seat of Federal Government. Every Welshman makes straight for the Congressional library where the brothers Roberts are librarians. They have five million volumes on 170 miles of shelves, cared for by 700 assistants. It was with awe I touched a sample of the 450 bound volumes of George Washington's letters and despatches; the same with the writings of Lincoln, Jefferson, etc. Here was the original MS. of the Gettysburg speech; the signed Declaration of Independence; Jefferson's Bible; Washington's Bible, and the Biblia Latina, worth 850,000 dollars. That library system is the most efficient known to man. I was invited to put an assistant to the test, and, playfully, asked him for a copy of my latest book, *Jesus the Agitator*. In less than three minutes the book was placed in my hands.

I interviewed Chief Justice Charles Evans Hughes, of the Supreme Court, a Welshman, related to Principal Howell Harris Hughes, Aberystwyth, and considered by some to be the strongest brain in the country. He came within an ace of the Presidency in 1924, and now occupies a unique position where he openly defies Roosevelt himself. We spoke candidly about American law and justice. I referred to Sacco and Venzetti, Tom Mooney and the Scottsboro negroes; but the great judge was noncommittal, and reminded me of the peculiarities of State and Federal law in America.

Senator James Davies was the next to take me in hand. He was Secretary of State for Labour over a period of ten years, and founded the Order of the Moose, over which arose some trouble. I was lavishly entertained at his palatial home next to the British Embassy; he lent me his car and driver, and introduced me to several influential people.

I was anxious to meet Senator Borah, who, at that time, was likely to be nominated by his Party for the Presidency. He was chatty, though wary, and placed his office and secretary at my service. That is how I sat in Congress for a time, and in the Press Gallery.

I realised that politics is a paying business in America. Each member of Congress is paid 10,000 dollars a year, and an extra 4,000 dollars to pay a clerk, and is given two rooms for his private use. A comparison of emoluments received by M.Ps. of various Parliaments is interesting:

U.S.A.	£2,000
Canada	800
Irish Free State	360
France	560
Belgium	300
Australia	825
Great Britain	600

Cabinet Ministers in America are chosen by the Executive and are usually outside Congress; every office is a reward for political service rendered at elections. Change of President causes a reshuffle in every branch of government service; policemen, postmen, teachers and even judges depend upon politics. Consequently, there is a temptation to make hay while the sun shines; graft is often practised. One official admitted that he spent 12,000 dollars when soliciting votes to place him in office. If I remember aright, his salary was about 10,000 dollars; he would feel justified, therefore, in recouping his losses.

When judges have to solicit the bloc votes of gangsters a price is demanded, and must be paid. Political alliance with crime halts the policeman, and cripples the judge; it supports bribery, perjury and gangsterdom. Ex-convicts are sometimes made policemen. The system of graft prevails even in prison.

A most impressive personality is John L. Lewis, President of the Miners Federation of America. Lewis is, by now, the supreme labour leader of the U.S.A.; he has fought the big motor magnates even, and won. A man of boundless energy and soaring ambition, his immediate object is to unify American Labour; and then, perhaps, this Welshman may occupy the White House as President of the United States! In 1932 he was a Republican, and campaigned for Herbert Hoover against Franklin Roosevelt; now he is a favourite of the President. He has a fine home outside Washington, is a voracious reader, fond of the English classics, and all out for the sit-down strike.

"But you see, Howard, American Trade Unionism is fifty years behind Wales,"—that was his parting word as he pushed two thick cigars into my hand.

Through Lewis I was introduced to Miss Perkins, Federal Secretary for Labour, one of the most brilliant intellects of our generation. She served as State Commissioner of Labour in New York when Roosevelt was Governor, and he took her into his Cabinet at Washington. In private life she is Mrs. P. C. Wilson who has a grown-up daughter Madam Secretary Perkins resembles Miss Margaret Bondfield with whom she has much in common; she made it easy for me to inspect pits and factories, and the great motor plants of Detroit.

Senator Borah introduced me to Edgar Hoover, head of the G—men, and, probably, the most remarkable man in America, certainly the most popular. Formerly he was a Government Departmental chief receiving some £1,800 a year. Now he can get whatever salary he cares to ask. He is the one indispensable public servant in a country that has no permanent Civil Service. He wields Federal powers in the detection of crime. This, under him, has become an exact science. For a whole hour he harangued me upon what he regards as his mission in

life ever since the Lindberg case; it was a most telling
sermon.

When we remember that there are, on an average,
36 murders a day in America, and that 150,000 assassins
remain untraced, it will be seen how formidable is the
task before Edgar Hoover. His pet aversion is the sob-
politician who secures probation or parole for criminals;
no fewer than twenty per cent. of the murderers are
offenders on parole.

A man may be sentenced to twenty years imprisonment, but if he has sufficient " pull " he can get out on
parole in six or twelve months.

It is unsafe though to commit even a minor crime
in New York without a capital of at least 500 dollars,
because that city has a stringent code. The fourth conviction for felony, for instance, means a " lifer." But
graft can overcome that even.

Under the Sullivan Law possession of a gun is criminal. Yet there are 1,000 shootings a year in the city of
New York alone.

Here is a cutting from the *Daily Telegraph* for July
19, 1937:

> " Once a year Mayor La Guardia of New York goes
> out in a boat, and helps the police to dump into
> Long Island Sound weapons captured from gang-
> sters in the previous 12 months.
>
> When the ceremony took place the other day,
> the cargo included:
> 2,350 pistols and revolvers.
> 2,376 shotguns and air rifles.
> 814 catapults. knuckledusters. knives, swords and
> similar weapons."

During three years 157 policemen were received into
the penitentiary of St. Quentin *as convicts*.

Formerly the tough guy was the hero of young America; thanks to Edgar Hoover, the G—man is now the
ideal of youths in search of adventure.

The Chief of the Staff took me round his Bureau.
There were over seven million finger prints indexed, and,
whilst I was in the room, a request arrived from Scotland
Yard for one print.   It was wirelessed to London within
ten minutes.

The science department kept me occupied for an hour.
I watched scientists reconstructing crimes from small
clues, analysing bloodstains, ex-raying a parcel at the
bottom of which was seen a bomb, and in another a
small revolver fully loaded.   The museum proved exciting.   One saw all the stages which led to the capture of
Dillinger, public enemy number one ; and Hauptman, the
Lindberg baby kidnapper, etc. One exhibit was the core
of an apple which had a tooth dent in it ; that dent was
the means of bringing a murderer to the Chair, after ten
years chase over eight thousand miles.   The G—men
never give up a chase.

The shooting gallery was a long-range underground,
where the G—men practise shooting with all sorts of
weapons ; two paper-men, riddled, according to my
requests and directions, were autographed, and given
to me as a memento.   Every G—man is an expert shot,
and he shoots to kill.

Kidnapping, murder and bank robberies are now
Federal crimes, and G—men can pursue a criminal
through all the States.

All the time I was in America I wore my clerical
collar.   Protestant ministers rarely do so in the States ;
but I found it advantageous.   When leaving the Dodge
Hotel for the Department of Justice I took a wrong
turning, and lost my way. Accosting a passer-by, I told
him of my trouble.   "And has his Reverence lost his
way," replied the son of Ireland, "we shall soon settle
that." Hailing a taxi, he handed me in, and began talking about "dear Old Ireland."   Not one word could I
get in until we reached my destination.   It was useless
offering to pay the fare ; my loquacious benefactor
knelt on the pavement with : "Your blessing, Father."

So placing both hands on his shoulders, I murmured:
"My blessing upon you, my son," and hastily departed.

Scores of American policemen, yes hundreds, if not
thousands, are Irish Catholics, who revere the round
collar. I had only to stand a minute or two at a busy
street-crossing before all traffic would be stopped by a
big bobby who came to lead me safely across.

"Dare I go to the Italian quarter to-night?" I asked
one friend.

"My dear sir," was the reply, "with that collar on
you could go to Hell."

American hotels provide excellent accommodation,
though they are expensive. Each bedroom has a
writing-desk and 'phone, and bath. But, however
excellent their coffee, Americans cannot brew good
tea. They place a bag of tea to hang inside the cup,
and then pour hot water—seldom at the boil—over it.
At Washington I asked for a second bag, and even a
third, in the hope of getting one decent drink as at home;
by the time a fourth bag arrived I could taste nothing but
bag.

If that is America's best in tea I can understand the
Boston row which precipitated the break away from
England; England quarrelled with America over tea.

I visited the Ford theatre in which Lincoln was shot,
and the house in which the Liberator breathed his last.

The Franciscan Monastery and the Church of the
Immaculate Conception (cost 65 million dollars) are
worth making the journey to see them.

From Washington I went on to Wilkes-Barre, a min-
ing centre which had suffered from the floods that
wrought such havoc during the spring of that year.
Colliers there are good workers, and fond of fighting.
The two rival Unions were then at variance, and the
Italians were active with knife and bomb.

Judge Jones had just escaped being blown to pieces
by a bomb sent him through the post. A fortnight

previous the daughter of one neighbouring judge had been bombed in her motor car.

My host took me to see the renowned reformatory, Kislyn; and I questioned the boys and the warden during the afternoon. The system is not on time limit; a boy is retained until he wins 1,100 marks for good conduct. Some succeed within one year; others take as long as eight years. Delinquents who escape usually return of their own accord; society is against them. The warden called a cheer for the visitors before we left; but we were greeted with a chorus of groans. Judge Jones had committed all those boys to Kislyn.

I travelled by night bus from Wilkes-Barre to Syracuse where I was due at the Presbyterian General Assembly next day. The moonlight was glorious, but I had never realised how many bones make up the human anatomy. I felt like a bear with a sore back when I arrived at the hotel.

The General Assembly of over nine hundred delegates was a fine experience. Each delegate, or commissioner, receives his train fare and four dollars a day expenses. The average cost of an Assembly is 73,000 dollars (£14,300).

The Presbyterians have 10,000 ministers and over four million members in America, with an income of twenty million pounds.

In 1920 our Welsh Denomination transferred 91 preachers, 114 churches, and 14,000 communicants to the American Body.

We had a Welsh dinner, where forty Welsh ministers met to welcome the stranger from Wales.

The 1936 General Assembly was noted because of the modernist split which had come to a head; seven ministers were ex-communicated. Their leader was Dr. Machen of Philadelphia; and thus was finally settled a seventeen year old quarrel.

From Syracuse I motored to Buffalo, where I had three hours' sleep before starting for Niagara,—a life-long dream come true. I spent eight hours in the most wonderful spot of America, if not of the world: the torrent of the immovable, the mystery of the visible, the roar of the inexpressible. It was all there when the first Red Indian stood in awe before the rapids. I was dumb beside my kind guide; the sight was so awesome and stupendous.

I should love to have seen the moon shimmering on the Falls, and piercing the perpetual rainbows; spirits of the mists would be abroad at such hours, and a man could then interpret the river's moan as it rushed towards the sea. Often shall I dream of it all in the years ahead. It was worth living for the one day I spent at Niagara.

I had three days at Detroit, the city of motor cars and Father Coughlin of broadcasting fame. The Plymouth, the Chrysler, Packard, and Ford have their plants in Detroit; it is also the centre for General Motors.

The population was 1,568,662, almost all of whom were interested in automobiles. Yet, although the motor boom was near its peak, I found that there were 18,000 families on emergency relief, a number equal to 72,000 people, at four a family; an additional 20,000 were employed by the W.P.A.

Some tough guys live at Detroit. One afternoon ten minutes after I had left, eleven gangsters raided a hotel, and relieved the guests of their wallets, and that during broad daylight. They belonged to the "Black Legion of Detroit."

I went through the Ford works, covering 1,896 acres of land, and having 96 miles of railroad. That day there were 21,800 cars belonging to workmen parked on the 76 acres reserved for that purpose. The minimum wage is six dollars (nearly 30/-) for an eight hour day in a week of five days.

Ford has coal pits, steel works, coke ovens, timber saw mills, 30 ships, and a mile and a half of docks.

N

His motto is, " There is nothing static but change," and this is put to the test in the experimental shops.

There is an output of 4,500 cars a day, 75,000 hands are employed. The pay sheets amount to 135,000,000 dollars a year.

Gwyn Evans and I were lent a car and driver for the day, and taken through the works.

The Technical School was interesting because people of all ages are found at the desks.

Henry Ford does not live entirely for the motor; he has a large museum exhibiting the romance of locomotion throughout the centuries. The library also in that building is valuable.

Greenfield village is a masterpiece of modern and ancient combined, and is a fine monument to the memory of Edison, the inventor, who was the early patron of Ford.

Lincoln is commemorated in a Flame of Remembrance, and a replica of the house in which the great President was born.

Ford has built and endowed a fine commodious hospital.

I visited the House of Correction belonging to Detroit; the population was 946; of those 250 were females, and there were two hundred officials. Warders carried no weapons, except when marching prisoners to or from the eating house, and to the sleeping quarters. Once only had there been trouble in the jail; and that was when a prisoner escaped on the very day before his release was due.

Capital punishment is not practised in Michigan; so there were 30 " lifers " in the prison. Three degrees of punishment can be inflicted within those walls. (1) Solitude, (2) Reflection between bare walls for four hours. (3) King Row,—standing for five hours between iron gates. Few men can suffer King Row more than once without going insane.

Inmates did most of the work inside. A negro was chief cook, a " lifer " at that, which means that he was in for murder.

The female quarters were a sanatorium of detached cottages, clean, bright, roomy, surrounded by gardens, and with no locked doors. Mrs. Campbell, the warden, treats crime as a disease; there is no penal atmosphere about the place. A woman prisoner is given a home and responsibility, and rarely betrays the trust; the few who break through the frail wire fence always return of their own accord.

There were 23 convicted murderesses; one half-caste had been declared not guilty of killing nine men; it was proved conclusively that she had poisoned only seven. Another woman was in for murdering six children. One had hacked her husband to pieces. . . .

The Temple of Remembrance outside Detroit is worth visit. But those cemetery touts!

I spent three happy days as a guest of Mr. and Mrs. Perrot who showered kindness upon me.

Then away for Canada whither I had tried to emigrate from Llansamlet thirty years previously. How silly seems the Customs' search beyond the Ambassadors' Bridge! But one is glad, and surprised, to think of the 4,000 miles of undefended frontier between America and Canada; evidently national safety is not merely a matter of guns and fortifications.

It was a monotonous train journey through hundreds of miles of waste land and forest, interspersed with hamlets and townlets. The country is too flat for people who have lived amongst the hills of Wales. I can understand the longing of compatriots for their Homeland. A prairie lacks the lure of the hills; yet the silence can be overpowering at times.

One tall Red Indian told me in New York that the noises of the city were not so audible to him as the stillness of the plains.

I was guest of the United Churches of Toronto. Their central office is a hive of activity, and the Rt. Rev. Dr. More arranged a luncheon for me to meet the clergy of the city.

At nearly every meeting of ministers in America and Canada I was questioned about the attitude of the home churches towards Modernism and Fundamentalism. My questioners were rather shocked to hear that British religionists had passed through that phase of thought fifty years ago, or more, and that they were concerned now with different problems, mostly economic. Amongst Protestants across the Atlantic the Pope, Darwin, and the Devil are amusingly confused just now.

When I visited the town hall of Toronto the Mayor informed me that our then Lord Mayor of Liverpool (Councillor R. J. Hall), was on a visit to that city, and was due at a public luncheon that very afternoon. Consequently I had to attend a civic and a church luncheon the same day. At the former function I met Lieut. Governor Bruce who invited me to Government House.

Chief Constable Brigadier-General Draper entertained me afterwards, and we cruised Lake Ontario which the chief engineer declared is 200 miles of fresh water between city and sea.

I was motored around the city and its environs, and on to Alda Farm, where 120 cows were housed in fly-proof sheds; insects are electrocuted at doors and windows; so there is no waste cow-energy through tail-flicking. Green grass and flowers always remain before the cow's eyes, and she is fed, cleaned, and gently milked to the accompaniment of radio music. With the result that an Alda animal yields twice the amount of milk got from an ordinary cow.

One hundred and fifteen pigs were fattening to music, and each animal had his own special run and sty.

Four hundred hens lived in wire cages, and never left them except to be treated or killed; each laid two eggs a day—to the sound of radio music, and in plenty of sunlight and false dawns. Everything was done on that farm to music.

"Music Therapy" was the discovery of Dr. Wilhain Van de Wall, who began to study the effects of music upon human beings some twenty years ago. It is reported that he quelled a riot in a New York women's prison, not by bullets, but with songs. His theory has been successfully tried in prisons, asylums, and hospitals all over America. Of late, people, like the owners of Alda Farm, are experimenting with music upon animals, and they find that it is an economic success.

Toronto was not all music; at the time of my visit there were some 100,000 citizens in receipt of charity of some sort; housing shortage was chronic, and the churches were greatly concerned. Civic administration was said to cost 30 per cent. of monies collected, and this was a sore point with my informants.

The United Church of Canada is a romance of our century. That experiment has lasted twelve years, but is not an unqualified success; the majority of Presbyterians still stand aloof. Leaders of the new Church feel driven towards the Episcopalian form of church government because of the difficulty of combining the "call" of the Presbyter with the "establishment" of Methodism and the "independence" of Congregationalists. Similar difficulties are encountered in United Churches elsewhere.

The then Moderator, Dr. Richard Roberts, and I addressed a huge Demonstration the evening before I left Toronto; and I shall always cherish happy memories of that city and its people. At midnight I left for Minnesota, a journey of 900 miles.

The Hiawatha streamline train from Chicago was the fastest I ever knew,—travelling an average of 90 miles an hour for eight hours. I found that the farther West we went the trains were swifter and ran more smoothly. Up North the rail tracks were rough and trains rather slow; jolting occurred on starting and when stopping; one missed the easy glide of our British trains.

After seeing a gangster film at Harrisburg I travelled in a "sleeper." At every stop during that interminable night I awoke screaming that the gangsters had got me; this afforded great amusement to the negro attendant.

But the "Hiawatha" was a dream of a train; we flashed like the spirit of speed through towns and stations with ease and comfort.

Minnesota is the "State of ten thousand lakes," and that day I saw some of them in their glory, especially during sunset and moonlight; there is no twilight in that part of the world. One felt the spell of the infinite, the silence, and the majesty of sky and earth.

A genial Presbyterian minister, Stephen Jones, and his wife met me at Minneapolis, and that kind physician Dr. P. M. Jones gave me a Welsh welcome. The doctor motored me to Mankato where I was due to preach at Dr. Morgan's Church. He was well versed in local lore, and showed me where the Welsh pioneers had settled amongst the hills, although the soil was stony and unproductive. Others were left in the richer plains; the Celt, like the Jew, always feels the lure of the mountains.

One shuddered beneath the tree where thirty Red Indians were hanged after a rebellion.

My medical guide told me the latest Lloyd George story then going the rounds in America. An English sailor was arrested during a drunken brawl, somewhere in Brazil. After sleeping his bout off, the Britisher demanded trial before the magistrates; but his request was refused. Repeated attempts were of no avail, week after week. At the end of six months the prisoner asked his warder for paper, pen and ink.

"What for?" queried the turnkey.

"To write to Mr. Lloyd George," replied the sailor. That night the Prime Minister, the Chief of Police, the Commander-in-Chief, and the jail Governor waited upon the Englishman, saying, "Please, sir, will you go out."

The district of Mankato was haunted with fear at the time of my visit, because sixteen lunatic murderers had escaped from St. Peter's criminal asylum, three days previously. Every householder was on the watch day and night, and guns were ready to hand.

I inspected the mill of the *Miss Minneapolis* where 160 people were employed producing 3,000 barrels of flour a day. We were surprised to learn that the ear of wheat passes through 125 machines extending a mile in length, and takes 22 hours to become flour. Asthma is the dread of the miller.

Minneapolis English churches close on Sunday evenings in summer; so about two dozen ministers attended my service, which for the occasion was English. Several of the clergy were of Welsh extraction, and joined us at supper.

The following morning we all went to meet, and to hear Kagawa, the great Christian leader from Japan. I consider him to be one of the three greatest living souls of the century; he is short of stature, frail and reserved. Every disability imaginable for an orator is evident in Kagawa,—with his hesitant manner, discordant voice, and very limited English vocabulary. He was the worst speaker I heard in America, and yet the most impressive of all. Kagawa has published 160 books dealing mainly with Christian co-operation.

I attended the degree ceremony of the Minneapolis University, where 2,546 students were capped in the presence of 30,000 spectators, assembled in a vast open-air stadium, at 8 p.m.; the brass band was deafening, but spot lights thrown upon the platform and played over the procession were really effective.

The larger American Universities provide excellent degree courses, and have thousands of students. There were over 12,000 in Chicago University that year. Medical science also is modern and very progressive in U.S.A.; their best clinics are really marvellous. But their so-called Higher Education and High Schools seem very primitive. They call a school-leaving certificate "graduating from High School."

In some of these High Schools Freudian psychology is the latest craze.

I preached at Columbia, where the Rev. Hugh C. Griffiths leads the Presbyterian flock; his first show-place was a cemetery, so typical of a Welshman.

Of interest was the dried-milk workshop and the pea-canning factory, where I spent hours questioning workmen.

Racine is a centre of factories. A Welshman was general Manager of Horlick's Milk Works. Owing to the lateness of my arrival I saw very little of the city; but Doctor Kendrick Roberts and his family were ideal hosts.

Very early next morning I left for Chicago. On the way one caught glimpses of miles of corn yellowing to the sun-kiss, orchards laden with luscious fruits, lakes like great seas upon which sailed huge steamers, and barques with coloured sails, forests dotted with Indian villages, prairies where roamed wild cattle, and perhaps, wilder men, lonely cabins and crowded towns—it was all very amazing and awesome. But I was leaving the West where I had heard no cuckoo, no skylark, no thrush, and I longed for an hour of twilight.

Some day I hope to return for a long journey beyond Minneapolis; from all accounts it must be wonderful. I should like to see more Indian villages and "reservations." One felt sad to think of the segregation of Indians in their own country. White civilisation (?) has decimated the Red Race; it brought diseases and customs, liquor and weapons which sowed death among a noble race. I was told of one tribe who are practising racial suicide; no children shall be born amongst them. In some parts allotted to tribes of Red Indians oil has been discovered. Consequently, Red chiefs are amongst the richest men in the Land of millionaires.

I reached Chicago on June 18th, and found that the Rev. E. Arfon Jones had scheduled every hour of my stay in advance. The chief reporter of the *Tribune* could not be shaken off without "copy"; but most of the stuff that appeared in his Paper concerning that interview was imaginary. He readily joined me in questioning the Chief Constable of Oak Bank, and the Staff at the Bureau. I learnt much about Prohibition and gangsterdom. Dillinger's armoured car was the Chief's trophy which he now uses to hunt criminals; he is proud of his collection of finger prints. I watched his assistants taking the prints of two suspects.

That night I preached at Hebron to a bilingual congregation.

Friday morning I was received by Mr. Kelly, the Irish Mayor of Chicago; he took office when racketeers had terrified the authorities. Each of his three predecessors in office had been bumped off for interfering with illegal traffic; but Kelly is a stranger to fear and was cleaning up the city. He conducted me into the council chamber to hear a very fine discussion about relief for the unemployed. At that time three cents were charged on every dollar's purchase in the city, and this went towards the fund for relief of the unemployed.

I spent two hours with Mr. Lyons, the Local President of the E.R.B. and he taught me a great deal. Ninety per cent. of the destitution throughout the whole State was found in Chicago; at one time, during the depression, the city spent 8,000,000 dollars a month on relief; most of the money went to negroes and their families.

Friday morning we visited Stateville prison. The "Murder in the Bath" had brought the place and the warden (Rayen) into notoriety the previous week. We inspected the cell and bath, and could imagine the sordid tragedy when one prisoner killed a homo-sexual fellow-convict. That murderer was exonerated by a Court of Justice.

There were 3,211 inmates at the time, a third of whom were coloured. Some were serving a 90 years sentence; and one was in for 199 years!

Treatment was not harsh, but solitary confinement had driven many insane. Circular cells are characteristic of that prison; the experiment is not a success. True a warder can see all the cells on one side; but the occupants of cells opposite see his back turned, and they give endless trouble.

During my return journey from Stateville, our sergeant driver was very silent and seemed sad. At last he turned to me and said:

"Padre, I saw a man in that prison who was a schoolmate, a playmate, a neighbour of mine. He became a gangster, and I, as a police sergeant, arrested and brought him to justice; he is on his way to the Chair, and I am a free man. Why the difference after so similar an upbringing?"

My voice must have been unsteady when I replied:

"So far as I can see, Sergeant, the only explanation is—the Grace of God."

"Padre, I think you are right," sighed the man by my side,—"the Grace of God. But poor Ted! Poor Ted!"

At twelve o'clock on Friday night Lewis Jones and I met the squad car which was to take us on a tour through the underworld of Chicago. I wished to know whether Edgar Wallace had exaggerated in his thrillers. Our immediate British predecessor to do that journey was the late Admiral Beatty who had married a Chicago lady. We had the identical car and the same escort.

The Chicago Bureau of Investigation has 34 squad cars in radio touch with headquarters whilst on duty day and night.

We had four detectives fully armed, and in addition, one loaded machine gun in the car. I was offered a revolver, but I feared to touch the weapon.

We started in China Town where lived 12,000 Chinese with their own Mayor, schools and temples. It would be unwise to carry money there, and much too risky for a stranger on his own. We entered several dens where

votaries of the poppy sought escape from reality; every
bunk was occupied; the whole environment seemed
fantastic and satanic to me.

An order was picked up to hasten about twelve blocks
away where a group of Asiatics were slashing each other
with knives; we were there in five minutes, and rushed
three Chinamen, besmeared with blood, into the bride-
well close by.   One Negro was discovered in that crowd,
and he was immediately raced out; as a trespasser, he
could be up to no good.   The Colours are not allowed
to mix at Chicago.

No sooner had we scattered that crowd of excited
Chinamen than another order came to go to Negro
Town where the 400,000 Negroes of Chicago dwell. We
were one of twelve squad cars in that area then; it was
the night of the Schmelling-Louis fight, and the coloured
population were excited all over the States.   There had
been riots in New York the previous night.   The Negro
boxer did not pull it off that time, although the whole
Press predicted that he would beat the German.   Consequently the black people were rather cowed and silent
in Chicago.   Our squad broke up several crowds, and
ran a few turbulent ones into the cells to cool them.
We interfered in three brawls.

The squad men were on good terms with the leaders
of Negro Town, but one detective always stood between
me and each man I spoke to that night; they were taking
no risks.

One Negro was discovered in the very act of slitting
a girl's throat,—she was a white woman; we discovered
three corpses during the night.

After leaving Negro Town we went to a few of the
night clubs where gangsters congregate.   Probably, many
of the overdressed, bestudded, and jewelled gentlemen who covertly eyed me had taken more than one
victim "for a ride," and would himself find a similar
expeditious exit from life, if he did not reach the Chair.
They all had a strained and furtive look, and carried a

suspicious bulge at the hip. Our guide knew each by name, and told us a few exploits imputed to some; the oldest of these desperate men could not be above thirty, and some were boys of 18 or 20. I noticed that each of the "Big Boys" had a body-guard watching every move; the Al Capone gang were there in force that night. And the women! they were dressed like queens, and knew how to show their figures to advantage. They played for high stakes, were aware of the fact, and paid the price.

But it made me sad and pensive long before we reached home at 4 a.m. Civilisation rests upon a volcano of bestiality and violence; the brute is only curbed, never really tamed. How grateful we should be for the men who risk their lives hourly in the underworld of our great cities. One hundred and ninety nine policemen have been murdered in Chicago alone since 1905. The public do not know the number of G—men who have fallen victims to the assassin's dagger. I never can forget squad I.B., car 1146, and shall always treasure the autographs of those four detectives; they belong to a noble band of heroic men.

New York is a twenty hours train journey from Chicago. I had spent so much money upon "sleepers" in which I failed to sleep that I determined to forego the luxury on my last trip; but it was painful trying to rest without a bunk; by the time I reached New York, Cynolwyn Pugh said I looked a real "down and out." That explained why the Negro outside-porter made no attempt to carry my traps. But a wash, a shave, and a brush-up soon put me right. All these amenities are available at every large station in America,—so different from English stations where passengers are made as miserable as the law permits.

The first thing I did afterwards was to phone to Mr. Rea Whitely, second in command to Edgar Hoover himself; he had received instructions from Washington to render me every help possible. So, within ten minutes,

a motor came for Pugh and myself, and we were taken
off to the palatial Bureau of Investigation. All the time
I remained in the city that car and driver were at my
disposal day and night. I went to almost every nook and
corner of the great city, and saw wealth untold brushing
shoulders with dire poverty; palaces and workhouses,
schools and churches.

I noticed that the poorer quarters in New York were
not so squalid as the slums of Liverpool; the scale of
living is higher in Harlem even than amongst our destitute poor. America is a newer country and richer than
Britain.

I wished to inspect Sing Sing, the best known prison
in the world. It was a privilege to meet Warden Lawes
who had written three books about Sing Sing and its
population of 2,450. We spent four hours within those
walls, and interviewed twelve representative prisoners;
on that day there were seven men and two women awaiting execution. Cynolwyn and I inspected the "Chair"
from which so many have gone to eternity. There is a
beautiful garden and an aviary beside the House of
Death.

A "Mutual Welfare League" of co-operation between
officials and prisoners is a great success in Sing Sing.
The punishment meted out to recalcitrants takes the
form of losing benefits. Visitors are allowed to mix with
prisoners without the usual glass or wire partitions found
elsewhere. In fact, the enlightened Warden advocates
greater liberties than this even; he hates capital punishment and insists that it is no real deterrent to crime.
As an official he has been compelled to watch over 200
people being electrocuted.

The prison consists of two parts, one very old, and
the other modern in every sense. I told the Warden of
my disappointment with the hundred-year-old cells still
in use. They are dark, narrow and unfurnished; the first
six months of imprisonment is spent in one of these; and

then, if he is still sane, the convict is transferred to the luxurious modern part.

Sing Sing is a mixture of the cruel and the sentimental. Nobody regrets this more than Warden Lawes.

Sentimentalism may prevail in the prison system of North America, but the further South one goes the treatment is correspondingly harsher; there are to be found the chain gangs and the torture of prisoners. Temperature has something to do with this, and so has the presence of a larger Negro population. In the North a Negro is treated as an equal. He can share trains, trams, cinemas and even some public appointments with the Whites. Not so in the South, where the Negro "must be kept under," and lynching is a common occurrence.

The detective who accompanied us to Sing Sing made strenuous efforts to get one prisoner to "squeal." A threat of the Chair even could not shake the determination of the hardened gangster who was only twenty-two years old. He seemed to dread his confederates in crime more than the House of Death.

Our chauffeur for the whole of that week was an educated Negro,—Nimrod Nisbet, who resolutely refused a gratuity, and had great ambitions to become a fully qualified G—man.

I spent my last night in America on Long Island with a nephew and niece of my wife,—Mr. and Mrs. Larson. They took me to an open-air concert at Jones's Beach. Over 150,000 people were present to hear the plaintive German music which made me want to cry; perhaps I was homesick.

I was among the first to get on board the *Aquitania* next morning, and glad to find my cabin where I wished for a long sleep. For two days and nights I did little but eat and slumber; and during the whole voyage took scant interest in my fellow passengers. I felt too tired to talk, and had no desire to make new acquaintances. Exhaustion of nervous energy made it impossible to absorb more impressions.

During three months I had been under the spell of immensity. No longer do I smile at the large talk of Americans; everything in the Old World must seem puny to people who speak in continents. Britain is infinitesimal to a man from the West; Snowdon resembles a molehill after the Rockies; our big buildings are insignificant beside the sky-scrapers of New York; our lakes are hardly noticeable to a man from Michigan; the robin redbreast in America seems bigger than thrushes in the Homeland.

America is the land of experiment. That explains its hustle and go; the static is unknown in the States; there is the restlessness of youth. They do not fear change across the Pond; civic laws are altered frequently. They have little patience with failures; nothing is final or ultimate (except the Constitution). That is why Roosevelt is so popular; he is not afraid of change and experiment; he had fourteen attempts at the New Deal; and each was declared unconstitutional by the Supreme Court. Now he attacks the Supreme Court itself. America is supremely individualistic; thus Socialism makes slow progress in the Western Democracy.

The conglomerate of nations admire, envy and pity Britain in turns. Listen to Upton Close:

" The Britain we knew was not a Britain to back down before the bluff of a Mediterranean upstart Caesar. It was not a Britain to implore a League of Nations to fight its battles for it, and then fear to lend the League assistance in doing so. It was not a Britain to answer Hitler's march to the Rhine with a questionnaire,—ignored. Nor a Britain to back down before an ultimatum from a puppet Spanish General. That Britain we knew was not a Britain to offer her coal mines in China for sale when a Japanese military junto had them bottled up.

We thought we knew Britain. Major Wearne, old chief of Reuter's News Service in China, used to offer at the club bars of China a toast to the 'Five Kings who would survive all monarchical overturns, —the King of Hearts, the King of Spades, the King of Diamonds, the King of Clubs and the King of England.' We agreed and drank heartily with him. A Britain that spewed out a most popular Prince, her most built up King, was a shocking surprise to us. Is England to-day coming or going?

We face the fact of a Britain wanting peace so badly that she is willing to be licked for it. She has taken lickings in the Mediterranean, in Africa, in Spain, in India, in Australia.

Britain's confusion remains a wide open bid to Japan, Germany and Italy.

Englishmen more than any other people know that the fruits of Empire are not worth fighting major wars to enjoy.

The monied class in England doesn't want war. Nor do the Labour and League of Nationites in England want war.

The people of England do not want war.

Great Britain to-day presents the amazing failure of a nation too civilized, too decent, to put its heart into a rough and tumble game of Empire bequeathed to it by less squeamish forefathers."

And here is a sarcastic note from E. L. Meyer:

"The semi-annual parade of our war debt defaulters was repeated Tuesday when all the world war debtors to the United States, with the exception of Finland, notified the States department that they could not pay their shares of the billion and a half instalment due. The debt will amount to 22 billion dollars with accumulative interest at the end of the 62 years period of payments established.

I shall try the token payment stunt on my butcher."

I append some pithy Americanisms heard.

" As snug as a bug in a rug."
" Slack like a Negro with money."
" Go jump in the Lake."
" He is just a pansy and can't take it."
" Go chase yourself."
" As cute as a bug's ear."
" Hold your horses."
" Hunk your doughnut in the coffee."
" Did you lock him one?"

And a few advertisements seen:

" Hurry up big boy, Hell ain't half full." (For motorists).
" Our hot dogs are not puppies."
" You can't beat milk, but you can whip our cream."
" Banks do not serve meals, why should we cash cheques?"
" Do not smoke cigars unless you have two."
" Do not divorce your wife because she can't cook; eat with us."
" We'll hold your horse, crank your car, nurse your baby, but we will not cash your cheque."

CHAPTER TWELVE

LIVERPOOL . . . . HOME OF EXTREMES

" Where the city of the faithfullest friends stands;
Where the city of the cleanliness of the sexes stands;
Where the city of the healthiest fathers stands;
Where the city of the best-bodied mothers stands;
There the great city stands."—*Walt. Whitman.*

WE moved to Liverpool in April 1927. Catharine Street Church, the mother English Cause of the Presbyterian Church of Wales, was built, in the first instance, for Thomas C. Edwards, a mighty preacher and ripe scholar of European fame, who became the first Principal of Aberystwyth University College, and, later, Principal of Bala College.

Two other pastors of this Church ended as college Principals—William Howells and David Charles Davies. Sir Henry Jones was invited to the pastorate of Catharine Street; but, at the request of Principal Cairns, he refused the call, and remained in Scotland. The church has great traditions and prestige, and I have spent eleven years of real joy amongst this people of Liverpool.

Fascism, Communism and active Secularism are very live issues on Merseyside, and I have had some exciting times through personal contact with each. Religious bigotry is largely responsible for retarding the progress of the Labour party in Liverpool; but the main obstacle is apathy amongst the workers themselves. Patience and an understanding spirit are essential in the service of the sons of toil.

During the winter months of 1932, Canon Raven and a few of us who were members of the Christian Industrial Fellowship conducted a study circle for Liverpool dockers. One night the theme for discussion was the *"Injustice of a means test for the unemployed."* Some hard things were said in unparliamentary language, until I put a blunt, but fair question to the meeting: "Tell me, comrades, did many of you vote for the National Government at the last general election?" There was a significant pause, and several men nodded assent. After a while I ventured to add, "Why not take your medicine without squealing then?" It is only fair to say that we did not quarrel over the business. Dockers never resent plain truths. They themselves freely indulge in the pastime of dispensing them.

During one strike, the Rev. Cynolwyn Pugh and I tried to persuade a group of dockers that conciliation was the sanest way of surmounting industrial difficulties. "Nonsense," shouted one man, "what did God do with the capitalists of Egypt when the Israelites left their bondage? He drowned the b—— lot; and that is the only way to deal with the swine." Our crowd roared with laughter, and we could do nothing else for a time.

I was persuaded to contest a Ward at one municipal election. After the adoption meeting, our comrades seemed to think that their responsibility had ended; all the work was left to about ten workers, six of whom were enthusiastic women. On election day I had to convey several members of the selection committee to the poll; they would not have troubled to walk the half mile to record their vote if they were not carried. Of course we were handsomely beaten. Perhaps it was worth while fighting that election to get the following letter from Philip Snowden, then Chancellor of the Exchequer:

Treasury Chambers,

Whitehall, S.W.

7th October, 1929.

" Dear Mr. Howard,

I write to offer you my hearty good wishes for your success at the impending municipal election.

You have a record of public service behind you which should entitle you to the support of all electors who wish to see the great powers of municipal government used to promote the welfare of the community.

I hope the majority of the electors will appreciate the fact that they have in you a Candidate who is so well worthy of their support.

Yours sincerely,

PHILIP SNOWDEN."

During October, 1930, I engaged in public debate with Mr. Chapman Cohen, president of the British Secularist Society, and brilliant editor of the " Free Thinker." This is how it came about. The Rev. Rhys Lewis, then pastor of Pembroke Chapel, was conducting a series of open-air services. A group of secularists caused considerable annoyance by interrupting, and issuing a challenge to debate. Lewis stood this for a long time, and, ultimately, determined to bring matters to a head. He asked me to accept the challenge, which I readily did. Next night saw a repetition of the row, followed up by the usual challenge. Then Lewis informed the delighted crowd that I had accepted, on two conditions:

(1) That the secularists secured their most prominent debater in the country. (2) That a charge of one shilling be made for admission, and the proceeds devoted to charity.

Mr. Chapman Cohen was their spokesman. The meeting was held in Pembroke Chapel, filled to capacity (1,000), and many people failed to procure tickets.

Mr. Artro Morris, a prominent Liverpool solicitor, presided, and the subject debated was " *That Christianity is a hindrance to Progress.*" It proved a tumultuous meeting which I thoroughly enjoyed. We had our clamourous supporters on each side, and they indulged in noisy arguments of their own; but, on the whole, good temper prevailed for the two hours' debate. At the close, Cohen, who is a gentleman, declared: " I have been in this business of debating for over thirty years, and to-night has been the best case ever put forward for Christianity in my hearing." He also paid the debate a high tribute in the " *Free Thinker.*" Both sides seemed satisfied, and my backers carried me out of the chapel.

I remember but one saying of my own in the meeting: " Speak up," cried an excited critic from the gallery. " Friend," was my laughing retort, " before the end you'll be begging me to shut up."

Another meeting I recall with pleasure was held amongst communists in Marmaduke Street. My theme was " *Christ and Poverty,*" and I spoke for nearly two hours. At question time, a young Jew asked, " Did not Christ say, 'the poor ye always have with you'?" " True," I replied, " but Jesus added, 'Me ye have not always!' We have poverty whenever we exclude Christ." The Hebrew was first to applaud.

In 1931, the Merionethshire Labour Party persuaded me to contest that seat at the Parliamentary General Election. Five other constituencies had been offered me; but out of sheer cussedness, it seems, I chose the most difficult. That constituency covers an area of 500 square miles, and consists of scattered villages and a few small townlets. Festiniog is the most populous centre, and I was informed that there were sufficient quarrymen in that place, together with Penrhyndeudraeth, to win the seat if they so desired.

I found no difficulty with my elders at Catharine Street; they unanimously resolved to release me for the contest on condition that I retained the pastorate whether I was successful or not at the election. That was a most generous gesture, and amazed the general public. I know of no other church in the provinces to do it. Towyn Jones resigned his church at Cwmaman when he entered Parliament; Silvester Horne lived in London, as does Sorensen to-day; so that they could carry on their church duties and attend the House daily. The gesture appears more magnanimous still when we remember that practically all our church members are either Liberals or Conservatives in politics.

Merioneth Labourites were enthusiastic, and gave freely of their time and money; especially the teachers. A few of the scholastics were Welsh Nationalists, and returned spoilt papers at the poll; but the huge majority of them worked hard for me. I cannot forget the Bala contingent whose optimism was so contagious; and I admired the loyalty of the Festiniog men.

Ministerial brethren were timid, indifferent, or frankly hostile. Two only helped my platform: Edward Evans, Towyn, and Edward Powell, of Festiniog. It was a three-cornered contest. Sir Charles Phibbs, the Conservative candidate is a fine Irish gentleman, always ready for a fight, electoral or any other, so long as he has a share in it. He is kind, and very generous; the people get his money, but refuse to give him their votes. At Corwen fair he lent me his motor car as a platform; we were quite friendly.

Sir Haydn Jones, the Liberal candidate, had held the Seat for over twenty years. I regretted putting him to the trouble and expense of an election; but it was good propaganda for the Cause; and when the present member retires the Seat is likely to go Labour.

The result was (1) Jones, (2) Howard, (3) Phibbs.

That experience was invaluable for insight to human nature. During elections one finds the best and worst in men. People will sacrifice much for their Party at such times; and, on the other hand, there is a spate of falsehood, and mis-representation. Staid citizens feel licensed to prevaricate; and men renowned for piety and straight dealing in ordinary life can stoop to meanness unbelievable. Pity the candidate who fails to make allowances for the times! he is likely to get embittered and lose faith in his fellowmen. Welshmen, of all people, are rarely normal during a parliamentary election. I have always taken things philosophically, and been amused. When a church elder offers to speak for a candidate, and on the very next evening calls him a traitor and a cad, as happened to me, what is a person to do except laugh and enjoy the joke! But I do detest the publicity that is inseparable from elections, and I think that canvassing for votes is humiliating and demoralising.

It was during the 1931 election that I first met Sir Oswald Mosley, then an erratic, brilliant, aristocratic Labourite; James Maxton, so like Keir Hardie—minus the beard; and David Kirkwood, who addressed a great demonstration for me at Festiniog. The finest speech I heard then came from Fenner Brockway: it was a blend of passion and poetry, mysticism and statesmanship, and the huge audience burst into song as though at a religious revival. Grenfell was great; Rhys J. Davies refreshing; Soronsen persuasive, and Gordon MacDonald proved very inspiring.

I remember motoring Miss Margaret Bondfield to a demonstration at Towyn. Edward Evans presided, and kept the meeting going until our arrival, over an hour late. He prefaced his opening remarks by recalling the boast of the Liberal candidate in that very hall on the previous night: "I fear neither lawyer nor parson."

"To-night," said Evans, "we have a candidate who does not fear the devil himself."

A presentation umbrella belonging to Miss Bondfield was taken from our car whilst the meeting was on. Perhaps somebody was showing his disdain for Labour, and getting back a bit of his own.

The following morning, at six o'clock, I motored the
lady Cabinet Minister to catch a train at Bala. I still
remember that early hour when the country was at
its best,—a spread banquet of hawthorn and bluebell, fit
setting for the fairies' rendezvous the district is reported
to be. We recited our favourite poems, one for one all
the way, and found that our pet authors were the same : —
Sassoon, Flecker, Hodgson, Rupert Brooke, W. H. Davies,
Yeats, and Francis Thompson; for once, that tortuous
road was all too short.

Ruskin said that the most beautiful road known to
him was from Barmouth to Dolgelley, and that the next
loveliest was in the reverse direction from Dolgelley to
Barmouth. But Ruskin never motored over that road,
or his language would not have been so ecstatic. When
I campaigned, many of the Merioneth roads were death-
traps to motorists.

Our helpers, and many of my opponents, thought that
I was winning Merionethshire; but when I heard Philip
Snowden's vicious attack upon the Party I knew that
Labour would go down in most constituencies. Is there
another instance in British history where one speech
wrought such havoc on the fortunes of a great political
Party? The two men who did most to build up a Labour
Party had the greatest share in destroying the work of
their own hands and brain.

Three prominent politicians sat with me listening to
the results of that election coming over the radio, in
Maentwrog. At first, two of them were jubilant; but as
" Conservative gain " rolled in with monotonous regular-
ity, one turned to me and said: " This is tragic! Snowden has over-reached himself." I went down as one of
many, and in good company.

The physical strain of speaking and travelling over
that vast constituency was exhausting. Frequently I arrived in Liverpool at two o'clock on Sunday morning,
and was due in the pulpit by eleven. But the zest and
fun of it made life worth living. The comrades paid my
official expenses.

Labourites are taught to sacrifice for their convictions. I wondered at the way those quarrymen rolled up to give of their meagre wage towards defraying our costs, and feared lest some of them should actually deprive themselves or their families of the bare necessities of life. Their women-folk were as anxious to help as the men. Such generosity was in keeping with their traditions. In those parts of Wales the workers will give their last penny to further a Cause they believe in ; that is their history in education, Nonconformity and freedom. They build gorgeous chapels but live themselves in small cottages.

That Merioneth electoral campaign confirmed my faith in the innate unselfishness of man, and the wonderful nobility of the ordinary Welsh working class. It was a glorious revelation of altruism and unselfishness.

In 1934, I published " *Perarogl Crist,*" a biography of the Rev. William Jones, Morriston. The book was a labour of love to commemorate one who befriended me during my boyhood.

The same year I joined some social workers who were investigating casual labour in Liverpool. Nothwithstanding Trade Unionism, dock labour is still casual. Is it impossible to remove this curse of the docker's lot? So far, no remedy has been found or applied; and, candidly, I fail to see how shipping could be carried on under the present system, or lack of system, without a pool of surplus labour to draw upon as needed, and dismissed when no longer required.

Another fact to remember is that derelicts of all classes drift into the casual labour market, not only at the docks, but in other directions as well. The Trade Union " button " can be bought or cadged.

One cold morning in March, 1934, I joined a queue awaiting to be taken on for a job. I wore very old clothes, a cap, and an untidy muffler ; a clay pipe even was requisitioned for the day. As the supervisor selected one man after the other from our crowd, I trembled lest he should point to me; but, evidently, I looked too weedy and weak for the work, and he passed me by. Thirty men were chosen out of our group of eighty that morning; and it was a raw day. I went home to a good breakfast, fire and comfort. I wondered what awaited those rejected men. If Dante were here to write an "*Inferno*" to-day it would not be of hell fire and devils at the boil, but one of cold grates and empty cupboards, unemployment and the Means Test.

Unemployment is no new infliction invented subsequent to the war. As a problem of government and relief it has troubled Western civilisation for well over a century; but, of late, it has been acute and ominous; millions of men are now doomed to a life of compulsory idleness. So the State is facing up to the problem, and the conscience of nations is stirred. Conferences to discuss the question are being held in every industrial centre, and the Distressed Areas receive special attention.

On April 4th, 1935, I was invited to address a conference over which Dr. Havard, Bishop of St. Asaph, presided. Our public meeting was held in Zion Chapel, Wrexham. The bishop's speech was refreshing and greatly impressed the huge audience. Preparatory to that conference I perused all the reports and books dealing with the problem within my reach. But, wishing to get the human touch, a telephone request to a Salvation Army Captain in Liverpool, resulted in my introduction, next morning, as "down and out Jim," to an Irishman of equally meagre means who finds refuge in the hostel during his frequent spells of destitution. He is called "Tom" in the Army. There are 230 beds at that particular hostel, usually occupied by a nondescript collection of destitute humanity. I saw about 200 men in the common room, most of whom were as shabby and nervy as my partner for the day. At first, they seemed suspicious of the stranger, but soon got going on the Means Test which had driven scores of the younger men on tramp in preference to sponging upon relatives. My old clothes, and unshaved chin, evidently enabled me to look my adopted part; I was treated as an equal, and even invited to a share of one man's scanty meal. I determined to live as Tom lived, eat similar food, and act in every way possible as a brother of the road. So far as I know, Tom never suspected a parson in rags; if he did, he was too much of a gentleman to unmask me before others.

From that hostel we rambled along to the nearest Labour Exchange, and stood with the crowd there for about fifteen minutes or so.

"Come away, Jim, this is no place for us," said, or growled Tom, "these are b—— aristocrats." Thus I realised that there are four classes in the ranks of the unemployed.

(1) Recipients of full insurance benefit. These are alert, and, in the earlier stages, confident. True it may feel a bit undignified to stand in a queue, and have to answer inquisitive clerks. But "things will soon right themselves, and we are sure of a job long before exhausing our benefit." This is the attitude maintained for a few weeks.

(2) Men on transitional benefit. These are not nearly so cocksure. One finds incipient doubt, and something approaching fear; a man may not be needed after all; one loses interest in clothes and appearance, and he is shy of old associates.

(3 Unemployed on public assistance. The linen collar is now discarded; independence is a luxury one cannot afford; here is real dread of the future, and, in many instances, loss of confidence and self-respect.

(4) The down-and-out derelicts who are not mentioned in Ministry of Labour returns. Once in ten years a forgetful nation is reminded, by means of the Census, of these dwellers in the gloom. For this class there is no

dole, no transitional benefit, and no public assistance in
the form of out-door relief.

Tom, my mate of a day, belonged to this last class.
He was 29 years old, had left Ireland five years previously, never worked long enough at a stretch to secure
the requisite number of insurance stamps to qualify for
the dole, and had not gained a "settlement" in Liverpool,
although frequenting lodging houses here for several
years. Like about 6,000 of his compatriots, he haunts
the docks and lower part of the city in search of casual
labour which gets scarcer every year. Irish emigrants of
this type form a growing problem for our Poor Law
authorities in seaport towns.

We visited a hostel where another 200 or more unemployed were just finishing breakfast. In the majority
of cases the meal consisted of bread, margarine and tea ;
that seems to be the staple diet of the down-and-out.
Later on in the day I suggested a hot dinner (cost 5d.) to
Tom, and offered to foot the bill. "Nothing doing, mate!"
was the reply, " I haven't had a dinner like that for years.
I tried a free Christmas one at the Refuge two years
ago, and was ill for a whole week." As a result, I also
lived that day on the same diet as Tom,—bread, margarine and strong tea for breakfast and lunch; then, as a
change, strong tea, margarine and bread for supper.

Whilst conversing with two men at one Refuge, I
noticed certain signs of compulsory retirement from
ordinary society, and ventured to ask when last they were
in " quod." " Came out three days ago," was the ready
reply. " Not so bad this time, either; you see, it is the
easiest way to get lodgings, bed and good grub for the
whole winter. When summer comes we find a job
at harvest, or cadge our way and sleep out." Then, as
an after thought: "We've a good job on to-night, easy
money, and quite safe. Like to join us?" To my horror
that " job " was to be a burglary at the house of a friend
of mine ; and only after long persuasion on my part was
the project abandoned.

At one free library it was pathetic to see men crowding about the Ministry of Labour notices of vacancies. "See any chance of a job, mate?" I asked a middle-aged man who was laboriously copying out details from one board. "Job, did you say? Hey! Bill! Here comes Roosevelt and the New Deal!" Then to me, "Stranger, I have been trying for a job in this b——— city for over fifteen years."

Tom and I tried a warehouse, two factories, and three shops. "No hands required," was the monotonous response to our appeals. So back again to a cheap lodging-house where men sat, and smoked, and swore, whilst some played cards. A few seemed to desire solitude. Timidly, I joined one tramp, and asked, "Know any of this crowd?" "Not one," was the retort, and, looking me straight in the eye, "and 'A dos'nt want to know any b——— too!"

Solitariness is the tragedy of the not-wanted man; maybe, it ensures the safety of society. Men in benefit, lately, united with others who were on transitional pay to compel the withdrawal of oppressive treatment of applicants for relief. What if the down-and-outs of the whole country could unite? Hunger marchers have besieged Parliament before now, and may again.

When we passed the great provision stores, the cafés, and shops, I almost expected my partner to break a window and help himself to the delicacies so temptingly displayed before the eyes of hungry folk day and night. The honesty of the poor is a miracle. But, perhaps people like Tom lack the physical stamina necessary to break a pane of glass. Bread and margarine is poor diet to sustain the spirit of revolt.

We were out to find six pence, the price of a night's lodging and breakfast. As a last resort we would try singing in some side-street, outside the usual haunts of "slops." We offered to shovel a load of coal, to trim a hedge, to dig a garden, to sweep a path, to carry a bag, to stand watch over a motor car,—all in vain; we belonged to the great not-wanted; we were superfluous flotsam! The world could carry on without us.

Was it the coward in me that suddenly remembered the " one bob I had saved from a previous job "? After something like prevarication on my part (still unregretted), Tom was persuaded to accept a "loan," which will not be recalled.

And that was a typical day in the life of an unemployed man. Tom had been doing this tedious round for ten years by now. There have been a few breaks when he sold fruit on commission from a hired cart, and during a few weeks' sickness in an Infirmary. So far, he has not been convicted of crime; but I wonder how long he can resist the crooks who haunt shelters offering desperate men easy jobs with safe money! Thus the criminal population is recruited, jails are filled, and the gallows fed.

My last penny went for a tram-ride over our aristocratic route, No. 15. For a while I wondered why passengers moved away from me, and took out scented handkerchiefs. Then I remembered my old clothes, soiled boots, unwashed and unshaved face. More than that, the odours of the refuges that clung tenaciously to me did not recall the sweet perfumes of Arabia; not without reason was I given elbow room. But, with Carlyle, I marvelled at the difference clothes can make; the following week some of those folk would be listening to me preaching.

That evening I accompanied an important employer of labour to see Walter Greenwood's play " Love on the Dole," in which the tragedy and pathos of unemployment are depicted with a realism guaranteed to disturb and haunt the most complacent of men. So ended my imperfect day of helplessly witnessing the torture of the not-wanted. Aimlessness, frustration, blank despair, being not wanted at twenty nine years of age . . . . these constitute the horrors of twentieth century industrialism.

During 1935 I published *"Jesus the Agitator"* —
a sequel to *"Which Jesus?"* The book has had a wonderful sale throughout Britain and in America. Mr.
George Lansbury wrote an appreciative Preface which
I greatly treasure. The following review appeared in the
British Weekly, and is typical of a few score of such tributes the book received :

"'This volume of essays and addresses, by the pastor
of Catharine Street Presbyterian Church of Wales,
Liverpool, is a brave attempt to realise afresh the re-
levance of Jesus Christ to the modern impasse. Its
main theme, unifying all the separate discussions, is
the thought that Our Lord is the most disturbing
presence in history, bringing to religious and social
complacency not the peace of our desiring, but the
sword of His challenge. On a wide range of social
and personal problems Dr. Howard has much to
say which is stimulating and fruitful. The regimen-
tation of life, the lack of discipline which calls it
forth, the need of Sunday and the kind of quiet in
which we can be truly agitated, and the mechanising
of human relations, rendering us incapable of worship, are among his chief subjects. Whilst we feel
disposed to question one inference from some of
Luther's failures,—for the break-up of the social
whole of mediaeval Christendom began long before
the Reformation,—nothing in the book is more valuable than the wealth of historical illustration, especially that drawn from our own island story.
Above all, the author's textbook is the Bible. He
wanders at will through its pages, taking the spirit of
his Master with him in his interpretation.

A gracious Foreword by the Right Hon. George
Lansbury makes us hope that many who think with
him, as well as many who do not, will study Dr.
Howard's book."

Like every big city, Liverpool is the home of extremes. Wealth and poverty almost touch ; we have man-

sions and some of the worst slums in Britain; two huge
cathedrals are abuilding whilst some denominational
schools cannot find money for necessary repairs.   Over
2,000 half-castes, together with a growing coloured and
Asiatic population, etc. are pressing the native inhabitants outward more and more; then suburbia provides
new problems for a Distressed Area.

Liverpool is the great centre for football pools, dog-
tracks, horse races, racial feuds and sectarian riots.
Formerly, the slave traffic flourished here; traces of the
horror can still be seen in old parts of the city.   The
area used to be called the "Black Spot on the Mersey."

But that is only one side of the picture.

Liverpool has about two hundred cultural and philanthropic societies, great hospitals, numerous charities, and
an abundance of churches at work.   Our writers, edu-
cationalists, lawyers, preachers, industrialists and Labour
leaders are amongst the most enlightened and progressive
in the Empire.   Gladstone, Huskisson, Lord Birkenhead,
Martineau, Stowell Brown, Ian Maclaren, Sir Robert
Jones, etc., are names that will ever be linked to Liverpool; and I make bold to assert that there are equally
great characters living here to-day.   But we are too near
the trees to see the forest.   The "soul" of this city is
clean and noble.

I was asked once to preach a sermon upon, "If Christ
came to Liverpool."   The subject I spoke about was,
"What if Christ left Liverpool!"

The weeping Man of Mercy left Jerusalem of old
to its selfwrought desolation.   What if He no longer
trod the Mersey, and ceased to go about our streets
doing good and healing all manner of diseases!

An illustrious example of Liverpool idealism in
citizenship and industry is Sir Frederick J. Marquis.   He
is a Manchester graduate who settled in this city as
Warden of the Liverpool University Settlement, in 1908,
and, during the war, served on the War Office Army Contracts Department.   Subsequently, he became secretary

Sir FREDERICK MARQUIS

of Boots Manufactures' Federation; he then joined
Lewis's Ltd., and has risen to be Chairman and Manag-
ing Director of that huge concern and its associated
Companies. In addition, he is on the Directorate of
Martin's Bank, and of the Royal Insurance Co. Ltd.

Industry does not account for all the activity and interest of this one-time research student of poverty and
the poor. He has served on several Government committees; and it is a mystery to his friends how he has found
time to give to the Council of Art and Industry, the
Board of Trade Advisory Council, and the Royal College
of Art. He has been a member of the Councils of both
Liverpool and Manchester Universities, and still is treasurer of the former. Deservedly, he received a knight-
hood in the Birthday Honours List of 1935.

After much persuasion I got Sir Frederick to explain
his philosophy as an industrialist. For the sake of young
people who may read this book I quote his own words
in full.

"It was during the last year of the War that I began
to realize that the future of industrial relations
would not be a repetition of the relations of those
existing before the War.

For years people had looked on the squalor associated with poverty without any great amount of
concern; it was the order of things. The history of
the relationship between capital and labour had not
left a great deal to the credit of capitalism on either
humanitarian or strictly business grounds. In the
mass it had treated labour with somewhat less consideration than it treated machines, and it had done
little to secure that supplies of healthy and compe-
tent labour should be available for industry; it
had trusted to chance.

Before the advent of the new conditions caused
through the effect of war on conditions in industry,
we had assumed that charity of judgment and
charity of purse were sufficient to deal with most of

P

our social difficulties. Our industrial and our commercial life were both the victims of that delusion, and only the greatest employers of labour considered it necessary to understand their workpeople. Neither masters nor men were unduly disturbed about the conditions in which labour lived.

Nothing short of a cataclysm could disturb a people so contented with its own lot and the lot of others. But that cataclysm came. Whole populations were subjected to new conditions of life; men were trained and disciplined; women, who were wives, had regular and sufficient incomes; old ideas of comradeship revived; industry and commerce were enrolled for national needs. It became clear to thinking people that the danger point in the social life of the country after the war would be the problem of the relation of Capital and Labour.

A new Age was to bring in a new world in which the economic feuds that had embittered life should be healed, and the social rifts that had divided life should be closed; a world in which service willingly rendered should be generously rewarded, and a new sense of brotherhood should build up a new social order.

The economic welfare of the community after the war had to depend upon its productive capacity. Instead of being a lending nation we were faced with the prospect of being a borrowing nation; and a borrowing nation can only obtain a high place among the nations of the world by using to the full its capacity for production.

These were the conditions of industry as I saw them at the end of the war. My training until then had been gained in the slums of Liverpool, where, as a Warden of the University Settlement, I had made a study of the problems of poverty and endeavoured to discover its causes. It was my intention, after this period of training, to take up a political career, in the hope that the intimate knowledge I had gained on the subject of how the poor live might enable me at any rate to try to set in motion some legislative machinery that would raise the standard of life for the masses.

But these new conditions in industry at the end of the war seemed to me to offer a greater field for activity to this end than did the House of Commons. I began to wonder whether it was not possible to organise industry on a basis that would retain the efficiency necessary to secure profits, and still be able to secure that the people who worked should be well-founded in life.

I am bound to admit that I did not receive any very great measure of encouragement from my employer friends, and when one day one of them told me that if he put into practice the theories that I had expounded to him, and they failed, it would mean the ruin of his business, I felt that it was time to do something more than talk theory, and I accepted his challenge. I entered business determined to prove whether or not my theories were right.

Those theories were always to pay at least as high rates of pay as the highest paid by others for comparable work, and constantly seek to raise that rate. I was determined to introduce into the organisation with which I was associated the principle of securing the good health of every employee. I had ideas of welfare work, free doctors . . . . all with the object of preventing any employee from suffering unnecessarily ill-effects from the nature of his work. I was determined to avoid the tyranny often exercised, *not* by the boss, but by the employee's immediate superior. I made it a rule that no employee should suffer dismissal at the hands of the individual placed immediately above him; the case must always be made out to an impartial judge. Every person should have the right of appeal to the head of the firm, who should listen calmly and judicially to that appeal. No employee should be tempted or permitted to behave dishonestly; because it is my belief that no first-class service can be expected or obtained unless business is run on lines that satisfy the consciences of the employees.

I believe in time to come the larger organisations who are dependent on the productivity of their staff for their success—that is to say, people who have not been able to mechanise their business, so that the machine and not the individual, is in control,— will have to engage as labour controllers people who have made a deep study of those problems that are called the problems of industrial psychology. It is, I believe, of infinitely more importance to any business that there should be an informed and sensitive manager of personnel than that there should be a good buyer or a good mechanician. There is much knowledge among those who have devoted themselves to the scientific study of the emotions and their effects on physical disabilities, on labour wastage, on sickness absenteeism, that is not used in industrial control. If those of us engaged in industry were to give to this branch of science the same sympathy and support that we have given to the mechanical, vast new fields of knowledge would soon be explored. Then I believe we should get a new mental adjustment to our responsibilities, and the world, physically, mentally, and perhaps, spiritually too, would be better for it.

I believe that no greater social service can be rendered by an employer of labour than to organise his business so that the people he employs shall be prosperous and healthy, and have reasonable contentment. That is a real service, of greater value to one's country than legislation in Parliament; and, since it is based on personal responsibility, of untold value to those who practise it."

CHAPTER THIRTEEN

THE WELSHMAN AT HOME

"IF one wants to judge of a man, one must study him at home in his natural surroundings, when he is thoroughly himself. A man out of his own country is out of his element, not at ease, is less than his best."
—*Max O'Rell.*

NOTWITHSTANDING my passionate devotion to Wales and to the Welsh, I am not insensible to some undesirable features in our national life. A Saxon reared in Wales may regard his adopted Land and nation with some degree of detachment, if not quite dispassionately; he can be a candid critic as well. In this case, though, criticism is confession more than reproach. Delusion, not love, is blind to blemishes in one adored; true affection cannot be satisfied with the second best.

Sensitiveness to criticism, servility, and sectionalism are usually found in nations that have been long oppressed. It takes centuries of freedom to remove the effects of suppression.

Our people are very sensitive to every sort of criticism, and fiercely resent an aspersion, however slight or unintentional. We have no use for the cartoonist; Bertram Thomas and men of like genius are exiled. We take ourselves too seriously to enjoy irony and healthy caricature. Marchant Williams was rarely appreciated. "*Punch*" would not survive three numbers in Welsh. Emrys ap Iwan is praised immoderately since he died; he was equally blamed, when alive, for his pointed references to Celtic prevarication. Goleufryn and Beriah Evans were treated likewise for ridiculing national humbug, a salutary service still whimsically rendered by the

" Junior Member for Treorchy " through amusing articles in the *Western Mail*. W. J. Gruffydd, Tegla Davies and Saunders Lewis deserve thanks for demolishing many of our clay idols. But they are called traitors by deluded defenders of decadence. In fact, we are partial to writers who present us with romance in place of literal history. When Puleston Jones first listened to "*Wales*" (O. M. Edwards) read to him (being blind himself) he exclaimed: "Excellent, Owen, I hope it is true." But that book is good reading still.

If our young dramatists could get over their "*chapel cum deacon*" complex they might teach us to laugh at our national foibles and idiosyncrasies as do the Scotch and Irish. We should be a happier people then.

Why must the descendants of Howel Dda and of Llewelyn develop an inferiority complex when dealing with foreigners? Fluellen even would be an improvement upon Uriah Heap for those who speak the language of Owen Glyndŵr and Goronwy Owen. North Walians are more diffident than Southerners amongst whom the workers predominate, and may have a tendency to arrogance. But both servility and truculence are phases of an inferiority complex produced by an alien system of education and age-long suppression. We have been taught to emulate and fawn upon the foreigner, and the rich, and people placed in authority. Wealth and worldly power were made into tribal gods. Young Wales maintains that Midas is a very poor substitute for Saint David.

Clannishness and sectionalism are not the monopoly of one nation, and Wales is no worse than any other country in this respect. We are not fond of the "*dyn dwad*" (lit. 'the man who comes'), and we treat a stranger with great caution and reserve even after he proves his worth. Parochialism characterises a nation made up of small and scattered communities separated by mountains, and, in many cases, by rivers. National consciousness is spasmodic in Wales, and depends much upon the national anthem and absence from home — "*Gorau Cymro, Cymro oddi cartref.*" We find it difficult to practise unity in any sphere of life; secession is our popular pastime; we are adepts at sectarianism.

We rarely hear the cry "Wales for the Welsh" to-day, since we realise that it would go badly with our own people if other nations retorted in kind. Welshmen find their way to every country in the world, and occupy high positions in the professions, in commerce, and in industry wherever they go. Our chief exports are preachers, teachers, doctors and coal. A self-contained, independent Wales would be far from satisfactory if other countries closed their doors to our children. Several learned leaders of the Welsh Nationalist Party owe much to the education they received in England. Saunders Lewis was born and educated in Liverpool; Prof. Daniels and Prof. W. J. Gruffydd each had a brilliant career at Oxford.

Welshmen can revel in a world of make-believe; that, partially, explains our passion for poetry and myth; we are at home in the realms of fancy. For one whole week every year we luxuriate in music, poetry and pageantry; the National Eisteddfod rallies the nation, and seems to embody the hopes and ideals of an united Wales. But the practical results on the life of our people are not very noticeable outside the magic circle of the Gorsedd.

The Welsh love singing; it is their natural expression for ecstasy and grief, hope and despair. They sing in funerals and at weddings, beside the grave and at cupties. The "Three Valleys' Festival" in South Wales, and the "*Urdd*" competitive meetings (without prizes) may save Wales from commercialising her magical gift of song.

Psalmody festivals also are social and religious solvents. But, so far, our people have not given the world much original music. They seem satisfied with singing the works of foreigners. We have no Welsh equivalents

of Bach, Beethoven and Handel.   The history of our
nation, and our puritanic Nonconformity partly account
for this.   At last, Wales is regaining faith in her own
creative genius and destiny; much of this is due to the
young Welsh Nationalist Party, and to radio broadcasting.

Gwalia is the land of heroes, mystics and saints; her
mountains pierce the skies, and give sanctuary to
spirits of the mists.   Her rivers sing the way to their
ocean bed; her valleys are playing fields for fairies and
visitants from the unseen.

Englishmen belaud their kings and crowns. The Land
of his Fathers claims the love of a Celt.

When basking in the glory of a cloudless sun, or
during the hours of bewitching moon in alien lands, I
have longed for the tips of Rhondda and the chimneys
of Upper Bank, because they mean Wales to me.   The
silence, the strength and secret of Snowdon in my heart
mean more than the Alps, the Pyrenees and the Rockies to me.   The mighty Mississipi, the broad Hudson,
the graceful St. Lawrence never thrilled me like the
Towy, Clwyd or the Conway.   The dotted hamlets and
the little Bethels of Wales are more wonderful in my
sight than all the senate-houses, museums and cathedrals
I ever saw.

I love the Welsh people with their plaintive hymns
and songs that always end with a sigh; with their yearn-
ing for poetry, and preaching, and glorification of the
grave.   Tears express their pleasures; joy to them is the
acme of grief; a heartbreak means satisfaction for the
Celt. They are generous in great things, but, sometimes,
mean in things that are small.   They are capable of
mighty loyalties, and prove easy prey for demagogues:
they are both mystical and materialistic, loveable and
ridiculous in turns.   A Welshman embodies the incalculable in human nature; that is his charm and tragedy. On
the field of battle he is brave as a lion, and then he
cringes before a foreigner in times of peace; he will die

Principal H. HUMPHREYS-JONES

for a losing cause, and squeal beneath an imaginary grievance.

Writers and preachers are the pride of Wales at home. A representative journalist is E. Morgan Humphreys. I cannot call him a personal friend; twice only have we actually met, but, for twenty-five years I have read nearly everything E.M.H. has written for the Press. He represents the best Welsh journalism of our period, and, probably, knows more about literary Wales than anybody living to-day. His grandfather was that powerful preacher and author, Edward Morgan, of Dyffryn, whose printed sermons remain classics of Welsh sermonic literature. His great-grandfather, Richard Humphreys, also was a giant of the pulpit, and a prolific writer. The Rev. R. H. Morgan, Bangor, an uncle, wrote for the *Traethodydd,* as did the two ancestors named above. Edward Morgan edited the *Methodist;* and R. H. Morgan, along with O. M. Edwards, edited *Cymru Fydd.* E.M.H. was born into a family of writers, and, naturally, turned to journalism. He was for years editor of *Y Genedl, The North Wales Observer,* and *Y Goleuad.* As " Celt " he has been a regular contributor to the Welsh edition of the Liverpool *Post and Mercury* for many years.

Wales has produced several noted journalists in the past; but they have been either monoglot or free-lance writers. Our great journalists of to-day, men of genius like C. F. Elias and Edward James, confine themselves to either English or Welsh. But E.M.H. is a whole-time bilingual writer, and in this must be unique. His Welsh is classic, and the English he writes often reminds one of R. L. Stevenson.

Journalism is an exacting vocation, and I know that E.M.H. has sacrificed much for his convictions. If "Celt" had confined his activities to the English Press he might have been a richer man to-day, but Wales, in that case, would have been much the poorer.

I append a specimen of his descriptive writing: " *A Night of Fires*":

" The East was pallid, but there was colour enough in the West. The sky flamed into a splendour of orange and purple under a dome of intense blue, and, when the first magnificence had passed, some colour still remained, a sombre glow that seemed to intensify the coldness of the rest of the scene. High above, between the pallor of the East and the glow of the West, was a slip, a silver of crescent moon. All along the hillside on the other side of the lake ran a lurid wall of flame. The gorse had been fired, and as the darkness deepened the redness of the fires grew more intense. Presently, other tongues of flame showed themselves here and there along the side of the hill and on both sides of the lake, and, some-times, the acrid smell of the burning drifted across the road. On a far ridge of hill, featureless in the gathering dusk, ran a thin line of fire. The splend-our of the West grew dim. The ' red vast void of sunset' gave place to a smoky haze. The silver moon became golden.

We came to the foot of the hill and the level of the lake. There the wind found us again. Up on the sheltered road we had forgotten it, but, by the lake, it came from the dark emptiness, sweeping along the water and tossing it into waves by Pont Pen Llyn. It cut like a knife. There was no sheltered corner on the cold water, and there, with ruffled feathers, floated a solitary swan. Across the bridge there was a bend in the road. My companion and I looked back. There was a cold glint of light on the water, but everywhere else was dim and dark. The gorse fires could not now be seen; from be-hind the high shoulder of a dark hill rose two columns of smoke, shot with the red light of the un-seen flames. Nothing else in the valley could be distinguished. Snowdon and the Glyder had wrapped themselves in the snowstorm and the night."

I have heard good preaching in England, Scotland, Ireland, France, Switzerland and America; but found no equal of the Welsh pulpit for oratory, power and unction. Our language has much to do with this; it is poetical, musical and stirring when coming from a real master. Welsh cadences have a hypnotic effect upon listeners. An intonation, called *hwyl*, also plays a great part in Celtic oratory in the pulpit and on the platform. Our younger ministers discount, and sometimes, disparage *hwyl* as it was practised by the Fathers in the Welsh pulpit. But when it vanishes we shall miss something spell-binding and almost magical.

I listened to representative Welsh pulpiteers like Dean Howell (Llawdden), John Evans (Eglwysbach), Herber Evans, T. C. Edwards, and E. T. Jones (Llanelly), and they were mighty. Owing to personal contact, the one who impressed me most was John Williams of Brynsiencyn. He was not the deepest thinker, neither did he possess the most musical voice amongst the orators of his day. But he was a prince in the pulpit—tall, stately, dignified. He had a dark complexion, thick eyebrows, mobile forehead responsive to emotion, eyes that flashed fire at times, and side whiskers. With his turn-down collar and regulation white tie and long frock coat John Williams was massive, challenging and impressive. He displayed no jewelry; there was a puritanic atmosphere about the preacher which made one think of Knox. His was a deep, almost baritone voice of no great range, but always under perfect control; at zenith it reached a shout not a song. When he was really moved, his sentences flowed in perfect rhythm like an advancing wave, which, at its peak, breaks into cascades of ecstatic notes. I have seen crowds swaying under the Brynsiencyn spell. His Welsh was the

classic Goronwy Owen type, homely, yet pure, under-
standable by the peasant, and pleasing to the ear of a
scholar. He seldom preached for less than an hour, and
that was too brief for the crowds.

No Association was complete without John Williams
to preach at the principal meeting. For over thirty years
I rarely missed an opportunity of hearing him, and many
times we preached at the same service. Preaching
to him was a passion. He had modelled himself to the
pattern of John Elias, said to be the greatest preacher
since Saint David. If Elias was more powerful than
John Williams he must have been a remarkable creation.

My favourite preacher did not confine his activities
to the pulpit. He was a keen Liberal in politics, and
took active part during General Elections. At one time,
pressure was brought to get him adopted as Parliamentary candidate for his county. For some years he served
on the County Council.

Welsh Nonconformists in North Wales still cling to
the remnants of the Liberal Party. Two reasons ac-
counted for this alliance in the past,—a Cause and a Man,
Disestablishment and Mr. Lloyd George. The Cause
for which old Welsh Nonconformists fought is no longer
a live issue; but whilst the Man of Criccieth remains
North Wales will cling to him.

John Williams was a strong Disestablisher, and he
remained all through a most loyal supporter of his friend
Mr. Lloyd George.

My ideal preacher was a disappointment to many
when he donned khaki and became part of the military
machine. But we loved the man, and forgot our differ-
ences when he preached. How can one convey to English people an idea of the charm and force of those searching sermons delivered with the fire and passion of a St.
Bernard of the Crusades! A combination of Spurgeon
at his best with Parker on the heights, that, in my opinion, was John Williams in full stride. (Not always though;
he also varied). I have watched men weeping, laugh-

ing and singing beneath his spell. Once I remember the preacher himself collapsing under the strain when he motioned me to draw the service to a close. I could only weep. At such moments the depths of a soul were stirred and angels moved amongst men.

" Can a wavelet move the granite rock?
Will a limpet sink a Dreadnought?
May the decrepit idiot sweep back the main?
Does the express train divert from its course because of the barking of a cur?
Would your spittle extinguish the meridian sun?
When will a moth delay the dawn, or one croaking frog stop the inrush of Spring?"

That crescendo of defiance was hurled at his congregation, and we saw men pale with fear. Or take this warning:

" Sinner, you carry a sensitive plate in your conscience, and on it are recorded all the events, actions and thoughts of life, — sin committed, the Gospel rejected, the Blood despised, the Mercy you have refused. The plates are now in a dark room, but soon must they be developed, and woe betide you on the day of revelation."

Here is an appeal from the sermon on Barabbas:

" You must choose between a robber and the Christ. Accept Jesus and no robber will trouble you henceforth. Robbers of others will become your benefactors. Sickness can rob the ungodly, it will enrich the Christian; oppression impoverishes worldings, it brings wealth to the saint; death strips materialists of all, it ushers a Christian into the glory of his King. Listen to Paul defying robbers to do their worst: ' Who can separate us from the love of God in Christ Jesus? Shall tribulation, or famine, or nakedness, or peril, or sword! Who? Who? Who? (in ascending shouts).

Lest there be some unknown robber lurking in
the shadows between two worlds, I defy you also :
' or any other creature.' "

It is impossible to convey in words the cumulative force
accompanying that final triune " Who ! "

Yes, mine was an inestimable privilege to know and
to hear John Williams ; and I feel sad to think that no
longer shall I listen to my preacher friend playfully say :
" Howard, you wretched Bolshie, come to spend a few
days' holiday with us at home in Llwyn Idris."

CHAPTER FOURTEEN

TYPES

WEALTH of material is my difficulty in this last chapter. The few representative men chosen have been known to me for several years; my impressions come from personal contact.

Friendship.

National animosity and racial enmity are artificial excrescences deliberately manufactured and perpetuated for ulterior motives. Children are friendly irrespective of colour and creed; adults also forget their class distinctions in a crisis of fire, shipwreck, earthquake or war. Friendship is natural to man; kindness is human; love is a language understood by all. Life is not built on selfishness. The wonder of friendship is too often found amongst men for us to doubt its possibility and beauty.

When Montaigne wrote his great essay on Friendship he did little more than tell the simple story of his friend. "If a man should importune me to give a reason why I loved him, I can only answer, because it was he, because it was I."

My life has been blessed by some wonderful friendships; and one very remarkable friend is Henry Humphreys-Jones, proprietor and Principal of the Liverpool School of Pharmacy, where over three thousand students have passed through his hands. He is a Fellow of the Chemical Society, Fellow of the Institute of Chemistry, and a leading light in the pharmaceutical world, an ardent Welsh Nationalist, active Liberal in politics, and devoted to public service and social activities. Yet he finds time to discharge the office of elder at my church, and takes his share in the work of his Denomination. Here is a Welshman at his best in education. Many Celts adorn the teaching profession, but this man finds a mission in his vocation. Money, power and prestige scarcely count with him; they are means to an end — the making of friends and the spread of friendliness. Such a man has no time to talk about enemies; he is too busy adding to the number of his friends.

H.H.J. is of humble origin and glories in the fact; he shows it by helping people of similar upbringing. I have known several men whose college fees were remitted or reduced by the generous Principal. Many more necessitous students were not called upon to pay after leaving the School without discharging their debts. He always remembers associates of his poor days; and his name is blessed in numerous homes amongst the Welsh hills. This English educationalist remains essentially Welsh, and clings to his Welsh Presbyterianism.

In Liverpool, some prosperous Welshmen forsake the denomination of their youth and turn to English or Scotch churches for the sake of so-called " Society." They are rarely at home in those communities, and English folk secretly despise Welsh upstarts who are ashamed of their own nationality.

H. Humphreys-Jones is unaffected by this social swank; he loves his people and his church, and values his eldership more than any secular honour within reach. The prayer meeting is more congenial to him than a Lord Mayor's Ball; a church meeting is the tonic he seeks for his soul. He has a practice of finding impoverished ministers, and giving them anonymous help in the form of money or books. I dare not tell him of all the cases I know where money gifts would be helpful. The man is incapable of refusing an appeal for aid; and, frequently, he is imposed upon by people blatantly accentuating a Welsh accent. His generosity outstrips discretion at times. There are other generous members at Catharine Street; they have greatly enriched my life,

Alderman ELLIS DAVIES

and the civic life of Liverpool. When the time comes
for me to write the history of this church, I have plenty
of material in hand.

A minister's life can be very lonely, but I have been
fortunate in all my churches. My officers are friendly,
helpful, spiritual, and anxious to relieve me of all unnecessary worry, and the members are considerate and
kind. H. Humphreys-Jones represents all that is best
in this communion of saints. The Creator gave him a
great heart, broad sympathies, and a love that would
embrace the whole world. From Shillong, India, one
hears of him endowing a hospital bed. Principal Weston
reports gifts from the same source to the Baldwin High
School at Bangalore ; in several cities of America I found
his name associated with public benefactions. Why en-
large? Of such are the missionaries, philanthropists,
friends of mankind. "Some friendships are made by
nature, some by interest, some by soul."

This Welshman's gift to the world is soul-friendship.
I cull the following from a speech delivered by my
friend at a Presbytery meeting:

"We must not at any cost let go the moral and spiritual
gains of the past; they are our bulwarks against
barbarism, animalism and anarchy. We hear a call
to dedication to God and man.

Goodness is not simply repression. It is an urge
to positive living for the things that really matter.

We are not merely individuals, but members of
a society ; and we should be loyal to the Ideal Community, the fellowship of the Spirit, the Body of
Christ, the real living Church embarking upon the
great venture of transforming the world to God's
will."

Unselfish Service.

Prince and peasant claim to-day that they were born
to render service to mankind ; but, very often, this ends in

Q

lip-service. English boys are trained to rule; domination is their goal; each Public School boy in England is a potential viceroy. But W. J. Gruffydd maintains that service, not supremacy, is the soul of Welsh culture. Of this, Ellis W. Davies, Caernarvon, is an out-standing example, and representative of others one could cite from personal acquaintance.

This dark, short, Iberian type of Welshman was reared among Arfon quarrymen, and trained in Wrexham and Sheffield for insurance work. He then took first class honours in Law as a solicitor. From the very start he was a rebel against privilege and autocracy, and still is. Although for many years a radical Liberal in politics, he always had more affinity with Keir Hardie than with Gladstone, Rosebery and Asquith. Quarrymen and small holders have been his constant concern; for them he has pleaded, written and voted throughout the years. His startling series of Press articles upon *"The Poverty of the People"* did, for Wales, what Booth's *" Life and Labour "* accomplished in England; they also swept Ellis Davies into the House of Commons, in 1906, where his maiden speech dealt with unemployment and the condition of the Welsh peasantry.

During the following twelve years E.D. was a lively and agitating member on numerous Parliamentary Committees dealing with the Jury System, the Land, the Franchise, and the House of Lords, and proved more revolutionary than the most ardent of colleagues who claimed to represent Labour. He became an acknowledged authority on foreign affairs, and seemed destined for high office in the Liberal Administration.

Then came the War, 1914—1918, and Ellis Davies belonged to the small minority who pleaded for peace and reconciliation. The Coupon Election of 1918 left him with the army of the defeated. For five years he was outside Parliament. West Denbighshire then sent him back to the Commons, where he remained until 1929, when he retired owing to ill-health, devoting himself to the service of the poor of Caernarvon as Chairman of the Public Assistance Committee.

This Welshman sought no honour, title or office for himself or for a relative. Ellis Davies left the House of Commons unbeholden to any man. He had the courage to change his Party-allegiance after reaching middle age. What is more significant still, he joined the Labour Party immediately following the debacle of 1931, when Labour was split from top to bottom, and most Hendersonites followed their intrepid leader into the wilderness. But the losing side always attracts Ellis Davies. This son of the people follows his vision whether it leads to cross or crown. He neither waits for, nor expects, the plaudits of the crowd in the valley of decision, but takes his stand irrespective of consequences, and is always prepared to pay the cost.

Mr. Davies is a keen observer of events, and has kept a diary from the very start of his public career. When that is published readers will be treated to interesting sidelights upon the history of our times. I am allowed to quote one entry which has to do with myself, and may be of interest to others :

" 29th July, 1924.

To 10 Cheney Walk with J. H. Howard. Had breakfast with Lloyd George. Lady Carey Evans presided at the table. Her husband was also there. Howard was very frank. Said ' Labour ' had lost its faith in the Ll.G. of 1910 and of the ' Land Campaign '; and asked why he (Ll.G.) scrapped the Land Valuation? Ll.G. said ' I did not. The Tories scrapped the valuation. I only abolished the taxes. They were intricate, irritating and producing nothing; they were emasculated in the House before they were passed. I had a big fight for them in the Cabinet, much worse than in the country. On one occasion all were against me, but the Old Man (as he called Asquith) who looked round the room and said

'I think opinion is in favour of the proposal.'
Howard pressed the point of an understanding in
the constituencies. Ll.G. said it was desirable, but
the P.M. was against it; that Snowden, Buxton,
Thomas, Wedgwood, Clynes and even Wheatley,
and all the Labour members in the Lords were prepared for an agreement, but that the vanity of Macdonald prevented it. 'He is exactly like Wilson':
adding, 'Wilson was a big man but vain, wanted the
glory for himself.' Ll.G. told Howard, speaking of
his Coalition days, that he never mixed with the
other people; his friends were of his own class,—
Bonar Law, the son of a manse; Horne, another son
of a manse, was left an orphan, his widowed mother
having only £50 a year. Speaking of Bonar Law,
Ll.G. said 'I told him once that there would be a
revolution if the Land Question was not tackled.
B.L. smoked on and said, later, 'Maybe, but not in
my time'."

The interview referred to was significant in view of
the general election then impending. At that time, I, myself, innocently hoped that an alliance, if not fusion, between Labour and Liberal was possible; and that I might
do something to bring this about. The above extract
from Ellis Davies' diary shows the attitude of the Liberal
ex-premier.

On the following day I interviewed two Labour leaders of the Macdonald Administration, and put the question to both. "My dear Howard," replied one, "if it
were possible to get your great Welshman into our Cabinet his first question would be 'How can I get rid of all
these creatures?'"

I still believe that Liberalism and Labour are natural
allies. But the old leaders of both parties will have to
pass on before cordial co-operation between the progressive forces becomes practicable.

The following tribute to our mutual friend, Sir Ellis
Jones-Griffith, M.P., shows how discriminating Ellis
Davies is even in appreciation:

"The election of 1918 destroyed Griffith politically,
though he re-entered the House for a few months in
1923 for Carmarthen; but his soul was not there; he
seldom came down, and I do not remember seeing
him in the Chamber more than once or twice; he
resigned in 1924, and died in 1926.

Was he a failure? Witty and satirical, Griffith, according to Lord Snowden, was one of the two best
debaters in the House. I have seen him sway
an audience in the Caernarvon Pavilion at a
Temperance meeting as no one else did. It
was unforgettable; wave after wave of laughter
swayed the crowd, when, after having humour-
ously described a Tory demonstration at Plas
Newydd, he said solemnly: 'And there was
tea and speeches—*un yn rôt a'r lleill yn* rot.' Yet
as a politician he was without influence. Why? He
lacked courage; perhaps he had no deep political
convictions; indeed, I seldom heard him discuss political questions. When we met, in the smoking room
or in the club, his talk was of books, of poetry, of
hymns, of his own and other people's witticisms.
When in the mood he would quote Omar Khayyám,
sometimes in John Morris-Jones's translation:

' *Am ddau o ddyddiau ni ofidiaf fi,*
Am ddydd i ddyfod ac am ddydd a aeth.'

Often have I heard him quote his friend W. J.
Gruffydd. On one occasion, a number of M.P.'s
were travelling down to a conference at Llandrindod,
and when conversation lagged, he opened that
cavernous bag he always had with him, and threw
me Wil Ifan's poems followed by the sermons of
Edward Matthews, Ewenni, telling me to read the

sermon on '*Y ddafad golledig*,' adding, 'it is the best thing in Welsh literature.' In his later years, a solicitor had handed him a brief the night before the Assizes at Caernarvon. Griffith thanked him; but instead of having a conference asked him to call at eight thirty next morning. The lawyer went. Rather to his surprise he was taken up to a bedroom, where he thought Griffith would surely discuss the case. Not at all. Propped up against his knees in bed our Counsel had the Methodist hymn book, and for the next half hour the solicitor had to listen to his favourite quotations.

Such was Ellis Griffith. Physically handsome, intellectually of the first order, cultured, witty, honourable as few politicians I have known, needing sympathy and lacking encouragement, he has left behind him fragrant memories. Tried as few men have been, disappointed in his political friends, he did not become bitter; and as I pass along the Caernarvon-Bangor road I can never forbear to cast a wistful glance across the Menai Straits at Llanidan church, where, at the foot of the tower, he sleeps.

> " Here—here's his place,
> Loftily lying,
> Leave him—still loftier than the world suspects,
> Living and dying."

Co-operation.

Friendship and unselfish service naturally result in co-operation, and, ever since the days of Robert Owen, Newtown, the Welsh founder of the Co-operative Movement, there have been Welshmen prominent in that sphere far beyond the confines of Wales. Such a one is Rhys J. Davies, Labour M.P. for the Westhoughton Division of Lancashire. Although he has resided for the last quarter of a century in Manchester, he remains essentially Welsh. He was born in Llangennech, Carmarthenshire, in 1877, one of a family of eleven children. His father was iron-ore refiner, road mender and market gardener in sequence. Both parents were intelligent, monoglot Welsh. The M.P. himself learned English when over fifteen years of age. His varied career commenced in his working life as a farm servant. Indifferent health drove him to this at the expense of losing even elementary education. For the next ten years he worked underground, and studied during spare time. When twenty-two he failed by just two votes to be elected a local official of the Miners Federation; those two votes altered the whole course of his career. The local Co-operative Society had suffered a serious loss through theft. One of the employees had embezzled a considerable sum of money; Davies was told by the Committee of Management of the Society that the thief was " a clever, but not an honest man. We are looking for a man who is honest if not clever. Will you take the job?" Thus he became cashier of the Society at a weekly wage of twenty six shillings. On that income he married.

He formed the employees of the shops and offices into a Trade Union, and, after four years, was appointed on the permanent staff of the National Union of Distributive and Allied Workers at its headquarters in Manchester. In due course he was elected to the Manchester City Council, and served on that city's education authority.

The National Health Insurance Scheme became operative in 1912, and Mr. Davies formed an " Approved " Society in connection with his trade organisation. Membership of that Society now stands at forty thousand, and its invested funds amount to four hundred thousand pounds.

The declaration of War in 1914 placed this lover of peace in some difficulty. He opposed that war by speech and pen, and was known by all as an uncompromising pacifist. In 1918, he stood as Parliamentary Labour candidate for the West Salford Division, and was beaten, obviously owing to his anti-war views. But he won West-houghton in 1921, and has retained the seat at six consecutive contests. In the first Labour Government of 1924 Mr. Davies was Under Secretary of State for Home Affairs; and it is well known that were it not for his serious illness he would have held an important post in the Labour Government of 1929. He is an excellent negotiator, and a vigorous and eloquent orator.

Few Labour men have travelled more widely than Rhys Davies. He has visited Spain, Portugal, the Balkans, Hungary, and studied social conditions and the co-operative movement in America and Canada, France, Switzerland, Belgium, Holland, Germany, Austria, Czecho-Slovakia and Poland. He made a special study of the Polish Ukrainian conflict in Eastern Galicia; and was the official representative of the British Government at Geneva in 1924, and of the British Parliament at the Millenary celebrations in Iceland in 1920. Rhys Davies is regarded as one of our leading authorities on European Social Insurance Schemes.

"I am a Trade Unionist, a Co-operator, an Internationalist and a Socialist. Above all give me liberty or death. Some men go forth in search of wealth, and when they secure it, spend it prodigally. Others aim at achieving power, and when they have done so, use it mercilessly. For my part, give me the good-will of my fellows, and I am happy.

Governments could provide me with the finest raiment to wear, the most delicious wines and foodstuffs to feed me, and house me in the grandest surroundings. But if they took away my liberty of speech my soul would perish."

Statesmanship.

Until lately Wales harboured but few peers of the realm. We are a nation of cultured peasantry, lovers of our Land, proud of our language and literature, and satisfied, usually, with our station in life. Our Patron Saint is St. David the Preacher; our national emblem is a homely leek, and the elusive Dragon symbolises the natural reserve and mysticism of an average Celt.

But, during the last thirty years Gwalia has figured prominently in the Honours List, and we have many titled people now resident in Wales. Some of them have proved real benefactors, and their names are revered throughout the whole country.

To speak of North Wales alone, — the late Lord Sheffield did much for Welsh education; Lord Clwyd has a burning passion for temperance; Lord Aberconway was philanthropic at Oakdale and elsewhere, and the work of Lord Davies on behalf of peace is known throughout Europe. But the most remarkable peer known to me, in Wales, is Lord Colwyn, whose Welsh residence, " Queen's Lodge," is at Colwyn Bay. He belongs to the front rank of national leaders and financiers.

We cannot trace any Welsh ancestry for Lord Colwyn. Neither did he turn to Wales in search of a fortune in land, or coal, or shipping; his wealth was made elsewhere, and is lavishly spent in the Land of his adoption; he came not to get but to give. The natural beauty of " The Garden City of the North ' has an attraction for most Manchester folk, and Lord Colwyn early succumbed to its charms of wood and hill, its sea and far horizons; and nothing but duty can lure him from the serenity of Queen's Lodge where he usually spends weekends with his family, and entertains his friends.

A person is known best at home; and it has been my privilege to observe Lord Colwyn in that intimate circle. There is no ostentation or strain; the humble visitor is put at ease, and cared for as an equal. That inimitable hostess, Lady Colwyn, could make the most nervous feel himself an honoured guest. Her drawing room has been the rendezvous for organisers of all sorts of charities, and that at various hours of the day. Committees of Boy Scouts, Girl Guides, Church Guilds, Friendly Societies, and hospital bazaars, were welcomed and presided over by Lord and Lady Colwyn with all the tact and dignity usually exercised at Royal Commissions. I have met great statesmen in that homely atmosphere, and accompanied modest workers for charity to the Lodge; but every visitor was treated with courtesy and consideration.

Without being Welsh, this family have endeared themselves to our people; unversed in our language, they win Welsh hearts; aliens to our Land, they lead us in what is noble and unselfish; and they have added much to the highest life of the nation.

In one of his racy letters Horace Walpole says that the busy person can always find time to take on an extra duty; and that is verified in the history of Lord Colwyn. His activities in rubber, cotton, banking, and railway concerns alone would overwhelm an ordinary man.

I give here instances of a few public posts filled by Lord Colwyn through the special appointments of various British Cabinets: Chairman of Bank Amalgamation Committee, Member of Lord Balfour Committee, Chairman of Flax Control Board, Chairman of the Railway Committee, Chairman of War Contracts Committee, Chairman of National Debts Committee, Chairman of Joint Exchequer Board, Chairman of Dockyard Committee, Chairman of Arbitration Committee relating to finances of North Ireland and Great Britain, Chairman of Income Tax Committee, Chairman of Economy Investigation Committee. From careful enquiries made, I conclude that few men can have presided over more Government Committees than Lord Colwyn. "Are there not twelve hours in the day?" Evidently, Lord Colwyn fills every minute with disinterested service, and that without seeking emolument or praise.

And what of the statesman? In the course of my journalistic work I have interviewed all sorts and conditions of people,—Prime Ministers and gangsters, pugilists and preachers, Conservatives and Communists, and usually succeeded in getting the information I desired. But Lord Colwyn has not been officially interviewed, and absolutely refuses " copy " to a wielder of the pen. He will talk about everything but himself, and seems to enjoy parrying a questioner's attempts to get behind his defence. One fact is obvious, Lord Colwyn is no politician and still is a great statesman ; he takes no interest in the political game, and remains delightfully oblivious to the stratagems of every party caucus ; he has no desire to meddle in the squabbles of statecraft. At the House of Lords he sits on the cross benches, and thus reveals his detachment from all Parties. The strange thing is that whilst no Party can claim his allegiance, all Governments seem to call for, and receive his help. Conservative, Liberal, Coalition and Labour Prime Ministers have made use of his unrivalled knowledge, experience and tact, and honoured him as a great servant of the State. He received a baronetcy during the Asquith Administration, was raised to the Peerage when Mr. Lloyd George was Prime Minister, and Mr. Baldwin saw him made a member of the Privy Council. All sections see in Lord Colwyn the true patriot and an unselfish leader of men. Here we find a man devoid of personal ambition attaining national renown ; one who avoids publicity winning prominence. In him sheer ability and sincerity are honoured by contemporaries.

And now at the ripe age of seventy eight, and suffering from arthritis which has crippled him from the hips, but, to use the words of a Prime Minister, " in no other part, including the head," we see this unselfish British statesman discharging his manifold duties with a calm serenity which bespeaks of soul-anchorage in the Ageless and Divine. Such men are the pride of Britain, and a special joy to Wales.

Internationalism.

George Lansbury is not a Welshman ; neither does he live in Wales; but this son of England belongs to every nation ; the most remarkable internationalist of our century has a special message for the world to-day as a corrective to insular nationalism.

Much has been written about G.L.; and his Auto- biography was a best seller in 1936. Here I refer to a few personal contacts with this modern mystic in British politics. His booklet, *"Your Share in Poverty,"* takes its place in my study with *" Wealth of Nations"* (Adam Smith), *"Poverty"* (Rowntree) and *" Life and Labour"* (Booth). It is Lansbury speaking from the heart to the conscience of mankind, and with an irresistible plea for a crusade against destitution.

I met this Labour leader for the first time during the agitation over Poplarism. He was cheery and unem- bittered, and prepared, if necessary, for a second term of imprisonment. Lansbury never could speak unkindly of another man ; the nearest approach was one reference to John Burns, and that even ended with, " Poor old John."

Lansbury loves the House of Commons ; but his real home is amongst the poor of Poplar where he is idolised by children and derelicts ; he knows them by name, and is welcomed to every house and hovel. He talks about his constituents as though they were dukes or fairies. One day I motored him along the Wirral peninsula, and our company was kept in roars of laughter by his Poplar stories and Cockney songs sung at the top of an un- musical voice. The old pilgrim of 76 is as boyish as a first year student on vacation, and quite as optimistic and free of care. Nothing can quench his faith in God and man.

On the platform he preaches and does not orate ; that is the complaint of critics. But politics to G.L. is a crusade not a career ; an election means a moral test more than a Party bid for power. This explains the re- fusal to delay his resignation of the Party leadership until after the 1935 General Election; he readily admits that the refusal probably lost that election to his Party. But with him there can be no dallying with principle. Once he did compromise for the sake of the Party, and he cannot forgive himself for that. (*"My Quest for Peace,"* page 12).

What a crowded life Lansbury has lived since he and his family emigrated to Australia! How sweet a soul he has remained throughout so tumultuous a career! He seems to share Paul's secret of contentment in wealth and poverty, success and failure, joy and sorrow. When East London attended the funeral of Mrs. Lansbury, the huge crowds sang the Halleluiah Chorus!

To be in the company of Lansbury for one hour always cures me of despondency; he is so irrepressible, and bubbles over with optimism. My dog " Paddy " had time for nobody else whilst G.L. graced our hearth.

He is always ready to share his vivid memories about the great democrats of our generation—Jaurés, Bebel, Adler, Debs, Bernstein, Gomper, Tolstoy, Hardie . . . he knew them all. Lansbury has travelled in Canada, America, Australia, Asia, Russia and Egypt. To him, every man is a brother, irrespective of colour or creed; and he sees a sister in the most forlorn of womankind.

I have shared his platform, and with him visited many and various homes; we have been fellow-worshippers. The secret of his life is in his religion.

Some people call Lansbury an impractical dreamer. But, as Commissioner of Works, he proved one of the three real successes of Labour in office. He has a burning passion for peace at home and abroad. Total disarmament is his sole defence against aggression. He will not vote for armaments, and cannot support sanctions, economic or military; passive resistance and martyrdom are the only weapons acceptable to him. On our way over to America, Lansbury and Dr. Salter gave me a gruelling time whilst I mischievously argued against unilateral disarmament, and in favour of collective force

and action. They were very refreshing, if not quite con-
vincing, and several passengers listened to our talks.

G.L. believes in the efficacy of personal appeal, and
therefore, as unofficial ambassador for peace, he inter-
views democrats and dictators, monarchs and republicans
to plead for reconciliation and disarmament. All give
him a patient, and, maybe, a wistful hearing; because in
their hearts they must know that the Christian Socialist
declares the only real escape for a war-weary world.

Lansbury is unique in British Labour; and is the
affinity of Gandhi, and of Kagawa, of Tolstoy and of
Francis of Assisi. The Poplar prophet recalls mankind
to the mind, method and might of Him who said "Resist
not evil," "Love your enemies," "Forgive without limit."

In Goetze's great painting, *"He was Despised and
Rejected of Men,"* the Saviour of the world is depicted
as deserted and ignored by excited crowds rushing by.
Soldiers and statesmen, courtiers and peasants, scholars
and ecclesiastics hurry along with the heedless throng.
One uniformed nurse turns her face Christward, but she
also is walking away; Jesus is left by all. For me, the
most significant feature of the Picture is that Christ is
not nailed to a cross, but remains lashed to a marble
pulpit.

When last I spoke to Lansbury, his parting word was:
"Howard, it is time to loose Christ upon the world."

As I draw these reflections to a reluctant close, many
questions must remain unanswered. Retrospection brings
mixed feelings of gratitude and regret, of satisfaction
and wonder. One sees mistakes and providential escapes, and some mercy and goodness overshadowing
all. Surely there is a Divinity that shapes our ends, and
some plan emerges from this maze of things. Every
experience has a significance in the cosmic urge towards
that far off divine event to which the whole creation
moves. Consequently, what is past recalling should be
past regret, since we cannot undo a single act. "The
moving finger writes, and, having writ, moves on."

The future? Who can scan the hidden scrolls
of the coming years? Yet "faith has still its Olivet,
and love its Galilee." I expect an angel at each turning
of the Winding Lanes; my sense of wonder grows with
the fleeting days; one to-morrow intrigues me more than
ten thousand yesterdays, because glory lurks beyond each
setting sun. "God Himself is in every to-morrow, and
with each dawn comes that bright angel called Hope."

Remembering the brevity of life on this plane of existence, and the eternity of dreams that reach into the
great Beyond, I have learnt, from Richter, to end each
day with one long look towards the stars, and amidst
thoughts of the hills that are eternal.

INDEX

Adler, Victor, 269
Alda Farm, 212
America, 190 ff
Ammanford, 77
Anderson, W. C., 116, 159
Angell, Norman, 159

Bangor (A), 198
Bangor (W), 158
Barlow, Sir John, 156
Barmouth, 232
Bebington Hall, 130
Beddoe, Thomas, 65, 66
Belgian refugees, 130
Belgium, 178 ff
Bernstein, Eduard, 269
Bigland, Mr., 131
Birkenhead, 119 ff
Birth control, 124
Bondfield, Margaret, 231, 232
Bonymaen, 31 ff
Booth, Charles, 98
Borah, Senator, 204
Brace, William, 53
Briand, Aristide, 166, 177
Brittany, 171 ff
Brockway, Fenner, 231
Burroughs, G., 122
Burns, John, 128, 133, 268
Butler, Josephine, 104

Caernarvon, 81
Cannes, 165
Cardiff, 81 ff
Case, Sir G., 143, 145, 146
Case, Upton, 223
Catharine Street, 226
Cecil, Viscount, 164
Champness, Betty, 167, 168
Chavasse, Bishop, 155
Chicago, 216 ff
China Town, 218
Clemenceau, 178
Clynes, J. R., 55
Clytotheus, 199
Cockett, 15
Cohen, Chapman, 228

Colwyn, Lord, 164, 165, 264 ff
Colwyn Bay, 135 ff
Colwyn Old, 141
Colliers, 51
Conscription of clergy, 142 ff
Cook, A. J., 56
Coughlin, Father, 209
Cuthbertson. G., 153, 154
Cwmavon, 108 ff

Daniels, Prof. J., 247
David, Rees, 111
Davies, Daniel, 93
Davies, Sir D. S., 161
Davies, Ald : Ellis, 144, 146, 257 ff
Davies, G. Ll., 148, 150, 158
Davies, J. E., 92
Davies, Mary, 29 ff
Davies, Moses, 93
Davies, Rhys J., 262
Davies, Teivy, 92
Davies, Thomas, 29 ff
Davies, R. R., 93
Davies, Senator James, 202
Davies, W. H., 139
Davis, J. W., 193
Detroit, 209, 210, 211
Dickens, Charles, 201
Dinan, 172
Dinard, 172
Dolgelley, 232
Dolwyddelen, 138
Draper, Brig. Gen., 212
Dregneselin, 172
Dunn, Col, 154

Earle, Governor, 192
Edison, 210
Edwards, O. M., 246
Edwards, R. D., 93
Edwards, T. C., 227, 251
Elias, C. F., 249
Emmott, Lord, 164, 165
Evans, David, 93
Evans, Edward, 91
Evans, Philip, 93
Evans, S. T., 118
Evans, Captain, 199

R

Fascism, 227
Festiniog, 229
Ford, Henry, 209, 210
Fosdick, 192

Gantry, 131
George, D. Lloyd, 115, 127, 143, 147, 152, 177, 193, 214, 252, 259, 260
Gerlan, 153
Glasier, Bruce, 159
Gladstone, W. E., 97, 104
Goetze, 270
Granville, 196
Great Meadows, 196
Green, John, 91
Green, William, 195
Grenfell, David, 53, 231
Grey, Earl, 110
Griffith, Ellis-Jones, 261 ff
Gruffyth, W. J., 157, 246, 247
Gomper, 269
Gwili, 128
Gwynfryn, 76 ff

Hales, A. G., 167
Hall, Marshall, 106, 107
Hammond, J. L., 157
Hardie, Keir, 54-56, 116
Harris, Richard, 93
Harrisburg, 197
Hartshorn, Vernon, 118
Havard, Bishop, 234
Healy, Tim, 146
Henderson, A., 119
Herbert, E. J., 93
Herriot, 178
Hewart, Mrs., 167
Hiawatha, 214
Hindenberg, 200
Hodges, Frank, 56
Hoover, Edgar, 204 ff
Hopkins, Mrs., 110
Howard, J. H.
    Parentage, 14: boyhood, 20—32: in Llansamlet, 32 ff: working in pit, 45: at Gwynfryn Academy, 77: Newcastle Emlyn, 79: Cardiff, 82: Trevecca, 87; Swansea pastorate, 99: the Welsh Revival, 100—103: rescue work, 104-6: Cwmavon experiences, 108 ff: Birkenhead church, Brotherhood, and Board of Guardians,

121—129: Belgian refugees, 130: *Lusitania* week, 130: Colwyn Bay, 135 ff: awakening to Nature, 136-137: conscientious objectors, 142 ff: Kinmel camp, 153 ff: Coupon Election, 160: collecting for new hospital, 162 ff: travels on the continent, etc., 170—189: in America, 190—225: in Liverpool, 226—245: a Saxon's estimate of the Welsh 245—254: types of people met, 255—271.
Howard, Lydia, 14 ff
Howell, Dean, 251
Howells, Richard, 64
Hughes, Charles Evans, 202
Humphreys, E. M., 249 ff

James, Edward, 249
Japan, 200   fl
Jenkins, R. T., 157
John, E. T., 160, 161
John, William, 24
Jones, Arfon, 216
Jones, David, 21 ff
Jones, Rev. David, 93
Jones, D. Brynmor, 118
Jones, Edward, 49
Jones, E. K., 161
Jones, Gwynn, 150
Jones, H. Humphreys, 255 ff
Jones, Sir Haydn, 230
Jones, J. M., 150
Jones, J. N., 93
Jones, Jack, 164
Jones, Dr. Lewis, 195
Jones, Puleston, 246
Jones, Dr. P. M., 214
Jones, Stephen, 214
Jones, S. T., 151, 152
Jones, Viriamu, 82, 97
Jones, William, 109
Jowett, F. W., 159

Kagawa, 215
Kelly, 217
Kinmel, 148 ff
Kirkwood, David, 231
Kislyn, 208

Lansbury, George, 190, 239, 268 ff
Larson, Arthur, 222
Lecky, 106

INDEX iii.

Lewis, J. L., 195, 204
Lewis, Saunders, 246, 247
Lewis, Timothy, 157
Lindberg, 201
Liverpool, 228 ff
Llansamlet, 32 ff
Lledr Valley, 136
Loire, 176, 178
Lloyd, Sir J. E., 157
Louchere, 178
Lusitania, 130

Mabon, 53
MacDonald, Ramsay, 116, 159, 160
Machen, Dr., 208
MacNeill, John, 114
MacNeil, William, 113
Mainwaring, W. H., 24
Maltby, Dr., 158
Mankato, 214
Marquis, Sir F., 240 ff
Matthews, Edward, 59, 60
Maxton, James, 231
Merionethshire, 228
Meyer, F. B., 131
Michigan, 210
Minneapolis, 215
Miskin, 85
Morel, E. D., 133, 134
Morgan, Dr., 214
Morgans, Master, 21
Morris, Artro, 229
Morris, O. G., 122
Moseley, Sir O., 231

Niagara, 208, 209
Nisbet, Nimrod, 222

Painlevé, 177
Paramé, 172
Penn, William, 194
Perkins, Miss, 204
Pew, Big, 60 ff
Philadelphia, 194, 195, 201
Phillips, Evan, 80, 81
Phillips, John, 80
Phillips, John (Cwmavon), 114, 115
Pittsburg, 198
Price, Dr. Peter, 161
Prys, Principal, 88 ff
Prytherch, W., 119
Pugh, Cynolwyn, 192, 221, 227
Purdy, T. E., 162, 163, 166

Queux, William le, 167

Racine, 216
Raven, Canon, 158, 227
Rawlings, Dr., 107
Reconciliation, F. O., 132
Rees, Caradoc, 168, 169
Rees, Principal Thomas, 150
Refugees, Belgian, 130
Revival, Religious, 100 ff
Richards, Robert, 157
Richards, Rose, 107
Richards, Thomas, 63
Rivera, Primo de, 184
Roberts, Evan, 100 ff
Roberts, Richard, 150
Rowntree, 98
Royden, Miss Maud, 158
Ruskin, J., 232

Salem, 57
Salter, Dr., 190, 269
Samuel Walter, 24
Sanger, Lord George, 95
Scott, Anderson, 167
Secularism, 227
Siabod, Moel, 136, 138
Sims, Evan, 66 ff
Sims, G. R., 98
Sing Sing, 222
Snowden, Phillip, 116, 117, 159, 232
Snowdon, 139
Sorensen, 230, 231
Spain, 180 ff
Stead, W. T., 104
Steven, George, 167
Switzerland, 174-176

Tabernacl, 108 ff
Talgarth, 87
Therapy Music, 214
Thomas, Abraham, 25
Thomas, Bertram, 245
Thomas, Ezeciel, 62, 63
Thomas, J. H., 166
Tolstoy, 269
Toronto, 212
Traffic, White Slave, 124, 125
Trevecca, 87 ff

Universities, American, 215, 216

Vincent, Sir Wm., 166
Vladeck, 193

Walpole, Horace, 266
Warman, Dr. Guy, 126, 127
Webb, Sidney, 157
Wedgewood, 260
Western Mail, 246
Wheatley, 260
White, Graham, 129
Whiteley, Rea, 220
Wilberforce, 98
Williams, (Rev.) David, 68
Williams, O. R., 194, 198

Williams, David, 114
Williams, Dr. John, 119, 153, 155, 251 ff
Williams, Dr. T. C., 155
Williams, Marchant, 245
Williams, Judge G., 85
Williams, Richard, 85
Wyn, Watcyn, 77 ff

York, New, 192 ff, 220 ff

The Calvinistic Methodist Printing Works, Caernarvon.
Printed and made in Wales, Great Britain